D0435468

LIVING in the IMAGE of GOD

LIVING in the IMAGE of GOD

JEWISH TEACHINGS TO PERFECT THE WORLD

Conversations with
RABBI IRVING GREENBERG

As Conducted by Shalom Freedman

Foreword by Rabbi Joseph Telushkin

JASON ARONSON INC.
Northvale, New Jersey
Jerusalem

This book was set in 11 pt. New Baskerville by Alabama Book Composition of Deatsville, Alabama.

10 9 8 7 6 5 4 3 2 1

Library of Congress Cataloging-in-Publication Data

Greenberg, Irving, 1933–
Living in the image of God : Jewish teachings to perfect the world / conversations with Rabbi Irving Greenberg as conducted by Shalom Freedman ; foreword by Rabbi Joseph Telushkin.
p. cm.
Includes index.
ISBN 0–7657–9980–4 (alk. paper)
1. Greenberg, Irving, 1933– —Interviews. 2. Rabbis—United States—Interviews. 3. Judaism—20th century. 4. Judaism—Essence, genius, nature. I. Freedman, Shalom. II. Title.
BM755.G74A5 1998
296.8′32′092—DC21 97–27108
CIP

Manufactured in the United States of America. Jason Aronson Inc. offers books and cassettes. For information and catalog write to Jason Aronson Inc., 230 Livingston Street, Northvale, New Jersey 07647.

To our children, Moshe, David, Deborah, J. J., and Goody,
who have given us joy, love, and fulfillment beyond measure;
and to our children-in-law, Mindy, Jonathan, and Eric,
who have enriched our lives even more

—Rabbi Irving Greenberg

To
Bob (Moshe Ben Yitzchak Yehuda Leib
and Chaya Rachel) Brown
Teacher and Friend
His deep love and devotion to his family
His dedication to Jewish learning and life in Israel
His dignity and joy in Torah reading and as *Shaliach Tzibur*
His modesty, quiet humor, great intelligence, and kindness
Made his life a blessing to all those who were a part of it
Never was the biblical verse more true than in regard to him
ויברא אלוקים את האדם בצאלמו בצלם אלוקים ברא אותו

—Shalom Freedman

Contents

Preface

Rabbi Irving (Yitz) Greenberg has devoted his life to helping the Jewish people. His love of the Jewish people, his identification with their suffering, and their struggle for renewal and redemption is at the heart of his own life's work. His thought about the Jewish people has always been a courageous effort to describe and understand where we have been, where we are now, and what we must do to achieve that *tikkun olam,* that repair of ourselves and the world, which is our historical purpose and goal.

Rabbi Greenberg has, over the past four decades, published numerous articles and essays addressing the major issues on the Jewish communal agenda. His book *The Jewish Way (Living for the Holidays)* is an inspiring presentation of Judaism as manifested through the Holy Days.

Having admired and benefited from Rabbi Greenberg's work, I have long felt that his ideas are not well-enough known. This is due to the fact that some important ideas were unpublished and others were scattered in many different places. Therefore, during his sabbatical in Israel, I approached Rabbi Greenberg with the idea of doing a book in the interview format. This present work is an effort to provide, for his many students and readers, a general picture of his views on most of the issues he has grappled with over the years. It is to be hoped that gathering views on diverse areas between the covers of one book will allow his teaching to be more fully understood and to have even greater impact than it has had to this point.

This work is a series of conversations that are more "interview" than conversation; they are not so much a dialogue between Rabbi Greenberg and myself as they are an opportunity for Rabbi Greenberg to express his views. The structure of the work grows out of my questions, and the book has been significantly shaped by my editorial judgment and priorities. My own aim was to ask and to listen, and to learn as I have done over the years from the reading of Rabbi Greenberg's work. A transcript of each interview was made, and was then edited separately by myself and by Rabbi Greenberg.

Each interview is organized around a particular theme. The first chapter is concerned with Rabbi Greenberg's background and career. The next three chapters concentrate on the philosophical and theological foundation of Rabbi Greenberg's thought. First comes a chapter "On the Human Created in God's Image," followed by chapters on "Covenant: On the Partnership of God and the Human in History" and "*Tikkun Olam*."

Then come a set of chapters that focus on contemporary issues: "On the Role of Women in Orthodox Jewish Life," and "The Jewish Family in the Modern World." Historical questions facing the Jewish community are probed in the chapters "The Situation of Modern Orthodoxy" and "Of Land, Peace, and Faith." The chapter "On Leaders and Leadership" also deals with these historical issues, while providing an understanding of how Rabbi Greenberg has managed to balance the roles of communal leader and pioneering Jewish thinker.

In the chapter "On Holocaust Commemoration," Rabbi Greenberg, who has contributed to both the Jewish people's and the non-Jewish world's awareness of the unprecedented evil of the Holocaust, explains how the act of commemoration is not, as critics have argued, for the dead at the expense of the living, but rather is in service of the Jewish and human future.

In the final two chapters, Rabbi Greenberg speaks of his conception of "Israel, the Jewish Renewal, and the Human Future" and of his idea of "The Teacher of Judaism in the Modern Age." In these chapters, Rabbi Greenberg outlines his conception of the people of Israel's role now that they have reassumed power and responsibility in history. He expresses a vision of redemption, a picture of a world moving toward *tikkun olam*, toward a better situation for the Jewish people and humankind as a whole. In the

Afterword, he deals with the conflict between messianism and realism and reaffirms the conviction that we are living in an age of the beginning of redemption.

As one who has been privileged to learn from Rabbi Greenberg's work, I can only thank God for having been given the opportunity to participate in these conversations. My prayer is that they will, by furthering the understanding of Rabbi Greenberg's work, be a real contribution to the Jewish people's understanding of how to create, in covenant with God, a true *tikkun olam* in the generations to come.

—Shalom Freedman

Perspective

From 1992 to 1993, my wife, Blu, and I spent a sabbatical year in Jerusalem. We had thought that we would move to Israel before that time, wanting to engage in the creation of a vital Jewish society there. However, our unfinished work in the United States held us in its grip and we could not let go. Therefore, we sought a year's living to immerse ourselves in Israel again and to draw on its inspiration.

There were two work-related goals for the year. One was to write a book spelling out the concepts—creation, *tzelem elokim*, and covenant—that have been central to my thinking and teaching over the past two decades. Owing to the pressures of administration and teaching, very few of those twenty years' ideas have appeared in print. The second goal was to assess my past work, as well as to prioritize and develop a strategy for the next decade.

My sixtieth birthday was coming in 1993. Time was running out, and the projects I still wanted to accomplish seemed to outstrip the available time ahead of me. Also, I was feeling the shock and sting of the 1990 National Jewish Population Study, with its implicit message that all efforts to renew Judaism in America had failed to stem the tide of assimilation.

Although the year was truly healing, and I used the time to sort out my priorities, the writing of the book went slowly. While I wrote chapters and sections of various kinds and lengths, in truth, I could not find the overall voice that seemed right for the book.

Enter Shalom Freedman. My contact with Shalom had started a year earlier, when he sent me a wonderful manuscript called *Life as Creation*. I was able to help him find a publisher, and wrote an introduction for it. Unfortunately, the book never received the attention it deserved, but I deeply respected the caliber of his mind and work.

Shalom had heard various reports of my teaching, some of which were contradictory and others of which were negative. Since he had read my book *The Jewish Way* appreciatively, he wanted to interview me, using a series of questions he had worked up to clarify both his own concerns and my thinking. He offered to transcribe and edit the conversations and to submit them for publication. I would be given every chance to clarify and expand my words so that the ideas would be more fully developed than through presentation in an informal conversation or even in a lecture.

His proposal won my heart, for I knew that I could not finish the planned book before the sabbatical concluded and therefore would be facing another delay in getting my thoughts into print. Most of my newer ideas had never been published, or had been printed in obscure places. Some of the concepts had evoked considerable opposition, and my critics had already published powerful, all-out attacks. The sad thought had occurred to me more than once that many more people had read about my ideas as represented by bitter opponents than had read them directly. Rather than accept another decade of silence and one-sided attacks, I decided that Shalom's work offered me a chance to be read and heard through a sympathetic and direct representation of my ideas. While this was not a book of systematic thought, at least it would be an articulation of some central ideas in my own words.

Here, I wish to express my deep gratitude to Shalom for his initiative and for his great efforts. He has toiled long hours with no remuneration or recognition. He has done this out of selfless goodwill for me and for the cause of bringing these ideas before the Jewish reading public. I am unworthy of these efforts, but I am grateful for them. May God reward his deeds; may he receive a full recompense from the Lord, God of Israel, under whose wings he finds refuge.

The passage of time has not dulled my belief that we are living in one of the great moments of transformation and rebirth in the religious history of Judaism and Jewry. To live in such a moment is, in the words of Rabbi Joseph B. Soloveitchik, a *shlichut* (agency or mission). The ideas and policy recommendations in these conversations are offered as a way of understanding what might be the role of Jews and what values we should represent in our community's life and as participants in humanity's struggle for *tikkun olam.* These concepts are still in formation; I welcome critique and elaboration from others to bring out what is best in them and to separate out the dross.

A number of people have helped in bringing this book to fruition, and I thank them: Bambi Marcus, who typed many of Shalom's original transcripts and my handwritten modifications with amazing discernment; Koren Backstrand and especially Hannah Gastfreund, who patiently and accurately typed and retyped this manuscript through many editorial changes; Janet Kirchheimer, my long-time, outstanding assistant, who managed this and so many other projects skillfully, and for her editing as well. My wife and my colleagues at CLAL—and, over the past few years, the CLAL fellows—have been a continuous source of insight, stimulation, and helpful critique. Their influence permeates this book.

It has become even clearer to me in recent years that all of us live on God's *chesed* (covenantal love) every day of our lives. This *chesed* is not to be taken for granted. I hope to be sustained long enough to finish the other book and further projects and publications. In the interim, I am grateful for this opportunity to share my life experiences and thought with others.

—Rabbi Irving Greenberg

Foreword

I proudly count myself a disciple of Rabbi Irving "Yitz" Greenberg, the most influential teacher with whom I studied at Yeshiva University. Profound as Greenberg's impact was upon me in the late 1960s and 1970s, it has grown and grown since then. And I, of course, am one of just thousands whose thinking has been shaped by his extraordinary vision of Judaism, Jews, God, and humankind. Indeed, I believe that Greenberg's thinking is only beginning to make its impact, and that it will prove to have ever-increasing significance to Jews, theologically sensitive Christians, and open-minded secularists throughout the next century.

What distinguishes Greenberg's thinking as so consequential? For one thing, he espouses an ideology of Judaism and the human condition that is both passionate and tolerant. Passion and tolerance in and of themselves are not necessarily virtues. Evil ideologies, no less than good ones, have passionate adherents, while tolerance is often practiced more easily by those with no convictions at all.

However, the genius of Greenberg's passionate tolerance is that it is more than tolerant; it truly is rooted in an openness to learning from diverse people and ideologies, an openness that itself derives from his full-hearted acceptance of Judaism's teaching that all human beings are created in God's image. If each person has a spark of divinity within him or her, then many, many people will have something divine to teach.

Greenberg's openness to learning from and appreciating people of diverse orientations also stems from his ongoing reflections on the Holocaust. It is one of Yitz's great insights to realize that the Holocaust challenges and, to a certain degree, shatters everyone. For Jews, of course, the Holocaust challenges one of the most important statements made about God in the Torah—that He is a God Who acts in history. Christianity, which argued for two thousand years that it had triumphantly replaced Judaism, must confront the fact that the Holocaust was conceived and carried out in the midst of Christian Europe and by people who—though many were not Christians—were all children of Christians. Secularists, who might point to the Holocaust to argue that there is no protecting God, must confront the fact that the Holocaust was instituted and carried out in a secularist society; it was made possible by enlisting some of the most powerful concepts and mechanisms of secular modernity—viz., technology, bureaucracy, universalism. The most powerful ideologies spawned by secularism, Nazism (and communism, as well) lacked mechanisms to stop their adherents from becoming mass murderers. Indeed, Greenberg was one of the first to point out the moral dangers inherent in value-free secular education; he noted that, of the twenty-four *Einsatzgruppen*[1] leaders put on trial for their wholesale murder of more than one million Soviet Jews, nine were lawyers, two were economists, and one each was architect, professor, banker, high-school teacher, and dentist. The Holocaust challenged religious faith because God did not stop the atrocities, and it equally challenged secularism, whose adherents largely implemented the "Final Solution."

Another important element of Greenberg's thinking is his willingness to do battle against divisions that unnecessarily separate people. While he certainly acknowledges the existence of serious differences between believers and skeptics, he also insists that, in the aftermath of the Shoah, such divisions may be less absolute than is commonly thought. For example, because of the Holocaust, few believers can assert that their faith is never plagued by doubts. Thus, Greenberg asserts that "After Auschwitz, faith means that there are times when faith is overcome. . . . We

1. The German mobile killing units that followed the *Wehrmacht* (German army) in the former Soviet Union, murdering at least one million Jews from 1941 to 1942.

now have to speak of 'moment faiths' interspersed with times when the flames and smoke of the burning children blot out faith, although it flickers again. . . . The difference between the skeptic and the believer is frequency of faith, and not certitude of position."

Greenberg insists that we guard ourselves against the self-righteousness that denominations and religious groupings inevitably seem to inspire. This doesn't mean that people shouldn't belong to a denomination or to an organized religious grouping; on the contrary, Greenberg is a passionately affirming modern Orthodox rabbi. But his profound awareness that all truth does not reside in any one group is reflected in one of his wittiest remarks: "It is not so important which denomination in Judaism you belong to, as long as you're ashamed of it."

The meaning behind this quip is profound. Interdenominational acrimony is largely fueled by various Jews' tendency to highlight their movement's perceived strengths and the others' weaknesses. Thus, Reform Jews commonly dismiss Orthodoxy as fanatical, and view their movement as the only truly tolerant, open-minded one. Meanwhile, Orthodox Jews often seem to think of themselves as the only ones sincerely trying to follow God's laws, and commonly view the non-Orthodox as irreligious people who change the Torah's meaning to conform to their own convenience.

But since all the movements have failed to complete Judaism's task of "perfecting the world under the rule of God," it behooves all their adherents to speak more charitably of their "opponents," and more humbly of their own accomplishments.

This insight applies to different religions no less than to different denominations. Twenty years ago, Greenberg argued with Dennis Prager and me over what he felt were our unfairly harsh criticisms of Christianity. "It's wrong," he counseled us, "to take the best of your own tradition and compare it to the worst of someone else's." The comment affected us both profoundly, and has ever since guided us to a more comprehensive, nuanced, appreciative, and balanced understanding of Christianity.

In his openness to learning from diverse views, Greenberg hardly preaches tolerance without limits. But the boundaries he establishes are commonsensical and moral; they emanate, as well, from his deep love for the Jewish people. Thus, although a tendency has emerged in recent years in right-wing Orthodoxy to understand the Holocaust as punishment for Jewish sinfulness, Greenberg denounces such an explanation on moral grounds: "Now that [the victims of the Holocaust] have been cruelly tortured and killed, boiled into soap, their hair made into pillows and their bones into fertilizer, their unknown graves and the very fact of their death denied to them [by Holocaust deniers], the theologian would inflict on them the only indignity left: that is, insistence that it was done because of their sins."*

Greenberg's love for *clal Yisrael*, the Jewish people, was instilled in him in the learned Orthodox household in which he was raised in Brooklyn. Once, several years after World War II, when he was a teenager passing through an intensely religious phase, he made some highly critical comments about American Jews' irreligiosity. His staunchly Orthodox father was angered by his words: "You dare to attack Jews in the name of God? Tell me—of these two [God and the Jewish people], who should be more ashamed of their behavior over the past decade?"

This seminal exchange deeply and permanently affected Greenberg. In a powerful passage in this book, he explains the impact of his father's rhetorical question: "Without ever saying a word about the Holocaust, my father communicated that that was what he meant. God had not saved the Jewish people from the Shoah, but the Jews had remained faithful. . . . In stunned silence, I heard the message: *Don't you dare ever attack (or shame) Jews in the name of God. They deserve better from God and from you.*"

It is this appreciation for Jewish loyalty to the Jewish people, after God's seeming abandonment of them during the Holocaust, that enables Greenberg to discern a life of Jewish affirmation even among those whom others dismiss as leading "uncommitted" lives. Jews who celebrate a child's bar or bat mitzvah, even with gaudy parties, do so with an awareness that identifying as a

*Given polemicists' unfortunate tendency to use the Holocaust to justify positions they already hold, Greenberg has offered this challenging and moving guideline for Holocaust discussants: "No statement, theological or otherwise, should be made that would not be credible in the presence of the burning children."

Jew can and has led to death, and are making a profound, if hidden, affirmation of convenantal commitment. I remember thinking that Greenberg had gone too far when I once heard him speak of Jewish parents affirming the covenant by installing wall-to-wall carpeting in their homes so that their children would not suffer unnecessary pain when they fell. This struck me as far-fetched, but when my children were born, I had wall-to-wall carpeting installed. Greenberg understands such behavior as, in part, a response to the Holocaust. Because Jews had suffered such unnecessary and extreme pain during those years and children were the greatest victims of this pain, Jews were responding by trying to do away with preventable suffering.

An awareness of this sort of holy secularity is what lies behind Greenberg's affirmation of the work done by Jewish federations. Operations Exodus and Solomon (respectively, the resettlement in Israel of Jews from the former Soviet Union and from Ethiopia) and programs such as Meals-on-Wheels are more than kind acts of philanthropy; they are holy behavior. A half-century ago, the Nazis not only waged war on the Jewish body; they also tried to destroy the Jewish notion that human beings, because of their creation in God's image, are of infinite value. A major reason the Nazis used Zyklon B gas in murdering Jews was because it cost them less than a penny per person to do so. By expending enormous amounts of money and effort to save lives, the federation community is affirming—in the aftermath of Nazism's assault—the most important of Jewish religious values, the infinite value of human life.

Just as Greenberg's tolerance does not encompass those who would blame the Jews for the Holocaust, so it excludes those of the political left who hold Israel to standards that will ensure its destruction. After the Holocaust, the need for a Jewish homeland is so self-evident that one must question the goodness of any person who wants to see Jews deprived of sufficient military might to defend themselves ("No one should ever be equipped with less power than is necessary to assure one's dignity"). Greenberg has taught me that one of the Holocaust's most important lessons is that Jews must never again be so weak that their very weakness tempts others to destroy them. And while power must be used morally, it is immoral to impose upon Israel the kinds of limits that will guarantee its destruction. "If we Jews are five percent better than the rest of the world, we can be a 'light unto the nations.' If we are twenty-five percent better than the rest of the world, we can bring the Messiah. If we're fifty percent better than the rest of the world, we'll all be dead."

Finally, Greenberg is, and will remain, famous for his radical and controversial notion of "voluntary covenant." In espousing the idea that the Holocaust broke (or wounded) the covenant between God and the Jewish people, he is willing to say what many feel, certainly on an emotional level, but are reluctant to articulate: "Therefore, morally speaking, God must repent . . . for having given his chosen people a task that was unbearably cruel and dangerous without having provided for their protection. Morally speaking, then, God can have no claim on the Jews by dint of the Covenant." The covenant, therefore, "can no longer be commanded and subject to a serious external enforcement"; thus, it becomes voluntary. The miracle of the age, in Greenberg's view, is that "the covenant was broken but the Jewish people, released from its obligations, chose voluntarily to take it on again and renew it. God was in no position to command anymore but the Jewish people was so in love with the dream of redemption that it volunteered to carry on with its mission."

What is often overlooked is that these words, which appear harsh to some or radical to others, are, in fact, words of reconciliation and love between God and Israel. Greenberg concludes that, during the Holocaust, "the Divine Presence was in Auschwitz, suffering, burning and starving . . . ," that is, "sharing the pain in a way that only an Infinite Consciousness and Love could share." God's inaction was part of a greater divine *tzimtzum* (self-limitation) that is a call to humans to take full responsibility for the covenant. Furthermore, Greenberg insists that human voluntary acceptance of the covenant yields a loyalty that is, in fact, more internalized, more idealistic, and more steadfast than ever before. What is more, even though God is more hidden than ever, God is more present than ever. This opens the door to an explosion of holiness in the secular—further eroding the easy, but mistaken, walls and categories that separate the holy and the secular.

The book before you is not the book that systematically

articulates Greenberg's later thought with its emphasis on Judaism's vision of Creation and the image of God and his exploration of the centrality of covenant, Judaism's method of redemption and *tikkun olam.* However, until that book is written, this one will have to suffice. It is an important, very human introduction to Greenberg's life and thought. We should be grateful to Shalom Freedman for eliciting the thinking and placing it before the Jewish world. Jews everywhere are searching for a compelling retelling of Judaism's story; Greenberg's version embraces the entire tradition and encounters the fullness of contemporary experience without fear of their interaction and without flinching at the consequences. Whoever reads this book will be enriched.

A final thought: The world Greenberg strives to create is an ideal one in which people can learn good from each other. Small wonder, then, that SAR, the Riverdale day school created by Greenberg and his wife Blu's inspiration, is the sweetest Jewish school with which I am familiar. SAR's faculty does extraordinary work in communicating to its young students the ethical implications of what it means that human beings are created in God's image. My wife, Dvorah, and I joyfully send our children there, and this is just one additional reason that I regard myself as a disciple of Yitz Greenberg, a seminal—perhaps *the* seminal—Jewish thinker of our time.

—Rabbi Joseph Telushkin

Story

On a freezing cold, dark and moonless night, the traveller races his horse and carriage toward the shtetl when he wishes to visit the Rebbe. A heavy snow is falling. As they roll onto the last bridge over the river that is the entrance to the town, there is a man standing in the middle of the bridge holding a lantern. The traveller barely stops the horses in time to save the watchman from being trampled. He jumps out, much chagrined and apologetic, explaining that it never occurred to him that anyone, let alone a watchman, would be standing in the middle of the bridge on such a cold, God forsaken night.

After he dusts off the watchman and after his apologies are accepted, he offers the watchman a ride into town. "Listen," he says, "it is cold on the bridge. Let me make it up to you by driving you to your home or to some warm inn." The watchman refuses to leave his post and turns down the ride

"But why?" asks the traveller. "Why must you stay at the bridge even in such inhospitable weather? And what are you doing here anyway?"

The watchman explains. "The great Rebbe whom you go to visit believes with all his heart and soul, that the Messiah can and will come any minute, any day. But most people are home at night. Should the Messiah come at that hour, it would be wrong to let the redeemer feel unwanted, unappreciated, unanticipated. It would be terribly wrong that the Messiah proceed into town and go to the Rebbe all alone, unescorted and unwelcomed. Therefore, the Rebbe decided to station a watchman—namely me—on the bridge at all hours of the night. In this way, whenever, whatever day or hour, the Messiah arrives, the redeemer will be properly greeted and escorted to the Rebbe."

The traveller is moved by the simple faith and trust of the Rebbe and the watchman. He wants to help. He again renews his offer. "Let me take you to a warm inn. No one will come anymore tonight. It is too late and too cold. Let me buy you a hot drink and good lodging. In the morning you can resume your great task!"

"No," says the watchman. "The Rebbe pays me to be here at all hours. No matter when Messiah comes, I must be here to perform this essential task."

"My God," exclaims the traveller. "What incredible devotion to a task! The Rebbe must surely pay you a magnificent salary that you show such steadfastness to your work of bringing the Messiah to town."

"To tell you the truth," says the watchman, "the pay is lousy. But I like this work very much anyway because this is a good, steady job!"

1

Background and Career

Shalom Freedman (Q). Rabbi, I wanted to ask you some questions about your background and your parents' influence. Would you explain the kind of education you had?

Rabbi Irving Greenberg. Mine was a classic modern Orthodox experience. My parents were immigrants. Our Americanization pattern unfolded differently than other immigrants' children's experience mainly because there was more learning and piety in our home than in the average Jewish home, more than in even the typical Orthodox home. The learning was supplied by my father, who was a *talmid chacham* of awesome proportions (in the *misnagid* tradition). He taught Talmud daily in an immigrant congregation. The practice of the *chevra shas* (a friendship group that studied *shas*, e.g., Talmud, regularly) was itself a carryover from Europe. My mother was an unusually pious person. Many women who were observant like her were not as religiously and emotionally God-related as she was. To these influences I credit the fact that I did not follow the dominant path in the American-born generation, i.e., assimilation and rejection of observance. My parents sent me to a modern Orthodox day school (Yeshiva Etz Chaim in Boro Park) and then to an equivalent Orthodox high school (Yeshiva University High School in Brooklyn). Thus, my educational experience was in the upper range of modern Orthodox education in America. Under my brother Aharon's influence, I also joined Hashomer Hadati (later renamed Bnai Akiva); this religious Zionist movement provided me with an inspiring and nurturing youth cohort. Although I was a bit rebellious in high school (I felt that the administration was too bureaucratic and insufficiently caring), I do not recall any great dissatisfaction with my education.

Nevertheless, there were lots of flaws in that education; the weaknesses later showed up in modern Orthodoxy. A low percentage of my elementary-school classmates stayed Orthodox. The high school was particularly weak in that it never came to grips with the fact that it was offering general education as well as yeshiva learning. A lot of students were not interested in or could not follow the Gemara—yet Talmud constituted ninety percent of the yeshiva study. Many dropped out; perhaps most just sat around "bottling"—doing nothing (from the Hebrew word *batel*, unemployed). The religious atmosphere in the school was not bad, but when you went out in the street, the general environment was very magnetic. American culture was eons away from the school's religious concerns. Inside the school, the encounter with modern culture was all too shallow. In later years, I realized that the challenges were not understood in depth, so the "answers" given were superficial. When students grew up and experienced the general culture, undiluted and strong, many lost their faith or dismissed the yeshiva's answers as trivial. In later decades, the resurgence of the right-wing Orthodox posed new questions. Again, the surface answers of modern Orthodoxy often crumbled under the pressure. This was sad because, in many cases, at the depth level, modern Orthodoxy was and is right. But the education rarely hit that level.

Most debilitating was the shortage of human personal relationships and ethical models. There was widespread cheating on exams, but the religious leadership never challenged the behavior; nor did it offer alternative ethical guidelines. The administration was not very responsive; indeed, it was not even respectful of the students. The students were deeply attracted to Jewish activism. The administrators were *nudniks* rather than cooperative in the matter. Instead of seeing activism as a positive opportunity to confirm religious teachings, they ignored or harassed the students if they cut school or class to engage in demonstrations.

Most of the Talmud teachers were European. The main *rosh yeshiva* spoke Yiddish only. There was a vast cultural gap between him and the students; language was the tip of that iceberg. Sadly, when I came to teach at Yeshiva University, many years later, the same problem of Yiddish-speaking teachers existed. Fortunately for me, Yiddish was spoken in my home in my childhood, but a lot of the students then and later did not understand Yiddish at all. This compounded the difficulties of studying Talmud, and many students were turned off. Since Talmud took up four to five curricular hours a day, in essence, such students wasted their lives in the yeshiva. I was also fortunate in that Hashomer Hadati had a very strong youth cohort; the members were excited emotionally about Israel, which left a permanent positive effect on me.

The next major upgrading of my Jewish education was the result of a lucky break. When I graduated from high school, I planned to attend Yeshiva University. Through my father's connections, I was introduced to a *musar* yeshiva in Boro Park called Bais Yosef (Novaredok). Attracted by this refugee yeshiva with strong religious spirit and emphasis on *musar* (ethics and character building), I decided to study there. Thanks to its remarkable people (half were survivors of the camps, and a third were survivors of Siberia) and its strong *musar* component, Bais Yosef gave me a dynamic and very different, more moving religious experience than I would have received at Yeshiva University. Compared to Y.U., the religious educational experience was much less filtered by modernity, and my college experience (at Brooklyn College) was much less filtered by Orthodoxy. To the strong but independent pull of both educations, I credit my tendency to this day to go for dialectical approaches to religious questions rather than to reach resolved positions.

The main religious–educational influence on my life was my father. His impact is described in some detail in my book *The Jewish Way*. My mother also influenced me, but not so much intellectually. My father was a classic *misnagid*. The way he expressed himself, the way he expressed love to his children, was through learning. We learned together quite frequently. The association of learning and family-love was a very positive influence. Also, he rebelled against injustice and was a fierce fighter for the underdog.

Q. I also suspect that the importance of consideration and understanding the other person's point of view was something you learned at home.

Greenberg. Definitely. When I look back, certain amazing little experiences stand out. There was one Conservative congregation in Boro Park—Temple Emanuel. David Koussevitsky was *chazzan* there. Many times, on the way back from Beth El (my father's *shul*), my father would take me in to hear Koussevitsky. I do not think there were many other Orthodox rabbis from Boro Park who would have gone into that *shul.* Boro Park was not marked by the extreme *haredi* atmosphere that governs there now; still, going into a Conservative congregation was not standard operating procedure. By such simple, almost elementary gestures (not only taking me inside to hear the *chazzan*, but also showing respect for the service), he taught me an instinctive pluralism.

My father was critical of the religious anti-Zionist position. No matter how great a *haredi lamdan* may have been as a scholar, my father would brook no attack on Israel. He would go to the local Agudas Israel synagogue and sit in on learned discourses by such scholars. As a *talmid chacham*, he valued their learning. But he would rise and challenge them when they would criticize Zionism; this was something no one else dared to do. He had a sense of humor; sometimes, he would tell me with a twinkle in his eye that he would challenge their *chiddushim* (in the yeshiva style of the old days) in order to take their learning down a peg or two, and thus weaken their anti-Zionist influence. His model of "you shall show no fear of any man" (Deuteronomy 1:17) was a very strong personal influence.

Q. What made you decide to study history?

Greenberg. I always had a tremendous love of reading and learning, and a great intellectual curiosity. Somehow, history became the focus of these feelings because it covered so wide a range, especially intellectual history, which touched on literature, ideas, arts, economics, and so on. This specialty gave me a way of including all my interests in the course of study. Then, too, I attended Brooklyn College. My sister Lillian, who had been a history major, called my attention to the extraordinarily rich offerings of the history department.

One professor, Jesse D. Clarkson, had a tremendous effect on me. Clarkson's brilliant exposition of the impact of reality on ideas (and the frequent contradiction of ideas and reality) shaped my thinking. He would go out of his way to point out the contrast between how theory would portray reality and what the actuality was. In the 1930s, Clarkson had been a radical Marxist. By 1950, when I came to know him, he had already gone through the disillusionment process. He used Marxist insights to expose the socioeconomic infrastructure shaping ideas, but he also cut through Marxist categories and showed how they often obscured or distorted the reality. He showed us the devastating contrast between theory and reality under communism. He was years ahead of his time with regard to Marxism.

Clarkson taught "European History Since 1914" and Russian history. He sensitized me to the insight that it is not sufficient that ideas be credible or of logical construction; they have to enable people to cope with reality. He also showed exhaustively how good intentions can lead to evil. These teachings were very influential on my thinking. They also shaped my life's work. I have striven to articulate and teach ideas that help us build a better world, but, following Clarkson's warning, I have sought to develop and apply these ideas in ways that upgrade the real world. Clarkson showed how ideas—even good ones—can shield people from reality and serve as justification for cruelty and systematic evil. He showed a remarkable grasp of totalitarianism and its importance in the twentieth-century—and how it was embedded in the conditions of modern life. In a way, he planted the seeds of pluralism in me by showing how deadly good ideals can become when they are unchecked and totally in command of society or community. Those insights and teachings helped confirm my feeling that history was the right major for me.

At that time, I was planning a secular career because I did not want to make religion my profession. There is a tradition of not making the Torah into a source of livelihood. Furthermore, I was influenced by my father's struggle. Life was hard, although he never complained about money. I did not think that we were poor, although my parents lived very spartanly. They put their children through higher education—including graduate school at Harvard—without our having to take out loans. By living an extremely simple life, they could afford to do it.

My father always had this fantasy: that had he learned English, he could have become the American rabbi upstairs and "succeeded" in America. The rabbi upstairs in Temple Beth El spoke English and was well paid; my father taught the *chevra shas* [Talmud study group] downstairs in the Bais Medrash and was paid pennies. So he always pushed me to become an "American rabbi" and thus "succeed." I reacted against this push because, by implication, it put my father down as a "failure." So I resisted the idea of being an American rabbi for a long time. I imagined that I was going to get ordination simply to please my parents, especially my father, but I would not practice the rabbinate. I would get the learning done—that was expected anyway—and get the *smicha.* Then I would work in academia in a secular profession.

The professional model of college Jewish studies never crossed my mind. Of course, this was in the early 1950s, when Jewish studies hardly existed on university campuses. I studied general history (but not Jewish history), both at Brooklyn College and at Harvard. Looking back, I can observe that my university career was lived at the fault line—right at the chronological seam—when Jews changed over from the self-denial and anonymity of the '50s to the ethnic self-expression of the '60s. I walked this way toward self-assertion personally. I started with a major in general, i.e., "universal," history. Then I went to Harvard because I wanted to attend *the* American school, the acme of the American experience. Then, right there, I had a surprisingly strong religious reaction. When I arrived in Harvard Yard, I was not a little awed by the statue of John Harvard, 1935, and all that; still, my immune system kicked in.

Q. Was there a *minyan* at Harvard in those days?

Greenberg. There was a *minyan* at Hillel, but everything Jewish was marginal. The classic example: when I arrived, no one told me, but I just knew that you could not wear a *kippah.* It bothered me a lot because I was Orthodox; I did not want to walk around bareheaded. So I wore a hat and took it off when I went into class. As soon as I came out of class, I would put the hat on again. It was awkward, it was uncomfortable, but what could you do? I would go to faculty–student receptions and hold a drink in my hand all the time because I would not drink it without covering my head and making a *bracha.* I remember my first encounter with Oscar Handlin. He was the pride and joy of the Brooklyn College history department because he had made it to Harvard. He was the great man. At the first reception I went up to him and said that I was from Brooklyn College and that Professor Madeline Robinton of Brooklyn College (my advisor) had insisted that I look him up. It was like a vision of death for him.

Q. He didn't want to be reminded?

Greenberg. He gave me a brusque, almost brutal response. I must have caught him at a bad time. To be fair to him, he later came out of the closet and became more avowedly or visibly Jewish. (Needless to say, he was always hopelessly Jewish—in accent, dress, bearing, image.) It bothered me the whole time that I could not be myself. Only after two years or more did I finally say to myself: "Look, I have a right to do it"; then I put the *kippah* on. That was in about 1955. I met my wife, Blu, in the middle of 1955. We went out, and I wore a *kippah* in the theater. Many years later, after we were married, Blu told me that the *kippah* had bothered her; she had felt that I should not breach public etiquette. Most of the Orthodox fellows just did not wear a *kippah* in public.

That coming-out was a key transition for me. By then, I was looking to emotionally connect with and serve Jews. I never thought of going into Jewish studies, even though I met the distinguished scholar Harry Wolfson at Harvard. In his work, Wolfson demonstrated that Jewish thought—especially Philo's—had shaped the Church Fathers' thinking, and through them, philosophy. Despite the significance of Wolfson's work, the area of Jewish studies was not recognized at that time as a distinctive academic field. Wolfson himself was a former Eastern European *yeshiva bochur* who lived and acted like a Marrano in many ways. He was confused as to his Jewishness, unable to represent and articulate Judaism—yet clearly he was being seen and judged as a Jew. Yet I was searching for Jewish identity expression; I still wanted to do something Jewishly. Instead of studying Jewish, I became involved with the Young Israel of Brookline as their rabbi for two years.

When I chose my Ph.D thesis, I picked a *hoch* American topic, and worked with a *hoch* American professor. My topic was Theodore Roosevelt and Labor, it focused on the progressive critique of laissez-faire. The topic had religious overtones, i.e., social gospel issues. My faculty mentor was Professor Frederick Merk, who had been a primary pupil of Frederick Jackson Turner, the classical scholar and secular theologian of the American frontier. Arthur Schlesinger, Jr., would have been a natural as my thesis mentor but in doing my M.A. work, I found him to be both domineering and partisan. He did not handle evidence objectively, and did not give the students enough leeway to follow their own insights. Of course, every historian does this to some extent, but he did it heavy-handedly. So I sought out Merk. Merk was a self-restrained thesis mentor; he was deeply interested in his students, but he allowed them to find their own orientation. (That, by the way, is my image of how God teaches—self-restrained, allowing humans to choose.)

At the last minute, I had a chance to stay on at Harvard. Merk suggested that I do some research; he believed that he could get me a fellowship. But then, just before the summer of 1959, I heard that there was a new dean at Yeshiva College. In the back of my mind I had this fantasy about Yeshiva University. Ever since Bais Yosef had planted its ideas of being a missionary for Jewish education, I had thought that Yeshiva University would be an appropriate place for such work. Y.U. represented the religious and secular brought together. Of course, I had mixed feelings about Y.U. The fact was that I had opted not to go there for my college studies—partly because Bais Yosef was a greater magnet Jewishly, partly because Brooklyn College seemed to be a better college. Still, I heard that the new dean intended to shake up and upgrade Y.U. He was looking for new faculty who would offer personal religious models. In the summer I called him up. He offered me a job, and I accepted it on the spot. In retrospect, I realize that that constituted opting for a career in which Jewish expression would be central. I would teach American history, but since I would be at Yeshiva University, I thought that I would get a chance to express my religious interests as well.

In a way, by going to Y.U., I was going against the grain of my own thinking. Theologically speaking, I already had this idea of secularization, i.e., that my life would express religious values, masked by a secular career setting. By choosing Y.U., I shifted to a more overtly religious setting. Clearly, the choice reflected unmet needs to work with and realize my Jewish religious urges. On the other hand, ostensibly I came to teach American history and general history. Incidentally, the college focused on the sciences and on premedical training. The history department was very small, but it grew; the courses we offered (such as "A History of Civilization" and "Intellectual History of Modern Culture") gave me a chance to have some religious influence on students.

Then, in 1960, a group of Orthodox college students started a project at Columbia University to serve their intellectual and religious needs. They were struggling with the challenges to faith as well as such practical questions as getting kosher food, and so on. As they developed their program, they heard from other Orthodox students around the country who needed help. They convened a weekend to explore whether there might be room for a national organization for Orthodox students facing the challenge of college. College and the intellectual challenge of modernity has been one of my areas of interest from the beginning. The interaction of modernity and Judaism has been seminal for the past two centuries, and it was the key to the Jewish future. Somehow these students invited me to speak at that *shabbaton.* I gave a very strong talk to rally the troops. They decided to found an organization, named, at my suggestion, Yavneh. After the destruction of the Temple, Rabbi Yochanan ben Zakkai had transformed Judaism intellectually and institutionally—preserving and renewing at the same time. It seemed to me that, after the destruction inflicted by the Holocaust, Jewry needed another Yavneh to renew Jewish life and religion as one. I became deeply involved with the new organization, serving as its key adult advisor. In retrospect, I realize that Yavneh gave me the outlet to express Jewish interests that Yeshiva University did not. Y.U. continued to prefer that I teach American and general history. As far as the administration was concerned, my Jewish interests were my private business. Y.U. was a different world.

In 1961 to 1962, I received a Fulbright fellowship to teach American history at Tel Aviv University. That teaching took up parts of two days a week. Suddenly, I was seized with a reading frenzy. During the year, I spent the bulk of my time studying about the Holocaust. When I came back, I decided that I was going to do more Jewishly. The first step was a determination to teach a course on the Holocaust. The Dean strongly resisted this new course, fearing that it was not academic enough. After a two-year fight, I won the right to teach about the Holocaust (although I had to promise to teach the course under a different title: "Totalitarianism and Ideology in the 20th Century"). It was sad and funny at the same time that at Yeshiva University, no less, there was such resistance to teaching about the Holocaust.

Then, in 1965, the Riverdale Jewish Center congregation asked me to fill in for a short time while they waited for an incoming rabbi to take up the position. But then this rabbi decided to withdraw, and they asked me to stay on. Without planning a switch in a career path, I took on the job as a temporary arrangement, but ultimately stayed with the congregation for seven years. Again, I had gone against the very grain of my thinking. In fact, I ended up being the one thing that I had said I would never be: the rabbi of a congregation.

In the 1950s, studying at Bais Yosef, I was fascinated by the model of Rabbi Israel Salanter. He had planned to "pass" as an accountant and live a hidden religious life rather than serve as a rabbi. Then he concluded that a crisis—the encounter with modernity—was looming, and that he had no right to sit it out and live a fulfilled personal religious life while Jewry disintegrated under the impact of assimilating forces. He determined to face the challenge of modernity, and therefore took up the role of rabbi and educator in the Jewish community. In a way, I modeled myself on that paradigm. When I graduated from Bais Yosef I decided to face modernity, in part by pursuing a secular career. In academia, I would beard the lion in his den, i.e., face modernity in its pure form. This was a personal solution. But just as Salanter came out of the closet to deal with the central crises of Judaism, i.e., modernity, so I was feeling that I must confront the issue more directly. As Y.U. resisted this change in my teaching direction, I found that the *shul* was providing an important new outlet for me.

The push for a course on the Holocaust was my turning point. Had Y.U. let me do more and more Jewishly, I probably would not have gone to the *shul* at all. Ironically, when I became Rabbi at RJC, the balance of power with Y.U. shifted. They began to let me teach more Jewish subjects because they feared that I would pull out of Y.U. altogether if they did not become more forthcoming. There was a leading layman at Y.U. named Ludwig Jesselson who belonged to RJC and became enamored of my views. They feared that Jesselson would be shocked if I left Y.U., so they began to allow me to teach straight Jewish courses in the history department. By then, however, I could teach college only part-time owing to the demands of the rabbinate. So I found that my career path was going "backward." Moving from the secular to Y.U. and now to the overtly religious setting—it seemed to me to be going backward.

Q. Backward and forward at the same time.

Greenberg. My own thinking, then and now, suggests that we need forms of religiosity that are less formal, less institutional, less separated from the general culture. I would have been interested in exploring how to be Jewish in a secular setting, but I never had the chance to act out that impulse.

Q. You told me that soon after came CLAL. But I think I didn't understand what you meant. You wanted very much to set up a retreat center, and that is the thing you did not accomplish that most disturbs you, correct?

Greenberg. The Riverdale Jewish Center allowed me to apply my religious thinking to building community and to create a day school with a positive synthesis of general culture and Jewish tradition. But the deeper issues of modernity, post-Holocaust existence, and so on were so complex and so multifaceted that I felt that a *shul* could not be an adequate vehicle for tackling them. So when the opportunity arose, I went to City College to found a

Department of Jewish Studies. There we started CLAL, which at its inception was called the National Jewish Conference Center. We had every intention of setting up a retreat center as the primary vehicle for our work, but we had trouble fundraising. Since a conference center seemed to be beyond our means, and since we were still trying out what types of programs might work best, it seemed prudent to put the retreat center on hold and to focus on developing various programs. However, I did not dream then that I was actually determining the fate of the project. In my mind, I was not giving up the idea of a retreat center; I was only postponing it. But once you make a decision like that, it is almost a final decision.

First, I was consumed with the struggle of establishing CLAL (then NJCC). That was a real struggle. Over the years, we developed various forms of outreach teaching without a site, but with limited resources we were unable to create an actual retreat center. In 1979, after years of trying to do both NJCC and City College, I had to make a choice. I realized that I had to make a total commitment to NJCC (by then called National Jewish Resource Center, NJRC) if it was to survive. So I gave up the professorship, tenure, everything to focus on building CLAL. About three months after I gave up the tenure, we went through a crisis that almost killed NJRC. I swore to myself that I would never get myself into such a situation again. It took three years to rebuild. To survive, we cut NJRC to the bone; it became almost, but not quite, a one-man operation. This was back in the early 1980s. Then NJRC grew and became CLAL—The National Jewish Center for Learning and Leadership. By 1986, we felt that we had grown enough to try to establish a conference center. Many of the lay people were nervous about the idea. Some of the key leaders were strongly against it. But I pushed very hard and did some fundraising. We raised $2 million dollars in pledges, which was the condition for gong ahead. Then we hired a full-time person to bring the object into being.

Within a year after we took on this conference center we faced several problems. CLAL had grown nonstop for five years. A cash flow crisis occurred and major cuts had to be made in the organization. We had to give up the plan for the conference center. We had to sell the site we had purchased. We had failed to create a retreat center. Moreover, CLAL's lay leadership was twice burned and gun-shy. To compound the resistance, over the last five years the community has become more skeptical of such ideas. The net result is that there is a real possibility that one of the central institutional goals of my life may never be reached.

This situation is very frustrating personally. From the beginning, CLAL's mission was suffused with the idea that Jewry was involved in an historic change. Starting in the 1980s we talked in terms of a "third era" in Jewish history. The new era would demand that we revamp old institutions and create new ones. Personally, I identified two new institutions that were paradigms for the "third era." One was the Holocaust Memorial Center. By the 1970s, I was convinced that Yad Vashem should not be the only primary Holocaust Memorial Center; rather, there should be such institutions in all major Jewish communities. Only such a new, dedicated "sacred space" (whose holiness was hidden behind its secular form) could do justice to the impact and transmit the memory of the Holocaust. The space would communicate memory, but also the need for new Jewish responses such as taking power, renewing life, and so forth. For years, one of the key divisions of CLAL was "*Zachor*: Holocaust Resource Center." *Zachor* combined Holocaust education with theological exploration—and with teaching the idea of the need for Holocaust memorial centers. CLAL's other division we later named *Shamor*; it was focused on learning for leadership. Out of *Shamor*, we hoped to persuade the Jewish community of the need to create retreat centers everywhere for learning and religious experiences.

As it turned out, in 1974, a young Atlanta lawyer was deeply affected by CLAL and its programs. The man, Stuart Eizenstat, had made a connection with Jimmy Carter, and ended up being one of his key operatives. When Carter was elected president, Eizenstat became Chief Domestic Affairs advisor. He was instrumental in the establishment of the President's Commission on the Holocaust, which led to the creation of the United States Holocaust Memorial Council. Over the course of fifteen years, the United States Holocaust Memorial Museum was established. The leaders of U.S.H.M.M. raised $150 million to create a brilliant, overpowering Holocaust Memorial Center. (Other communities that CLAL worked with also created a number of Holocaust memorial centers.) Now, there are two megacenters (in Los Angeles and Washington) and one more emerging major museum in New York. There are also five full-sized substantial memorial centers in Canada and the United States. There are probably twenty such centers of a more modest type. Thus, the model of a new "third era" institution has been definitively established.

Unfortunately, however, the other major new institution that I believe is central to the new era, the retreat center, has gotten nowhere. This is crazy. Given a choice at the beginning, I would have chosen to create the retreat center. Life comes ahead of death in Judaism; creativity is given priority over mourning. Due to an historical fluke—and my limited fundraising capacity—only one needed institution has been successfully established. The U.S. Holocaust Memorial Museum's creators tapped into the mechanisms of fundraising and recognition and successfully pulled it off. But the other equally (or more) needed institution is as yet unaccomplished.

Mind you, I become angry when people attack the Holocaust Memorial Museum as if this building represents death, not life. Properly understood, the Holocaust stimulates us to respond with more life. And I reject as just plain erroneous the claim that fundraising for Holocaust memorials takes away more from Jewish education and other priority areas of Jewish life. We need both types of institutions, as well as many others. However, I am tormented by the fact that the Holocaust memorials have been established—some with better taste and judgment than others—and the retreat center has not been. I remain convinced that one should not pit the retreat center (or Jewish education in general) against the Holocaust Memorial Museum; but the imbalance bothers me deeply.

If Jews are going to survive—and I believe that they are going to survive—there will be a Holocaust memorial center, and a retreat center, in every major Jewish community. Still, I must confess that it is far from certain that the retreat center will be created. Over the course of brooding and sorting out my life during a year's sabbatical in Israel from 1992 to 1993, I determined that I shall again push for the creation of a retreat center. We shall see what will happen.

One lesson that I have learned from these contrasting experiences is not to overrate the impact of my own ideas. History, events, and communities use people. In the case of the Holocaust Memorial Museum, people were ready for it, so my ideas were used effectively to generate and sell the project. In the case of the retreat center—more Jewish, less sellable through the prestige of the presidency, less able to meet the need to impress gentiles, and so on—the community was not ready yet to support it adequately. Ideas often lose out to reality; that is one of the insights that Jesse Clarkson taught me!

Q. Tolstoy's idea is that the closer you are to moving history, the greater the tool of history you are.

Greenberg. This is true. I believe that it is the mission of the Jewish people to be a force in history. But often they are used by others for their own purpose—good and bad. Still, I do not blame all my setbacks on the recalcitrance of history. Part of the fault lives in my own failures of judgment. One example: I was so convinced that the Holocaust and Israel were turning points in Jewish history that I never imagined that the counterposition could ever become so strong. When we started CLAL, I was convinced that my position within Orthodoxy was solid, so I sought to push the envelope further (toward pluralism, egalitarianism, and so on). I never dreamed that the modern Orthodox position from which I was jumping off was going to be so weakened and even disintegrated by pressure from the *haredim.* There was a classic misjudgment on my part.

I considered the *haredi* position to be comparable to Rabbi Eliezer ben Hyrknos'. In the talmudic story, Rabbi Eliezer sought to bring a divine heavenly voice to prove his argument. Of course, he could not win, because once the context of prophecy was over, heavenly voices would not be heard—or listened to. But I was wrong. Despite my conviction that the Holocaust and rebirth of Israel threatened *haredi* credibility, the reverse happened. The *haredi* position took over much of modern Orthodoxy, leaving me isolated. If I had to do it all over again, I would have made two great efforts sooner. One would have been to push for the retreat center; the other would have been to try and build a modern

Orthodox base in a much more thorough fashion, instead of assuming that it was going to maintain itself. The collapse of modern Orthodoxy has hamstrung CLAL's work in many ways.

Q. And now you are giving more time to your writing and your creative work, and less to CLAL?

Greenberg. The purpose of a sabbatical year in 1993 was to sort out my life and what is left of it. The decision to take a year off was a result of several factors. One was my "mortality crisis." I never had a mid-life crisis. (Perhaps I prevented it by leaving the synagogue for City College and starting new directions in my life.) Nor did my fiftieth birthday bring any special angst with it. Somehow, perhaps in anticipation of my sixtieth, the classic mortality syndrome struck. It dawned upon me forcefully that I am not going to live forever; yet there are a lot of projects and goals that I have not accomplished. In 1991, I did an informal inventory and realized that I have a good twenty years' worth of organizational projects in mind and a book-to-write inventory that could also take twenty years. Yet there was no guarantee that I would have even one twenty-year quota of years left.

That set in motion a strong personal ferment, which was further compounded by the shock of the National Jewish Population Study. The NJPS results were not so surprising; when CLAL was founded, we had projected such developments. Reading the NJPS material, however, it dawned on me that I had been so preoccupied with building CLAL that I had lost sight of the big picture. I had projected a polarized Jewish community in which a rising curve of a renewing community would intersect with the downward slope of disintegration. In my mind, I imagined that the lines would criss-cross with 40 to 50 percent (or more) of the community in the camp of renewal, led by a strong religious, creative, constructive avant-garde. In retrospect, I was wrong. The disintegration came quicker than the renewal. What is more, I felt strongly self-critical because I had allowed my own personal CLAL agenda to skew my vision of what was going on in the community at large. CLAL was growing and "succeeding" so I projected that the overall community of renewal was growing well, but it was not. I felt like the surgeon who reports that the operation was successful, but, by the way, the patient has died.

Q. You mentioned that you wrote an article in 1968 in which you indicated that you understood the kind of role the campus was playing in assimilation even then.

Greenberg. That article was a projection of the future, but I did not keep my eye on the ball. The studies of college-student patterns done in the 1960s showed that college graduates were exhibiting intermarriage patterns at 40 to 50 percent of all marriages. Over 90 percent of American Jews were going to college; the number increased sharply in the 1960s. That meant that once the marrying cohort was 100 percent graduates, intermarriage would soar. Furthermore, the college experience was uncovering the utter unpreparedness of Jews for living in a truly open society. CLAL was started to help the community upgrade its educational system and inner life in order to hold the loyalty of its people. Unfortunately, the community did not respond strongly enough. CLAL's pleas that all the groups stop fighting and work together to upgrade Jewish life by learning from each other also were little-heeded. Obviously, no one person or organization can cope with such an overwhelming transformation. But I blame myself for slipping into complacency—or for being so preoccupied with CLAL's survival that I lowered my guard and failed to speak out as sharply as needed about the cultural deterioration and the community's inadequate response.

In 1992, I asked for a sabbatical to try to recover my balance and reconsider my priorities. I also wanted a chance to review CLAL and community strategies to see where the most promising upgrading could be undertaken. I also wanted to assess how I could constructively use whatever years God will still spare me. All humans are given a limited number of years. *Merubim tzarchei amcha,* says the *piyyut.* The needs of people are limitless; there is so much that needs to be done. There is no time to waste—and it would be a betrayal to use the years to do harm. So I felt a great need to plan and maximize the contribution I can make over the next few years.

That year of reading and thinking and walking the streets of Jerusalem with my wife, Blu, was very helpful. These were some of my tentative conclusions. I hope—I believe—that CLAL is strong enough to make it on its own, even without me. Therefore, to keep CLAL going in its present track for another ten years would not be the best use of my time. If I were ten years younger, I probably would not feel this way, because CLAL is an outstanding project. I love working in its programs and with its faculty and lay people. This does not mean that I must leave CLAL, but it means retiring from the presidency and concentrating my limited participation on training teachers, writing, and community consultation.

What else do I feel is urgent? The creation of a model retreat center is a central, worthy challenge. Is it worth spending the next ten years in America doing that? Good question. I cannot answer it yet. But this is Option One. Option Two is to focus on innovation in the American Jewish community. Can we get the whole community to strengthen its outreach capacity in a substantial way? Can we develop new institutions with more powerful impacts on people—young adult centers, new kinds of day schools and high schools? Can we make breakthroughs in training? Can we upgrade rabbis and professionals? Can we create a powerful presence in the media? This is Option Two.

Option Three involves Israel. I have always wanted to live in Israel and work here. Part of the shock of my mortality crisis is that I wanted to get to Israel in full vigor and not when I am physically and emotionally spent, like people who have gone to Israel to be buried there. So I wrestle with the questions: "Dare I wait any longer? How much longer?" I would like to see American Jewry create a network of study opportunities in Israel—like non-yeshiva yeshivas—for every kind of American Jew. In fact, I believe that I could help train people to set up and teach in a variety of settings. Could CLAL do some of this? In Israel? I hope so. If not, should I imitate Abraham and leave my familiar world and go to Israel? Surely, this is worth considering.

The main alternative to all these options is my writing. There is a tremendous backlog of unpublished ideas. Perhaps I should give up all organizational work and write for this generation and the next. Is this the right thing to do? Or is this a coward's way of giving up on the community in its present crisis? My instinct is that this writing scenario also points to Israel; it would be easier to sit and write uninterrupted in Israel.

Q. It takes time. You're thinking it through. I wanted to ask you, and this is a question many writers won't answer, about the book you are thinking through now. Is it an extension of *The Jewish Way*? I had the sense it might be about the whole concept of *tzelem elokim,* which is so central in your thought.

Greenberg. In a way, *The Jewish Way* is my more traditional book.

Q. I wish that I had had *The Jewish Way* in my university days. The combination of presenting the philosophical basis of the Jewish religion and combining this with the valid account of what it is to experience life, to really live as a Jew in accordance with the Jewish calendar, makes it, I think, perfect for young, questing minds.

Greenberg. [In September 1993, *The Jewish Way* appeared in a paperback edition.] The new book attempts to present a theology of Judaism through an historical analysis of the development of the covenant in Judaism. In a way, it seeks to delineate Jewish history as the forging furnace, or, if you will, the area where certain central Jewish concepts are developed and acted out; this parallels *The Jewish Way,* which sought to offer a theology of Judaism through analysis of the holidays. That the human being is in the image of God is portrayed as the foundational principle of Judaism in this new book. This is one of two books that I feel contain my central theological insights.

The third volume that I would like to write would deal with the theology and psychology of everday life. That book also would build on the basic idea of the human being in the image of God. It would depict the humanization of the person through the process of *halachah,* from birth to death. The thesis is that all *mitzvot* and religious practices are attempts to shape human beings in the image of God by developing their capacity for relationship, for understanding, for competence in the context of the value and dignity of the individual. This third book would go through the life cycle from eating, to speech, to adult relationships, to sex; it would go from childhood (circumcision) to bar and bat mitzvah, to marriage, to middle age, to old age and death. As in *The Jewish Way,* I would try to show the inseparability of observance and theology. As in *The Jewish Way,* I would seek to capture the psychological and existential concepts that undergird the *halachah,* which, after all, seeks to develop people's capacity for living.

Q. I believe that such a book would be of great help to secular Jews who do not have any real understanding of how the Jewish way can give meaning to life in the modern world.

Greenberg. I do not kid myself in thinking that all secularists would become religious—if only I could show them the goodness of Judaism. However, a book like this would be helpful to them and to observant Jews. In my judgment, the Orthodox need help to recover the worldview and power of the faith almost as much as do the secularists.

This talk about books that I would like to write dramatizes the painful choices that I face. Each of these two books could easily take years to write. But there are other books in my brain calling for my attention. The topic of religious unity and pluralism has gone off the agenda of the Jewish community for the past few years. Yet, it is as urgent as ever. I would like to write much more about the religious divisions and what can be done about them. Then I would like to write more about the *halachah* and its role. In my view, the *halachah* is the Jewish method of *tikkun olam;* it is not just a legal system or a set of commandments. Then, too, some years ago I translated into English the writings of Rabbi Israel Salanter, one of the most seminal and least understood figures of nineteenth-century Orthodoxy. I would like to publish those works with a biography in stories modeled on Buber's *Tales of the Hasidim.* This is a writing program for ten years, full-time—assuming that I can continue to think and write at full throttle—but I am not getting any younger. CLAL and other community needs bring tremendous demands with them. At this point, I am very torn. I do not know what is the best way.

One consideration that I wrestle with is the question of how many lives are changed by writing. Let me confess that one of the reasons I wrote *The Jewish Way* is that Blu's experience with her writing instructed me. As I traveled the country, I was amazed by the number of people who came up to me and said, "My life was changed by your wife's book." I would come home and give her these reports each time. The more it happened, the more I said to myself that I had completely misjudged the capacity of writing to reach people. Through speaking, you can reach only a limited number of people, particularly if you are not a celebrity—and I am not. By contrast, books reach a much wider number of people. The more I listened to those people, the more I felt that I had to make an effort. For two or three years I made that effort; it consumed almost all my time, outside of my administrative and teaching obligations at CLAL. While I was happy to finish *The Jewish Way* and was somewhat pleased with the result, I was frustrated by the fact that it had a limited impact. The book fell somewhere in between the straight scholarly and the popular. Owing to the philosophical elements, it did not reach a truly wide audience; yet it proved difficult to get reviews—or even to be taken seriously—in academic journals.

Now I wonder whether giving up organizational work and turning to writing full-time would constitute running away from history. Working for CLAL or starting up other organizations (as well as writing columns of commentary on current policy) makes me feel that I am fighting for Jewish survival now. I fear that my books are a bit ahead of their time, and that it will take years for them to have any effect. So if I turn to writing, am I abandoning the current fray and hoping that future generations will bail me out? If I do turn to writing, will I just be fooling myself? Will I be appealing to an unborn generation because I have failed with the existing one? Or is writing for the next generation the true covenantal move? Does it represent my recognition that I could not finish the work, but that one who believes in the *brit* must trust the future generations and give them strength and nurturing to take up the cause effectively?

If I had my druthers, I would like to do both writing and organizational work. But I do not know whether I can do justice to both. I feel very strongly that I would like a chance to train additional people. The cause and views I represent should not depend on my own personal accomplishments or on any one person's writing, for that matter. Let others join in; let there be a school or a cadre of workers, and the accomplishment will be far greater. The good news is that there is an emerging consensus in

CLAL to step up the training aspect of the organization, even to turn it into the nucleus of a movement.

Q. The whole question of how a book influences is difficult. I was just reading a survey of Israeli writers who are almost unanimous in claiming that their political writings have no influence. On the other hand, ideas do change the world.

Greenberg. We need new ideas as well as new institutions to deal with the ongoing crisis of Judaism and modernity. The realm of ideas is the area to which I feel I can contribute the most in the long run, but as to whether ideas or institutions would be the way to help the most—I just do not know. Looking back, I regret that creating CLAL has taken the lion's share of the past twenty years of my life. I do not have hard feelings, but I feel a sense of annoyance. CLAL should have been created many years before, and not by me. If it had already existed, I would have gone to work for it. This would have saved me ten years of my life. I am not sorry that I did it; I just wish it had gone easier or that others could have done more of the work.

Look at the United States Holocaust Memorial Museum. I spent a year on that project through the President's Commission on the Holocaust. I was offered the chance to stay on as Director of the United States Holocaust Memorial Council, but I declined because I felt that CLAL needed me. Thus, others created the museum. Still, it contains 90 percent of what I would have wanted to accomplish if I had served there. Ideally, CLAL should have taken a year or two or three, maybe more, but not seventeen years more. Looking back, two decades was too much of a commitment; this was not the most efficient use of my life. I would have done better if we had found somebody to do the administrative work and the fundraising—on a better scale than I have done. Then I would have been able to teach more.

Q. We had spoken earlier of this crisis of Diaspora Jewry. Since your return to America have you seen any sign of the community reacting to the statistics of the latest population studies? Has there been greater support for your own idea of setting up retreat centers for Jewish life and study?

Greenberg. CLAL is doing better. Part of "doing better" is that its ideas, which had been creeping into acceptance, are suddenly more credible than ever because of the "shake-up." The immediate benefit in terms of CLAL's work is that there is greater understanding and support. American Jewry is beginning to repent of its past assimilationist behavior. But is there a total transformation of the American Jewish community yet? No. Are there any breakthroughs? It is too early to say. I am hopeful for some breakthroughs. The community is in ferment.

Let me give an example. CLAL has a contract to offer a multiyear, wide-ranging education program jointly to the rabbinic, lay, and professional leadership of one community with the goal of restructuring the institutions and their relationships to enable fundamental change. This is what I mean by transforming the community. It is not enough that the *shul* become more Jewish; the Jewish community centers, the Federation, the family service agencies, and so on, must also become more Jewish. This experiment will be a wonderful model—but we are talking about only one community, one scholar. There should be tens of scholars in every community. In all of CLAL we have eleven full-time scholars and fellows (plus fourteen part-time associates). This represents growth, but there should be eleven such scholars in every community—not just in the whole nation. This is a measure of how far we are from a total communal transformation. So your question really means: Is the glass one-third full, or two-thirds empty? The outcome will determine that. The change in American Jewry can be compared to a deathbed repentance, but it is not total by any means.

Q. Repentance? On the part of whom?

Greenberg. The community is waking up. It has been waking up for thirty years now. There is more of a sense of urgency now, and there is more talk about the need for total change. Is this enough to stem the assimilationist tide? Twenty years ago, I was more optimistic because there was a gradual positive change under way. However, the change has been so slow. As a result, the erosion has been much greater than I expected. Will there be true repentance? Will Reform overcome its instinctive universalism and commitment to public schools enough to create a system of day schools for its rank and file? Will unaffiliated Jews plunge into deeply meaningful Jewish experiences? Will Federations reconstitute themselves into true communities and incorporate Jewish learning into all that they do? Stay tuned. As of this moment, the answer is "Not yet."

Q. Do you believe that the connection to Israel can be the saving grace for American Jewish life?

Greenberg. Israel is a great resource for American Jews. Love for Israel brings Jews together. The Holy Land is a place for intensive Jewish study and religious experience. When Israel performs well, it is a magnet for American Jewish identity. When American Jewry develops a total program of renewal that will successfully stem the erosion, Israel will play an important role educationally and spiritually. Israel's model will be highly influential. But is a good image for Israel enough to change the spread of assimilation in the United States? Even if Israel were a one-hundred-percent positive model, that would not be enough to shift the tide in America. People cannot live totally vicariously.

This is not to deny Israel is a major focus of Jewish identity. The talk for the past fifteen years of erosion in American Jewish feelings is an exaggeration, in my judgment. Most of the "erosion" was on the surface. Deep down, there is still a very strong base of support for Israel. Israel remains one of several religious-cultural factors that must be upgraded in the battle for Jewish renewal. I would like to see Israel become a greater resource for American Jewry. Most, if not all, American Jews should study and spend time in Israel. Obviously, we will have to set up programs to enable this to happen. Such new programs are necessary and possible, but it is going to take an all-out effort and major money to accomplish what is needed.

Q. Do you feel that the American Jewish community is reducing its support for Jewish causes?

Greenberg. There are ups and downs from year to year. The long-term philanthropic trend is still inching upward. At some point, if you lose enough of the second and third generations of wealthy families, this will translate into an absolute decline in fundraising. But this has not happened yet.

In the last twenty years, American Jewry's wealth has grown by a factor of zeros. People who were worth $10 million in the 1960s are worth over $100 million in the 1980s and 1990s. There has been some economic setback in the last five years, but in the overall picture, there has been a huge jump in Jewish wealth. Some of the UJA campaign's loss in givers was offset by achieving greater access to this massive new money. Most of the campaign's growth in recent years has come from the expansion of large gifts. At some point, that curve of giving level, which is going up, will meet the down curve, which is the loss of givers in these superrich families to assimilation and intermarriage. Remember that the Jewish superwealthy are able to go into any social, cultural setting they want to. America is open to them. If we do not upgrade their Jewish loyalty and identity soon, the amount of American Jewish giving will start to decline.

Q. I think there are figures showing that the American Jewish community, despite its being the most generous in America, still gives a very small percentage of its income to Jewish—or, for that matter, general—communal causes.

Greenberg. In general, Jews give more proportionately than any other group—except maybe for Mormons. The capacity to give is there. In the long run, however, the will to give Jewishly has to be there also. One of the ironies: Jews become more assimilated, then the Jewish tradition of *tzedakah* is less of a motivating factor to give. Of course, when people have megamillions, they can give generously, but what they give may shrink in comparison to what their resources are.

In the past five years, there has been remarkable growth of family foundations. A number of them are giving significant priority to Jewish concerns. Take the Wexner Foundation, which focuses on lay and professional leadership, or the Mandel Foundation, which concentrates on Jewish education, especially personnel, or Michael Steinhardt's *CHAver'm kol yisrael*/Jewish Life Network, which deals with populations at risk and with needed new institutions. This is a very promising development. It will take multibillions to upgrade Jewish education in America. Furthermore, high tuition discourages a lot of people from sending children to day school, so underwriting costs could help expand the system tremendously. Yet initial research shows that the megagivers are not convinced that this unprecedented upgrading of the internal Jewish life can and must be done—let alone that they are ready to cooperate fully, pool resources, and underwrite such global needs. It will take a lot of further upgrading of public opinion and understanding to accomplish such a massive change in philanthropic priority.

Here is my summary of where we stand. Both in America and in Israel, the Jewish people is better off—economically and politically—than it has ever been in its history. With all the drawbacks and problems, the deeper truth is that Jews have not enjoyed this level of freedom and the benefits of power probably for two thousand years—maybe never before. From this truth flow two questions: Was the Torah meant to be meaningful only when we were persecuted? Is Judaism the religion of only a poor and struggling people? If this were true, then we are doomed to lose the loyalty of most Jews who are overwhelmingly concentrated in lands of freedom and zones of affluence. Rabbi Akiva Eiger, one of the halachic greats of nineteenth-century Germany, petitioned Napoleon not to emancipate the Jews for fear that equal rights would set in motion a social process that would lead to apostasy and disintegration of the religion. His insight into potential consequences may have been right, and perhaps a significant fraction of Jewry then might have agreed with him. But Napoleon (and, for that matter, the processes of modernization) were not deterred by such objections. Now the Jewish people has tasted the fruit of modernity and found it "pleasing to the sight and good for the eating." The vast majority of Jews will not agree voluntarily to return to poverty or to pariah status in order to avoid the "temptation" of acceptance and assimilation.

In principle, I object to the claim that Judaism can be convincing only when it is guarded by the protective tariff of gentile hostility and cultural inferiority. The concept is not very flattering to the quality of Torah. The alternative explanation of the erosion of loyalty to *yiddishkeit* is that we are the ones who are incompetent. Perhaps the Jewish people became so competent at playing the game of living in an environment of persecution and hatred that it does not know how to play the game in freedom and power. We all have had similar personal experiences; one is so good at a certain game that one wants to play it that way—even when it is inappropriate. When our son was a little boy, he would tell a joke and we would laugh. So he would want to tell it again. Everybody is that way. However, we are currently being wiped out in this cultural game because we are not supposed to play the same way as in the past two thousand years.

I believe that it is God's will and the eternal goal of the Torah that we learn how to play the religious game as a free and powerful people. We should welcome this stage of our convenantal road. If you were given a choice to appear in an epic play—there is one act in which people get abused and undergo great suffering, in the other act, characters enjoy freedom, affluence, and choice—in which act would you rather appear? The sad truth is that too many of our spiritual-cultural and communal leaders would rather go on playing the survival game under conditions of hatred and marginal existence. That is the power of conditioning. They are surprised when the masses do not listen to their messages. I believe that we can shake off the conditioning of two thousand years and learn to play by the rules of freedom and power.

Q. You've spoken about the Jews in this regard as possible avant-garde of humankind, in their being successful in the modern world. Most people would, at least in socioeconomic terms, like to be where the Jews are now. I wonder, however, about our paradigmatic role when I see so much suffering, chaos, and disorder in the world in places where Jews do not have a major role. In Somalia. In Yugoslavia. In fact, in all of Africa.

Greenberg. This is a fair question. Jews are 80 to 90 percent concentrated in lands of freedom and classes of affluence, whereas a majority of humanity still lives in poverty. That makes us a little less central as an avant-garde than I would like to be. Yet, even in this situation, there is much that Jews can do. Israel, as a nation, was able to organize help and supplies for Somalia and

Rwanda in a way that the American Jewish community was not able to match. There will be more opportunities for Jews to help the poverty-stricken world majority—and this can serve as a paradigm for all the affluent nations.

After 1967, Israel was cut off from Africa because of Arab pressure. Earlier, in the 1950s and the early 1960s, Israel had played a great role in agricultural aid. (This was part of the Third-World tragedy. Misled by its leadership, the Third World supported the Arab–Communist attack on Israel.) After the Third World abandoned Israel, the Jewish state was not in a position to be of much help to those nations in the 1970s and 1980s. Now, with possible peace on the horizon, I would like to see Israel put a percentage of its GNP into helping other nations. The percentage should grow as Israel's margins of security and affluence grow. Israel can send a Peace Corps to help development in various areas of the Third World.

The day may come when Israel will be in a position to send soldiers to help out where there is a need for international military presence to save the peace—as was needed, for example, in the former Yugoslavia or in Haiti. Up to now, Israel has not sent troops—for good reason. Israelis and Jews worldwide have felt surrounded by enemies. It is tragic that the world, acting through the U.N., has not put its collective foot down and stopped the ethnic cleansings and mass murders. It can be done. I do not think that it would be as hard as people believe; in fact, the lack of action reflects lack of will: The world powers just do not want to do it. If Israelis had the margins to operate in a peaceful world, they could do in Serbia what they did in Entebbe—i.e., go to the capital of the enemy and take charge to save lives. Israel may yet have to take out Iran's nuclear centers—and thus protect itself and the whole Middle East—even as it destroyed Iraq's Osirak reactor and saved America and Saudi Arabia from grave dangers that were to surface later.

Of course, there is a lot of unfinished work in Israel. Jews cannot become the police force of the world; Israel is still a small country. Still, as security and living levels improve, Jews should give a growing percentage to help other people, as well. Judaism taught us that we have to help ourselves first. But as we get stronger—as Israel gets closer to a potential peace in the Middle

East—we are taught to extend family help to a wider circle. By this principle, Jewry has to devote more resources to helping others. When it does so, it can become a teaching model to the industrialized world. We are the people who teach all nations that the obligations do not stop at the national boundary.

Q. Do you think, in the light of Jewish economic success in the Diaspora especially—and this is undoubtedly related to certain values in our religious tradition—that one way of helping the world might be through proselytizing? I know that this is putting the cart before the horse; but, by adopting Jewish religious values, other peoples might adopt those values that improve their economic situation.

Greenberg. I feel very strongly that proselytizing is a good idea, with one condition. We must not adopt the approach that the other religions have no validity or that a person cannot be saved unless he or she is a Jew. This would contradict the dignity of others. I prefer Isaiah's vision that even our worst enemies may be elected by God to experience redemption and to serve as God's inheritance (see Isaiah, Ch. 19). But if by proselytizing one means offering a model that people can identify with or become a part of, the answer is: Yes, we should proselytize. If there were a hundred million Jews in the world, other nations would not attack us so readily. Now (when there are only four million Jews in Israel and twelve million throughout the world), aggressors are less hesitant to attack. So there is real self-interest in converting others to Judaism. Above all, Judaism's critical task and goal is to be a model for the nations. God has called Israel to witness to the world. If we believe that Judaism is a world religion—as I do—then it should play a world role, through cultural and religious outreach as well as through humanitarian aid and political involvement.

One of the key ways that Judaism has witnessed has been through other religions, i.e., through Judaism's influence on Christianity and on Islam, as well as on Western culture. There is no reason that, in this more open world, Jews should not influence people directly, in terms of their becoming Jewish. And if they do not become Jewish, they may be influenced by Jewish models. Incidentally, a lot of Christianity's appeal in the nineteenth century was that the local populations saw it as the vehicle of Western technology and economic success. The same holds true for Mormonism around the world today. Mormonism is growing enormously—in part because of its message, in part because of an active missionary program, and in part because native populations see Mormonism as bringing with it the gifts of the West, gifts of the body as well as of the soul. If Judaism and Jewry can be a vehicle of upgrading economically as well as spiritually, that would attract many people. Such upgrading would be great for the world—and for Judaism also.

2

On the Human Created in God's Image

Shalom Freedman (Q). Rabbi, you are known for your gift for making friends and pupils. What is it in your conception of human relations that enables you to do this?

Rabbi Irving Greenberg. The central anchor of my thinking and of my life is the concept that the human being is created in the image of God. (In Ben Azzai's view, this is the great principle of the Torah.) Because humans are the image of God, they are endowed by their Creator with three intrinsic dignities: infinite value (the image created by God is priceless); equality (there can be no preferred image of God; that would constitute idolatry); and uniqueness (images created by humans from one mold resemble each other, but God creates God's images from one couple or mold, and each is distinct from every other) (cf. *Sanhedrin* 37A). All of society—economics, politics, culture—must be organized to respect and uphold these three fundamental dignities. Since the world is not yet structured to sustain these dignities, we must perfect the world. In the interim, we must act to respect these dignities to the fullest. We must also establish a process to move societal conditions and individual behavior toward ever-greater respect for these dignities. This is the guiding principle of the *halachah* and the ultimate goal behind all *mitzvot* and religious behaviors.

The principles of human infinite value, equality, and uniqueness not only regulate the realm of society and collective behavior. They are equally the ethical principles that are meant to govern all human relationships. The religious goal and test of all relationships is that they reflect—and nurture—the image of God of the human beings involved. The key to friendship and love is to recognize uniqueness and value in each person; I must "hear," "see," and respond to the distinctiveness of this person before me at this moment. When people receive a distinctive hearing, they speak distinctively; then their uniqueness evokes unique response and love from the other, and the cycle of growing love is established. Furthermore, all communication takes place in the context of relationship. The more the other person treats you as an equal, the more equal you feel—and the more willing you are to say things you would not say if you felt unequal. This creates the basis of a fuller, more integrated, and more satisfying relationship. Again, the cycle of dignity and equality reinforces ever-growing friendship and feelings of worth.

In the covenant, God models such behavior. One can have all the power in the world, but the more power one possesses, the less one will receive love—because others are so intimidated by power that they won't express what they really feel. So, in the covenant, God renounces power—takes on limits and equal standing with the human partner—so that humans can relate with integrity and love to God.

I have always set my goal to try to act covenantally with people, to listen to their own distinctive voice, to recognize their personal qualities, and to learn from their unique insights. People absorb and give back the response that they get. To the extent that people feel that you value and appreciate them, they reciprocate.

One reason I love my wife is that she actually practices such values. She will remember that eighteen years ago at this wedding you wore a black dress with a yellow scarf; I never recall such details. She gets to know all the shopkeepers and people we meet in a very distinctive way. She will remember that so-and-so's grandchild is going to become bar mitzvah next week. People sense that kind of response, and respond to her. They feel treated like a *tzelem elokim* (image of God), and they respond by recognizing her as a *tzelem elokim.* In sum: The encounter with the infinite value, equality, and uniqueness of the other evokes reverence and love for him or her.

Q. In reading your work, and in reviewing the other interviews, I did get the distinctive feeling that the dominant note of your thought is your desire to influence people for their own good. I have often sat in on the lectures of Rabbi Steinsaltz, and I have the sense that what he is really concerned with, returns to again and again, is the idea of how the human can best worship God. Now, I am not posing these as opposites; obviously they contain and complement each other; but it does seem to me that your desire to help humanity is central to your thought. And that even when you spoke about a crucial life plan for the years ahead, the key priority was the question of where you could do the most good. Would you say that this is a fair description of your basic attitude?

Greenberg. The principle is clear: If you "know" somebody, you want to help them. (In the biblical sense, to "know" means to encounter, experience, love. By extension, knowing is also used biblically, to mean intercourse.) When you feel the other and their needs, you want to help them in your bones. In turn, such attitudes nurture people and enable them to blossom even as the sun makes a growing flower bloom.

The two early major influences on my direction in life were important sources for the idea of the centrality of helping people. In my study years at Bais Yosef (a *musar* yeshiva that grew out of Rabbi Israel Salanter's nineteenth-century renewal movement for Orthodoxy), the yeshiva stressed character-building and ethics. The students studied *musar* writings (both intellectually and existentially), including Salanter's own writings. A powerful central theme in Rabbi Israel Salanter's thinking was that you express your relationship to God in your obligations to your fellow human beings. As Salanter put it: The other's physical [or material] well-being is my spiritual responsibility.

The other influence was my father's burning commitment to help people, especially the oppressed and the underdog. He held this very passionate—almost angry—position that after the Shoah one has to particularly treasure Jews and defend them, even against God. Jews deserved compassion and healing—and they needed such treatment. Once, as a teenager going through an intense religious phase, I was criticizing the nonobservance and assimilationist tendencies of Jews. As I rattled on, my father suddenly flared up. "You dare to attack Jews in the name of God?" (Angry pause.) "Tell me—of these two [God and Israel], who should be more ashamed of their behavior over the past decade?" Without ever saying a word about the Holocaust, my father communicated that that was what he meant. God had not saved the Jewish people from the Shoah, but the Jewish people had remained faithful. Jews had renewed and intensified their Jewish commitment. In stunned silence, I heard the message: *Don't you dare ever attack (or shame) Jews in the name of God. They deserve better from God and from you. Pick a bone with God, if you feel so fired up with piety and prophetic passion.* Of course, he said none of this in words then; he said it more explicitly at other times. The depth of anger and accusation and compassion that was revealed in that minute left an impression on me that has never disappeared.

The Gemara makes the same point. Religious service is not so much intended to satisfy God, who, in a way, doesn't need the gratification; the real obligation is to be kind or helpful to God's creatures—who need it. This defense of the people, Israel, was a very strong theme in my father's life, and appeared in all of his *psakim* (rulings). He viewed the responsibility of the *posek* to employ the *halachah* to help people, to relieve people's pain. Therefore, he was highly critical of *chumras* that inflicted avoidable burdens and of rulings that caused pain to people when there were alternative imaginative possibilities to mitigate suffering. He believed that *halachah*, as a system, has to be directed properly. *Psak* is never an objective exercise. This view was almost the opposite of Yeshayahu Leibovitz's idea that there is no human reward or humanitarian purpose to *halachah*; it is all selfless worship of God. My father's approach was that the last thing one should do is to glorify God at the expense of humans. Rather, one must help people, even "against" God. He did not really believe that such *psak* was against God; rather, this was what God wanted. He was dead-set against an halachic authority who comes in the name of the law and insists that people have to do such-and-such even if it is very destructive to them.

I remember one case of an Orthodox family in which the wife had come from a somewhat less Orthodox background. The husband was a forerunner of the *baal teshuvah* trend, i.e., he became more and more traditional and strict beyond the law in observance. There was no *eruv* in those days in New York, so taking a baby carriage out of the house was prohibited halachically. The wife was very upset. She felt that it was not good for the baby to be kept indoors all day, so she took the baby carriage out every *Shabbat.* Such action constituted *chillul Shabbat,* and the husband became very angry. The matter turned into a bitter fight, and it was harming the relationship; indeed, it was rocking the marriage. The couple came to my father. Well, the law is the law; he could not make believe that taking out the carriage was not against the law. But he stretched the *halachah* (though he had a halachic basis for this). He convinced the husband that there is no real *rishus harabim* (public space) today (a place that, by strict definition, 600,000 people have to pass through regularly each day). Thus, the wife's sin was *not* as grave as the husband felt it was. (The gravity of the act was disturbing the husband and driving him to more and more aggressive arguments with his wife.) My father was "countenancing" the woman's violation of *Shabbat,* de facto. Seeing that she was not going to stop, he made the *averah* (sin) less severe in her husband's eyes so that he would live with it—in order, so to speak, to save the marriage. That incident left a strong impression on me because he had gone beyond what was legally justified in order to help people.

As I look back now, almost fifty years later, I feel that this model gave me the psychological freedom to think in terms of pluralism. When I see Reform Jews doing their service on *Shabbat* (thereby also committing some Halachic *chillul Shabbat* such as lighting the candles or playing the organ on the day itself), my father's model enables me to not have the instinctive feeling—which most Orthodox Jews feel—of anger or rejection. I experience it not simply as a gross violation or some willful rejection of God's word; I also recognize that, in a certain way, it is an alternative model. One can disagree with someone else's religious behavior without rejecting the other—especially by not judging them and condemning them in the name of God. Furthermore, just as the *halachah* says that to save a life one can "override" the prohibition against carrying or traveling, so out of respect for human dignity one can give the quality of life of the other person weight in arriving at the *psak*. This implies giving halachic weight to people's feelings and priorities.

Q. And this attitude, no doubt, has gotten you into trouble?

Greenberg. There is no question that such views upset some people. Let me return the favor: In my judgment, the upsurge of *frumkeit* of the past thirty years has led to a halachic brand of "legalism," too often the enemy of *mentschlichkeit.* The classic case is the toleration of widespread *igun* [women being anchored without a *get*] on grounds that, legally, nothing can be done.

You know that some people have charged that I am too sympathetic to Christianity. In Jewish–Christian dialogue circles, I go out of my way to show the religious value and love implicit in *halachah* because I believe that Jewish law is an expression of love and covenant. But I have come to see that the Christian criticism of legalism has a grain of truth in it. If you don't watch your step, the process of law turns into pure legalism, almost indifferent to the human cost. Of course, not all law is legalism. . . . Legalism is the breakdown, the corrupt form of a valid religion based on law.

There are precedents in the *halachah* for increasing the legal "weight" of human pain. One of the most dramatic examples is in this very area of avoiding a situation of *igun*—a state where the woman is trapped, unable to free herself for remarriage and for entering into a decently fulfilling human condition. To avoid *igun,* the rabbis rewrote the book on witnesses and evidence—validating a woman's testimony to the fact that the husband died even though women were not permitted to witness in all other areas of traditional law. They also accepted the testimony of one witness as proof—though normally two is the minimum. There is also a precedent that a *derabbanan* (a rabbinically enacted *halachah*) is overridden for the sake of *kavod habriyot* (human dignity). (Admittedly, there are cases of not overruling the *halachah* because of human dignity—such as the ruling that a person should strip himself in public if he discovers that he is wearing *shatnetz* [clothing of wool and linen] rather than continue to violate God's laws.)

Then there is the principle of *hefsed merubeh.* In some cases, if the person can manage financially without a questionable chicken, we rule that it is *treyf.* But if it is a heavy financial loss for the person, the same chicken is ruled kosher. Now we should push these precedents further. After the Shoah, the value of *tzelem elokim*—of nurturing the infinite value, equality, and uniqueness of every person—is critical. Such confirmation is the only credible statement about God one can really make. This is the true glorification of God in an age when God is profoundly hidden, in a time when there has been a serious assault on the credibility of faith because of the great destruction of human life.

The way to restore credibility of belief in God—before one talks of worship—is to reduce evil and suffering by restoring the image of God. To restore the image of God means bringing out to the fullest the individuality, the equality, and the value of every human being. It follows that this consideration should be given a heavier weight in *halachah* or *psak* than in the past.

Historically, after destructive assaults on Jewry, great messianic outbursts have followed. It was as if the spiritual leadership understood that the balance between the power of redemption and the power of destruction had been shifted or destroyed; therefore, restoring the balance and credibility of faith demanded strong counter action. In the same way, the image of God has been so desecrated in our time that it is hard to talk about and affirm God. Yet, the most incredible and powerful way to uphold the Divine is to affirm and reestablish the value of the human being in God's image. Otherwise, the destruction of the image of God (six million dead, tortured, etc.) shouts down all talk about God. In this generation, the most important way of renewed talking about God is to help human beings rebuild the value of humans. That must be accomplished not only by using classic *psak* to advance this goal, but by engaging the *halachah* to the limit and beyond to confirm human dignity.

Q. Rabbi, I have difficulty with some of what you said. I keep thinking of the Kotzker Rebbe's "God is wherever you let Him in." And I know that many Jews live today with not only a sense of hidden God, but also a sense of God nearby. Another point: The redemptive actions of history you also point to in your writing, such as the rebirth of Israel—don't they show God active in history? Personally, I see my own life as being guided and directed by God. Sometimes it is as if the whole world was created for my sake, though I know, too, that I am a handful of dust. I really do believe that God guides, that there is personal providence, *hashgachah pratit.* I think I sensed that you yourself had this kind of feeling, and that you did talk about getting what you felt, at a certain point, were signals from God. While I recognize why, at certain times, people would need to talk about the absence or hiddenness of God, my own experience is of the increasing presence of God in my life.

Greenberg. The foremost expression of *hashgachah*—Divine Providence—is God's action in history. The Exodus was and is the classic statement of God's presence and care. The Exodus—at least retrospectively—manifestly exhibits God's intervention. But later events, such as the Purim salvation, in which God's hand is present but far from hidden, also have become cornerstones of Jewish faith. The process of redemption will not cease until the whole world is redeemed.

I believe with complete faith that the rebirth of Israel in this century is another one of those decisive turning points in history. But I also believe that God now acts primarily, at least on the visible level, through human activity—as is appropriate in a partnership whose human participant is growing up. God's "direct action" is all but invisible in the modern Israeli Exodus event. The human activities—armies fighting, diplomats negotiating, media covering, the wounds, the deeds, the suffering, the lucky breaks—are what is visible. This does not mean that God may not pull strings and create environmental or probability factors that affect the outcome. But the primary thrust of God's action is now directed through human acts. This does not diminish the religious significance of the redemption—or our obligation to acknowledge this gift from God.

On the other hand, to say that Israel is God's act in history—in the way that Gush Emunim people do—is close to offensive. A lot of secular, as well as religious, people died in those

Israeli army battles. Therefore, to give all the credit to God is like cheating these people. In this age, the only credit God wants—and properly gets—is, so to speak, for being with and holding the hands, for creating the framework for the people who are doing these acts of historic significance.

A second point about *hashgachah. Hashgachah* means that God is with us; God is interested in and concerned about every detail of our lives. There is not a moment in life that is cut off from God. But *hashgachah* is not to be interpreted as meaning that God is doing the fighting and, therefore, is guaranteeing the outcome for us. We no longer have the covenantal right to draw the same conclusion as does the Book of Judges—that if there was a good outcome, God did it because we obeyed; and if there was a bad outcome, God inflicted the bad result on us because of our sins. The interpretive rules have changed as the covenantal roles have changed, and humans have taken on more responsibility. This is God's will; this is the intended outcome of the covenantal partnership. This religious understanding has profound implications for human behavior. The concept that "God will do it for me" is the least acceptable version of the meaning of *hashgachah.*

Hashgachah means that even if I am given a bad hand to play in life it is my mission to play it well—and I will not be alone. Suppose that one is given a terrible sickness, or is born in the generation of the 1940s in Nazi-occupied Europe, when the primary choice is how to die with dignity; God is with one even then. I say this with a full heart. I believe that God was in Auschwitz. I believe that God was in the gas chambers with the Jewish people. But I do not believe that God inflicted those gas chambers on the Jews because they were sinful; nor is it proper to believe that God blew up the gas chambers, so to speak, at the end of the war, or that God miraculously stopped the Arab tanks in Israel. The Divine asks humans to stop the evil ones. Full responsibility is given to the covenanted human partner to redeem history—under and with God's *hashgachah.*

Hashgachah taken on the surface level can lead to mistaken and sometimes even destructive conclusions. *Hashgachah* means that God is behind the Jews in reconquering Israel. But it does not mean that Jews cannot lose even if they take a reckless or politically or militarily nondefensible position! It is true that God is with us; it is true that God wants us to reconquer Israel. But that Providence does not exempt us from making reasonable projections as to what we are militarily and diplomatically (humanly) capable of accomplishing. We cannot write a political or military check that is not backed by the bank balance—with the claim that God is going to cover for us.

This view walks a thin line. One cannot function by pure rationality. There is an appropriate role for faith and hope and courageous risk. And there is the intangible element of help conferred by Divine presence. But that extra margin must be treated as a very narrow one. To say that we are fully responsible means that we are fully responsible to deal with the situation with our best judgment—assuming no miracles and no *Deus ex machina.*

How can one think of giving back a sacred piece of land? The answer is: If in the best human political or military judgment that is necessary, for saving lives or making peace, then one must take full responsibility and do it. Even if that decision is the wrong one, God approves of it because it reflects the exercise of mature judgment in a spirit of full responsibility for the covenant.

This position contradicts the argument: "God will come to our rescue, if we show steadfast faith." Others argue that all of Zionism's accomplishments defy probability and rationality, but God accomplishes it all miraculously—so we must continue on this path. May I offer something I learned from my CCNY experience? I was certain that God was with me; I thought that the inheritance left to City College was a Divine signal to start CLAL and take on the task of equipping Jews to deal with modernity. It turned out that the signal was not that clear-cut—nor did it guarantee success. *Hashgachah* is subtler and more hidden, and therefore should not be invoked simplistically. But with this understanding, there is *hashgachah* in daily life and every step of our way. *Hashgachah* means the blessing of a universal and continuous presence of God's love, God's judgment, God's calling.

Q. I believe that people of political views very different from yours (I am thinking of Rabbi Rabinovitch of Maale Adumim) also expressed the idea that there are no guarantees, that God did not guarantee that we are necessarily going to be victorious in our present political struggle. But I believe that many of us feel that there are situations even in ordinary life when there comes what might be called "special" or miraculous manifestations of God. There are times when God seems to give us some special power or help.

Greenberg. There are times when you are carried through life beyond your normal capacity. This is part of *hashgachah.* There are times when your situation shifts—beyond your capability to affect it—in your favor. At such moments one has a right to affirm, trustingly or hopefully, that *hashgachah* is operating. But God helps those who help themselves. If you make realistic projections, then *hashgachah* pulls you through. But you are not exempt from making responsible projections. The more reasonable people's interpretation of God's acts in history, the more acceptable I find their views. I affirm that God is operating and transforming events in Jewish history miraculously now. But that fact cannot be allowed to hide or distract from the tremendous shift of responsibility for *tikkun olam* toward the human side. There is a greater role for the human agent of the covenant in the present historical situation.

Q. But how do we precisely understand this in various historical situations? Take, for instance, the Six-Day War, which many Jews saw at the time as an act of miraculous Divine redemption. Where is God's part in this, and where is man's?

Greenberg. It is very hard to draw precise delineations. That is another reason that we should welcome multiple views. I believe that the Six-Day War was a redemptive victory, accomplished by God and humans in covenental partnership, comparable to the great biblical events of Redemption. (1967 is part of the larger process of the rebirth of Israel, which is comparable to the biblical Exodus itself.) However no one can give a definitive answer because there is no clear revelation anymore; the age of prophets who are unequivocal Divine spokesmen is over. (Even then, usually, there were counterprophets with countermessages. Learning what God was doing was not so simple then, either). Since God no longer sends prophets with definitive messages, there are pluralistic possibilities of understanding—and the number is expanding. You have to make your best assessment and act. You live by that best judgment, but you allow for the others to correct or to supplement your own interpretations.

Not only is pluralism valid and necessary, God affirms it. If I exercise my best judgment and make an error, then I am not condemned by God. An analogy: If a subordinate or colleague makes an error in judgment in carrying out a good responsible and responsive policy, then any good executive knows not to come down on the person in that context. You ask the person to review and learn from the error. But if you give people responsibility and then condemn them every time they make an error, then you are not giving them responsibility; you are merely covering your own back. God should be credited with being a decent executive. God has given humankind a genuine delegation of authority. This includes the right to make misjudgments. Those who make misjudgments do not delegitimate themselves. They should be tactfully and supportively criticized. And we should work to ensure that errors are corrected. But that is quite different from saying that the other (erring) people are delegitimated.

So there is no clear answer to your question—how to tell exactly God's role and how humans should act in history now. Here are some guidelines: Use your best judgment. Use the past models. There are no self-articulating guidelines and parameters from the past revelations, only models that you apply now as best you can. Isaiah saw the restoration of Israel as God's work and proclaimed Cyrus, the Persian emperor who made it happen, to be God's Messiah. Others—and, later, Jewish history—disagreed. Today, we have no prophets to give us an interpretation. All the more so today, we must allow for various judgments as to correct policy or what God—or humans—hath wrought. Every religious person who wants to serve God's purpose should welcome pluralism as likely to prevent or minimize errors and provide the widest range of insight into what God wants right now.

Q. So you mean it's for the individual to judge and decide in most life situations what God wants of him?

Greenberg. No individual is an island unto himself or herself. The individual should not live in a solipsistic, atomized world. Most of us live in communities; therefore, you want to decide in the context of communities, if at all possible. There are also inherited parameters, law and practice in accordance with Jewish custom. These are fundamental models that are not to be dismissed. But no one can give a computer-programmed, "objective" answer. It is possible that the community errs, or that the official authorities err. The individual has to make a judgment, and cannot hide behind the community standard, either. The individual should defer, give weight, give respect to community values if for no other reason than all of us live in community. But when the individual genuinely believes that the community is in error, it is part of personal moral responsibility to stand up and say so, or to actively disagree, or to create alternative models.

3

Covenant: On the Partnership of God and the Human in History

Shalom Freedman (Q). A central concept in your thought is the interpretation you make of the traditional Jewish notion of "covenant." You connect the covenant with God's willing act of self-limitation. If I understand you correctly, you also connect the concept of covenant with what you call God's increased hiddenness and yet increased presence through time in history. Can you explain this further?

Rabbi Irving Greenberg. One of the central and distinctive ideas in Judaism is the concept of *brit*, or "covenant." Covenant is nothing less than *the* method whereby the world will be perfected, according to the Torah.

Through the process of covenant, Judaism strikes a distinctive balance between the two approaches to human history. On the one hand, there has been a tendency to conceive of God as the all-powerful Father who controls everything. Islam sometimes approaches fatalism in its emphasis that the will of Allah prescribes every dimension of human existence. Other religions also place enormous emphasis on trusting God absolutely. Accordingly, some religions view the practice of medicine as encroaching on God's prerogatives. This one-sided position is represented in Judaism, too, particularly in medieval Judaism. Thus, Nachmanides considers medical practice to be the fallback position, a decline from the ideal world in which God served as Healer of the Jewish people.

This tendency, taken to excess, is the root of the famous Marxist critique of religion as "the opiate of the masses"—because such teaching encourages people to passively accept their fate rather than to try to change the political–economic system. In this approach, humans find their reward not in this world but in the world-to-come. Improvement in the lot of the average person will come not in this life, but rather in some future messianic age. In this religious scenario, God often begrudges human strength and capacity; the highest religious virtues are passivity and obedience to God.

The other polar position is expressed in human rebellion against fate (particularly strong in modern times). Some of the most powerful trends and thinkers of the past two hundred years called on humans to "get rid of" God, so that humanity could finally come of age. (Marxism, Communism, secular humanism, and existentialism come to mind among the movements.) In this view, human power is the key to liberation; human self-affirmation takes the form of overthrowing God. Marx rejects religion for the sake of economic redemption; Freud slays the Father for the sake of psychological liberation; and both Nietzsche and Sartre proclaim absolute human autonomy for the sake of cultural freedom. All these theories share the notion that if only humans become self-reliant and powerful enough, then history will be perfected. God will be revealed to be an illusion.

Both of these polar positions have generated destructive side effects, historically. The first one has encouraged billions to remain passive amidst suffering and to accept their fate. By encouraging flight from the vale of material existence, religion allowed Mammon and other gods to control this world. Religion became the escape; God was the One who calls on humans to evade confronting the outrages of contemporary society. At the other extreme, especially in the modern age, glorification of human power has led to new idolatries, totalitarian states, and worship of the Führer and other dictators. Human power, out of control, has polluted and destroyed the environment. This century has been marked by killing on a mass scale as never before.

Judaism offers a dynamic, healthy balance between these two

poles and thus avoids the excesses of each. The Torah insists that there is an Ultimate Power. This world is not an accident; it came into being by the will of a Creator God. This God wants the perfection of the world and the triumph of life; God is on the side of humans. God cares and wants to help, but God wants humans to take power and responsibility as well. This concept is expressed most dramatically in the concept of *brit.* God entered into a covenant (a loving commitment) with humans. God will help, God will accompany, God will be involved in every aspect of this effort to perfect the world (the process of *tikkun olam*). But there must be an active human role in this battle. Human beings are partners with the Divine. God will not give us a perfect world on a silver platter; humans must take responsibility. In this conception, the process of perfection is a constant struggle—never ceasing, never "fixed," never to be taken for granted. Ideally, this joint action–relationship steers us safely between the Scylla of human passivity in the face of suffering and the Charybdis of human arrogance that has generated the kind of runaway, megalomaniacal power that threatens the planet.

There is another powerful dynamic in the concept of *brit.* The covenant idea teaches that, ultimately, humans are not alone. Still, God is not blatantly manifest in the world, but must be discovered. God is not self-evidently present, but must be sought out behind—and within—the veil of reality. This hiddenness reflects not God's lack of concern, but the way in which the Divine, lovingly, acting pedagogically as a great teacher, tries to evoke constantly increasing levels of human participation and human responsibility in the process of *tikkun olam.*

Biblically, the fact that God is not fully revealed is a characteristic of existence from the very beginning. However, God's hiddenness—an expression of divine self-limitation—increases as humans become more capable and more powerful. This *tzimtzum* (self-limitation) is not an abandonment of humanity; it is for the sake of humanity. Modern cultural critics and sociologists point out that the God Who came down at Sinai, the manifest Divine hand that split the Red Sea, is not encountered today. They argue that this proves that the miracles were illusions and that the Bible is a book of primitive fables. I argue that there is a history of the relationship between God and Israel; indeed, of the partnership between God and humanity. The present absence of visible miracle does not turn the faith that is found in the Torah into an illusion; the change reflects the fact that God has increasingly self-limited and has become more hidden as part of a process of human maturation.

In the biblical Exodus, the Jews are saved by the initiative of God. They do little. ("God will fight for you; and you shall stand silent" [Exodus 14:14].) But when God is overwhelmingly present, when there are visible miracles, the human is "intimidated" and turned into a dependent. As God "withdraws" into the natural, the sense of human competence grows. As the Israelites grow up to their responsibilities in the covenant, they become more active. Then God becomes more hidden to allow humans the freedom to act. By our time, God is so hidden that some humans misinterpret this phenomenon as posing a question as to the existence of God. But the positive side of that hiddenness is that humans cannot use religion as a crutch. Since God is not a *Deus ex machina,* humans become more responsible.

In my view, this hiddenness is what the Kabbalah means by the term *tzimtzum. Tzimtzum* is a reflection not of the absence or weakness of God, but of God's voluntary and loving self-limitation in order to help humans take full responsibility for their actions. As time goes on, God's increasing self-limitation means that humans take primary responsibility for the outcome of history—and, thus, of the cosmic process as well.

Q. Rabbi, could you relate more specifically the terms of God's relation to humankind in the Noahide covenant, and to the Jews in the covenant at Sinai?

Greenberg. The covenant is essentially an affirmation of human dignity and human capacity. The very fact that an Infinite Power gives up the power to transform the world unilaterally—or overnight—is a remarkable compliment to humanity. The first part of the book of Genesis tells us that God relates to the whole world. At first, as it were, God almost forces people to be perfect. When Adam and Eve disobey, they are threatened with death and are driven out of the Garden of Eden. When humanity sins, there is a Flood that almost destroys all of humanity. It is as if the Divine

Power is perfectionistic and demands that both humans and the world be perfect—or God will wipe out all existence.

According to the Torah, the emergence of covenant is a turning point in cosmic history, as well as in the relationship of God and humanity. God accepts humans with all their flaws, even their evil and their pettiness. God pledges to uphold natural law. Existence will go on in a dependable way, which means that humans will be neither rewarded automatically for good behavior nor punished automatically for bad behavior. Existence of natural law thus is a major expression of Divine hiddenness: One can believe and act as if there is no God, as if there is only a self-sustaining impersonal universe "indifferent" to humanity.

At the same time, Genesis teaches us that God has given up neither the Divine vision of a perfect creation nor the Divine love for humans. Rather, God has decided to work with full respect for human capacity and limitation all the way to the final perfection. In essence, the covenantal concept is a Divine pledge not to force humans to be free. The first covenant, the Noahide covenant, is made with all humanity. The paradigm of covenant reveals that God does not prefer the obedience of a perfect robot [which could be programmed to do just what God wants—this is the concept behind the classic idea of angels]. God has such love for humanity that God wants humans to do the right thing out of their freedom and dignity. God is not going to force good behavior. This means that God accepts the human right to sin. This freedom enables people to do all the terrible or disappointing acts—as well as to exhibit all the great behaviors—that mark human history.

The Noahide covenant expresses a primary turning point in the religious history of the universe. God commits not to coercively intervene in history, but to allow humans to become partners in making the world perfect. (Actually, the Noahide is a covenant with all living creatures. That is reaffirmed in Hosea, Ch. 2, where he speaks of a messianic renewal of the *brit* [covenant] with humans and with all life.) All are pledged to work for the triumph of life, to strive for the perfection of the world. The Noahide covenant is made with *all* of humanity because God is the God of all humans. Because all human beings are equal before God, they are equally worthy of participating in the partnership of God and humanity for the sake of *tikkun olam*—which will benefit all. Some of the covenantal obligations are to treat every human being as equal; to act as if the other is my brother, my sister, my child, for whom I feel responsible. People do not help immediate flesh and blood as a favor; they help because they recognize the other as their child, parent, spouse. That means they feel obligated. Similarly, every person should feel obligated to help the poor—as if each poor person is my child, a member of my family. In fact, says the Torah, we are all in one family; we are all children of Adam and Eve.

Where does the Jewish *brit* come into the picture? The Torah suggests that Jewry's role grows out of the logic of covenant. In order to protect free human participation in the covenant, God cannot force humans to meet their obligations. So how can God get humans to voluntarily do the most for the covenant? Out of respect for human beings, the best way to inspire higher performance is not to punish or reward, but to find humans to serve as pacesetters and as models. These pioneers will lead the charge. When they set a higher standard, others will learn from them and follow. In time, the others will set up their own further redemptive responses.

Election of an avant-garde is the purpose of the covenant of Abraham and Sarah. Thus, this covenant is best described as the creation of "lead" partners for the benefit of humanity. In turn, the Abrahamic covenant leads to the *brit* of Sinai, the covenant of the whole Jewish people. The Israelites hold themselves to a higher standard. Under the rules of the Torah, the Jews act now (or take upon themselves the obligation to meet a standard now) at a level of performance and intensity that someday the whole world will meet.

Under the covenant of Sinai, the Jews start to live up to a standard of responsibility and love in their own society that bespeaks the fact that every person is an image of God. Since all humans are *tzelem elokim*, we affirm that someday all of humanity will match these behaviors in every society. But for now, in this society at least, the poor will be helped as family. Every member of this people will be upheld as a creature of infinite value deserves to be.

Ideally, Jews should act this way toward everybody equally,

because all humans are in the image of God. But, in reality, one cannot perfect the whole world in one stroke. No one has enough emotional energy or financial resources to save the whole world. We cannot get to the messianic era overnight or in one generation. So where do you start? You start with the Jewish people. Start with one family (Jewry), one country (Israel), one city (Jerusalem), one building (*Beit HaMikdash*) as a zone of life, of peace, justice, dignity—and work outward from there; expand this process into the rest of the world so that the messianic dream can be turned into a living reality. This model, held up to the world, stimulates a re-imagining of the status quo. It spreads the vision of everyone being a *tzelem elokim.* By imitation, by internalization of these teachings, sometimes even by jealousy or competition, the process of liberation is speeded up everywhere. Thus, the covenant with Abraham and the covenant at Sinai constitute an attempt to intensify and speed up the process of redemption of the world.

The Jewish covenant is best located as a subpartnership of the Noahide *brit.* The Jews see themselves as pacesetting, or even managing, partners within the general partnership of humanity with God. The Jews' special role includes serving as teachers—about God—throughout the world. This we did through the Bible, through our tremendous impact on Christianity and Islam, and through Western culture. The second critical Jewish role is to serve as a model, to be the light to the nations. Whether Jews live as a minority among other people or act as a majority in the state of Israel, which has become the classic Jewish model in our world today, their example is studied and often followed. Finally, Jews labor as co-workers alongside the rest of the world for *tikkun olam.*

As we articulate and deepen our own covenant, we dare not imply that the other nations have forfeited their covenant. Quite the contrary. The Noahide covenant was never abrogated; the nations of the world continue their role in the Divine–human partnership. Christianity and Islam should be recognized and respected as covenantal religions working with God, inspiring humanity to *tikkun olam.* Other religions are less covenantal in their formal theological thinking, but they nonetheless have dignified roles to play in this world transformation.

Note that the dynamic dialectical model of covenant governs

the relationship of Jews and gentiles as well. God and humans share responsibility for *tikkun olam.* This means that each of the partners is independent; each one has a role of its own, yet each can influence the other. So Jewishness must be seen in terms of the universal and the particular. The Jews are very special. They do have a distinctive role in the world. But the rest of humanity has a special dignity and role, too, and each side can influence the other. The dynamic interaction of the two poles is characteristic both of *brit* and of Judaism.

Q. Rabbi, how do you relate these initial conditions of covenant to what you call the "broken covenant" in history? And how do you relate the covenant of Abraham and the covenant of Sinai to conditions of the world today? Is there some change in the historical response required of the Jews in this generation?

Greenberg. In the course of living the covenant, the Jewish people is exposed to history. This is one of the remarkable affirmations about Divine teaching as Judaism understands it. In spite of the infinity of the Divine, in spite of the infinity of the Torah, Judaism is not exempted or shielded from history. The very fact that the Torah teaches that redemption will occur in history (and not in the afterlife) means that what happens in this life has a powerful effect on the credibility of God and of the Torah. This point is stated not once, but repeatedly throughout the Bible. When Moses is told to liberate the Jews from Egypt, God promises, "I will take them from under the burdens of the Egyptians and save them from their slavery. I will redeem them . . . take them to be my people." *Then,* "you will know that I am the Lord your God" (Exodus 6:6–7). In other words, knowing God as God depends on the circumstances. It is true that slaves or poor people turn to God, but they do not really know God as God. They know God as some fantasy of relief from their suffering, as some straw to grasp at in history. The slave—as the soldiers in the foxholes—conceives of God as the tyrannical master before whom abject groveling may bring an arbitrary, one-sided grant of relief.

God really wants human service out of love—not just out of fear, but out of love. But only the free and the dignified can truly rise to the level of service out of love, for its own sake. Thus, God liberates the covenant partner (Israel is freed through the Exodus) so that the partner can begin to serve God out of dignity and capacity. Being free on their own land is the logical next step toward the freedom and security that form the infrastructure of human dignity and allow the partner to serve God at a higher level. In turn, the experience of being redeemed confirms the hope and promise of the covenant that ultimately there will be a universal perfection.

Since the covenant is entered into for the sake of a final redemption, then the covenantal mission must be passed on from generation to generation, or the commitment will die unfinished. Thus, every generation is bound up with—and dependent on—every other generation in the covenant. Every generation must review the covenantal obligation and mission. This ensures that its commitment is truly at a high level—strong enough to keep the mission alive and fresh. But the challenge of renewal—or death of the mission—is greatest when a crisis or disaster tests the credibility of the *brit.* This challenges the Jewish people to respond again.

In the course of history, particular crises have arisen and affected the Jewish experience of God. These are the moments of catastrophe that undermine the confidence Jews have that the world will be saved. When these major disasters occur, they seem to strike at the whole structure of faith. "Does God really care?" "Are we still the chosen people?" "Is the hope of redemption still alive?" These questions were asked during crises in previous eras of Jewish history.

The destruction of the Second Temple particularly serves as a paradigm as to what is occurring in our time. After the destruction of the Temple, the Jews went from their own land into a state of exile that lasted for almost two thousand years. Many Jews felt rejected; many concluded that God had lost interest in Israel. After all, despite a Jewish revolt to uphold the sanctity of Israel, God had not stopped the Roman conquest. The rabbis did not agree. They explained the destruction partly as a punishment for sin. Above all, they insisted that God's self-restraint (in not intervening and saving the Jews) was God's way of calling Israel to greater responsibility. God had become more hidden, in order that the Jews should now "discover" God. Instead of saving the day with visible miracles, God now showed the way through hidden miracles. This is the difference between Passover—the classic liberation holiday of the Bible—and Purim, the classic redemption festival expressing the hiddenness of God in the rabbinic age. In the Book of Esther, the name of God is not mentioned—yet the Jews were saved in the end. According to the rabbis, the Jewish people grasped that this was a case of salvation from God just as much as in Egypt when the Red Sea split.

The Babylonian Talmud makes this very point, then goes on to expand the significance of the new Divine limits. In retrospect, the covenant of Sinai was "coercive" because God first saved the Israelites with visible miracles. This made the Sinai revelation into an offer that the people could not refuse. Consider a bunch of ex-slaves in the desert. Who knew the way back to Egypt? They felt gratitude and obligation to God, who saved them. Of course they accepted the Torah. By that logic, however, the Talmud says, Jewry now lives in a time in which God does not split the Red Sea. Since God does not save with visible miracles, this would seem to imply that the covenant of Sinai is no longer binding. Nevertheless, says the Talmud, Purim constituted the ratification of the covenant of Sinai; Purim makes that covenant binding in a new way. By accepting Purim as the equivalent of Passover, the Israelites confirmed that they accept the covenant even when God is not performing visible miracles, even when it appears that human efforts (primarily) saved the Jewish people. Thus, Purim constitutes a major moment of reacceptance of the covenant [*Shabbat* 88A].

The subtext of this account is that the crisis was so searching and the catastrophe so testing of our faith and hope that the covenant could not have continued without the people of Israel intensifying the *brit* anew out of a deeper perception that God was present—albeit more hidden—in the world after the destruction. The further subtext is that in an age of such momentous destructions (or redemptions), we owe it to God, and to the covenant, to take the moment seriously, to consider again the nature of Jewish obligation and the human role in the partnership.

It is my contention that we are living in a similar moment of historic renewal of the covenant. In this generation, the Holocaust constituted a total assault—in a way, a successful assault—on Judaism, on the Jewish people, on the covenant. The covenant promises that life will win out, and that human life is infinitely valuable. In the Holocaust, we saw the reverse. Death won out; the Jews were condemned for the crime of being. Six million Jews were killed, and the existence of the Jewish people as a whole was endangered. A tragic event of such shattering proportions—that God did not stop—creates a crisis in relationship to God and the covenant.

Trying to express this crisis, I have used certain formulations that intuitively I think are correct, even though they are problematic. One of the images that I use is the implication that the covenant is *broken.* The word "broken" initially means that the covenant is wounded—just as the Jewish people was deeply wounded bodily by the loss of the six million. After all, if one-third of the people Israel is broken off from the body of the people and destroyed, how could the covenant of the Jewish people (which undergirds their being), and the Torah of the Jewish people (which shares their life), not be broken as well?

Well-meaning religious people insist that the covenant can in no way be affected by disaster. In fact, in the most extreme version, there are those who argue that the classic Jewish notion of punishment for sins applies to the Holocaust. Thus, in their view, the covenant is upheld. I find this theology outrageous—as if there is any crime or sin that would justify such a cruel catastrophe. Rather, this view convicts God of cruelty and hardness of heart that is unworthy of our loving covenant Partner. Ironically, people are driven to malign God because they are trying to uphold the seamless perfection of the Torah. In my judgment, this response to the crisis of faith—a crisis they must feel, otherwise they would not resort to so desperate an answer—is all wrong. Judaism teaches that the Infinite One limited God's own self and became involved in the world of flesh and blood. If God is linked to the Jewish people in love, then the Torah and the covenant share Jewish fate. If the Jewish people was wounded, then the Torah is wounded. That is the theological basis of the image of a broken covenant.

The term "broken covenant" is grounded in a play of words. Rabbi Nahman of Bratslav once said, "There is no heart so whole as a broken heart." Rabbi Nahman was trying to say that if you truly have a loving, whole heart and feel for people's pain, then when you see their suffering, your heart will be broken. So brokenness is a statement of a great, embracing "heart"; brokenness shows that you are a person of true compassion. If your heart is whole, i.e., unaffected, there is something wrong with you because you are not shattered by the suffering of the people.

My argument was that, after the Holocaust, Jewish faith was broken—but there is no faith so whole as a broken faith. After all, what kind of faith could be unaffected by such destruction of human and Jewish values? Thousands of synagogues and *sifrei Torah* were burnt. Jewish lives were turned into objects of such little value; to save zyklon B gas, the Nazis burnt Jewish children alive. Under these circumstances, for the heart of a faith to be broken is a sign of greatness, not weakness.

The term *broken covenant* is also a double entendre. Faith in the covenant is also broken in another sense. Consider the nature of covenant; it involves a pledge from both partners. God pledges to be with us, *to protect us, to ensure our life,* in return for our loyalty. In the Holocaust, the reward for covenantal loyalty was that such Jews were more likely to be killed. The Jews who were more assimilated were better able to escape than the Jews who were more observant. Deculturated Jews had better contacts with local populations; they were less visible as Jews. Note that ninety percent of the Jews who were most observant and most learned (as in Poland) were killed; Jews in the most assimilated countries (such as Denmark) more often escaped. Therefore, one can argue that the moral right of God to demand that the Jews observe the covenant has been "broken." But the same principle applies: The covenant is broken—but there is no covenant so whole as a broken covenant.

In my judgment, that is what happened. The Jewish people had every right to argue that if there was a quid pro quo for covenant, then Jews were released from their pledge. This parallels the talmudic argument (in *Shabbat* 88A), that if the Jews violate the sinaitic covenant, they should not be held liable, because its acceptance was coerced. In a world where God no longer intervened with visible miracles, then the Sinai revelation and Exodus redemption accomplished with manifest signs and wonders was no longer binding. It took Jewish insight (that God saves through hidden miracles) and a pledge to observe Purim (and thereby renew the covenant in a world of hidden miracles) to reestablish the authority of the *brit.*

By analogy to that talmudic argument, Jews today can say that the Sinai covenant was renewed in the Purim event because, after all, the Jews were saved. The authority of the Sinai covenant would not be binding in an age in which God no longer intervenes openly; what made it binding is that the Jews renewed the covenant at Purim. But what about after the Holocaust when the Jews were not saved? Perhaps the authority of the Purim renewal is binding in an age when God saves us, but is not binding in an age when God does not save us. This would be a persuasive argument, except for the fact that the people again renewed the covenant under the new circumstances.

In the retrospect of Auschwitz, the Purim covenant renewal is "coercive." (Gratitude for salvation leads to acceptance.) But in creating the state of Israel after the Shoah, the Jewish people ratified the covenant it had accepted already (in Persia and at Sinai). Thus, the Jewish people asserted that the covenant is binding even in a world where the outcome may be destruction (as in the Shoah), and not just salvation (as in Purim).

The language of "broken covenant" is an attempt to draw attention to the heroic renewal of the covenant in our time, especially as expressed in the recreation of the state of Israel and the decision of the Jews to renew Jewish life after the Holocaust. While terms such as "broken covenant" are upsetting to some people, these terms bespeak the enormous power of the covenant. The Jewish people showed love and faithfulness to the *brit* that far transcended any rational obligation.

May I add that talk about a covenant, broken and renewed, is in part a critique and challenge to those who would "uphold Judaism" and condemn the Jewish people in the name of God. To those who claim that the Jews are not observant enough, are not loyal enough, the answer is that the Jewish people deserves to be honored and celebrated in our lifetime for its faithfulness to God. The Jews could have argued that the covenant was broken, and walked away. They did not. They voluntarily stepped forward.

Even secular Jews took upon themselves the task of realizing the covenant.

One other paradoxical thought. Something that is "broken" appears to be less than something that is perfect. But that is not the Torah's teaching. The world was perfect before the Flood—but that perfection was not livable in human terms. Therefore, that "perfect" order was overthrown by God. Only when the perfection was broken—and God accepted humanity and reality in its brokenness—was the way paved to achieve the final, humanly livable perfection.

One can compare humanity's ultimate state to what scholars call "secondary naiveté." One loses the naiveté of childhood, when all those stories about God were so perfect and so literal. As one matures, one realizes that these stories were taken too literally—thus they become fairy tales. In the real world, you grow out of fables. Or, if you stay with the literalness of the stories, you become a cynic. Secondary naiveté comes when you grow up and renew your understanding of these stories' deeper truth. Thus, the brokenness paves the way for a much higher level of internalization and commitment to the stories.

Paradoxically the broken covenant is much stronger than the erstwhile "whole" covenant. Now that the worst has been done, now that the most terrible suffering has been inflicted on the covenant partners and they have persisted, then one can say that the covenant is truly indestructible. If that brokenness did not end the covenant, then surely it is much stronger than a covenant that is dependent upon victory and "unbrokenness" for its credibility and its binding nature.

Q. Rabbi, I see how that applies to that part of the Jewish people that takes the covenant seriously, that takes the destruction of the Jewish people in Europe seriously, those who are dedicated to doing what they can to ensure the continued life of the Jewish people. But what about that portion of the Jewish people that does not relate to the covenant, and that does not seem to be deeply affected by the historical losses or by the situation of the Jewish people as a whole? What about those who live by the religion of individual satisfaction without any real sense of Jewish communal obligation?

Greenberg. I worry about this group also. It is very troubling that, outside of Israel, the majority of Jews are unaffiliated. It is troubling that the triumph of individualistic values may lead to a point where many individuals no longer care about the Jewish people. The soaring intermarriage statistics show that people are more interested in their personal fulfillment, no matter what the effect on the community. This poses a danger to the viability of the covenant.

Still, I remain convinced that the commitment level of Jews is much higher than we think. Even when Jews have appeared to be estranged, they have surprised us again and again with their capacity for caring. In a crisis like the Six-Day War, these Jews came out of the woodwork. In many cases, the so-called assimilated Jews retain a deep feeling for Jewishness. Often, they do not know the covenant as a covenant; but they intuitively work in certain directions for *tikkun olam.* We must learn to give them the benefit of the doubt. Furthermore, most Jews, even though they are assimilated, do not hide their Jewishness, although they know that there has been a Holocaust and that they could be victims of such an assault again. To me that is a sign that, deep down, they have made up their minds. They are willing to risk martyrdom because they believe in the overall purpose of the Jewish people.

This is not to deny that there is widespread ignorance among Jews. But people often know more intuitively and unconsciously than they know intellectually. I do not mean to coopt all assimilating Jews, to imperialistically say: "I know what you stand for more than you do." Still, there is a bottom-line commitment and risk that they take upon themselves. This should not be eliminated from our calculations. Often, if we approach estranged Jews and articulate what we feel and share with them, they would say, "This is what I have believed all along." Even though they are not conscious of the covenant, if given a chance, if they could articulate what they are doing and relate it to what the Jewish people stands for, they would embrace it. Articulating that connection becomes our pedagogical challenge. We must not let ourselves dismiss other Jews or treat them with anger or contempt as if they are simply ignorant and estranged from the Jewish mission. Rather, we must dig deeper to summon up our love and their commitment.

It is entirely possible that we will lose many of the unaffiliated Jews. It is also possible that the non-observant affiliated and the unaffiliated are engaged in a search for a meaningful way of life, one they do not see exemplified in the living Jewish community. It's too early to say how much of their drift is conscious rejection of Judaism, and how much of it represents their feeling their way to a new articulation of the covenant that may end up, in fact, in a less observant lifestyle. I wrestle with these questions, and do not know the answer. I find it hard—almost impossible—to conceive that the Jews can live without the richness of Torah and halachic observance. Equally instinctively, I feel that it is too early to prescribe and say that observance is the only kind of Judaism that will survive. One must have a certain humility in making judgments.

Let me offer one last criterion for looking at Jews—once we admit that committed Jews, certainly observant Jews, are a minority of the Jewish people. I want to draw an analogy. (It is not entirely flattering; I did not agree with its initial use, but I think that we can learn from it.) In 1956, the Hungarian revolution was suppressed by Soviet armed forces; the Russians installed Janos Kadar as the new national leader. Kadar looked around and saw realistically that committed Communists were an infinitesimal fraction of the Hungarian people; yet, the Russians had clearly crushed any attempt to break away and would do so again. Kadar was convinced that there was no way out but to work for a better life from inside the system. Kadar sought some formulation whereby the people who did not agree with Communism would work within the system to make Hungary into a better society. (Eventually—he did not know it then, but we know it now—this led to the undermining of the Communist system in Eastern Europe.)

Kadar finally proposed a new national social contract. No one had to be a devoted Communist. You do not have to agree with the system that runs the society; behavior is what counts. As a responsible citizen, if you do not openly attack the system or try to destroy it by force but rather try to make this a better society, then you are O.K. If you are not against us, you are with us.

Now, I certainly hate and object to the Communists' use of force. But there is an important lesson here for observant Jews.

We are a very small minority of the Jewish people now. We should not go out and act—particularly as the Orthodox in Israel have done—as if we, the minority, are still the majority and every other view or party is an expression of deviance. We cannot act as if every other lifestyle is illegitimate. Sure, the non-observant majority can be patronized as if they do not know any better. In Israel, we have the power to suppress many alternatives; we have the political power to extort a monopoly in religion. However, this approach is a mistake. It bespeaks arrogance. In essence, it claims that we are the only way, that we have an exclusive on truth.

I would propose to Orthodoxy to set up a system in which "if you are not against us, then you are with us." If a person—or a movement—behaves covenantally and constructively, then treat them as a covenantal Jew or movement, whether or not they share Orthodox definition and commitment to the covenant. The fact that you are not formally embracing the Orthodox ideology, even the fact that you are rejecting the theory behind the ideology, should be ignored on the grounds that your actions speak louder than your words. You are not an enemy. This offers a model for the committed, believing, covenantal Jews to develop a more constructive relationship to Jews who verbally reject the assumptions or the theology of the Orthodox, yet are with us in so many constructive ways.

Incidentally, there is a much better chance to influence people or to bring them closer when you affirm them. Maybe, in taking this line, the Orthodox are also admitting that something new is being born that does not quite fit our categories yet, but which is not automatically negative. Rav Abraham I. Kook writes in the *Arpeley Tohar* that there are certain behavior patterns that are, in their external form, a breach and breakdown of the Torah's fence, but are in their result highly constructive. He applied this concept to the *chalutzim* (pioneers) of his time. We may have to apply that principle in a much broader way. This does not mean that we give a blank check to the non-observant and the assimilated. We have to challenge them—but we challenge them as partners in the system, not as a hostile group that we have to push out of the system.

Q. I wanted to ask you how you relate the notion of covenant to *tikkun olam.* I think that, as you see it, the fulfillment of covenant is the redemptive process that is *tikkun olam.*

Greenberg. The basic idea behind covenant is *tikkun olam.* God wants the perfection of the world. Rabbi Soloveitchik says (in *Halachic Man*) that, in creating the universe, God left it unfinished and flawed—to be completed by the human being. Kabbalah's explanation is that the world, as it were, broke down in the process of creation. There are many ways of formulating this insight. The main point is that the world is unfinished; there are serious flaws and evils within the natural world and in human society. The human mission, the covenantal task, is to join with God in perfecting the world. That is the connection between *brit* and *tikkun olam.*

The human role to complete and perfect the world means that the human being's own participation is critical to achieving a perfect world. Thus, one cannot be a full human being unless one becomes free, unless one becomes responsible. In the Garden of Eden story, God bestows Paradise on humans. But, in that setting, humans were immature, and the perfection was incomplete. Edenic humans never tasted temptation; they never struggled. God dreams of a human being in the image of God, functioning in freedom, taking responsibility for reshaping society to achieve universal justice and dignity. It is true that freedom can be used for evil as well as for good. Still, God is not going to force us to be good. In this partnership, God wants us to use our freedom to embrace the good maturely and voluntarily. Then we will use our growing power to work alongside God to perfect the world.

This is the history of the covenant. This is the history of the Jewish people and the rest of humanity. We have worked over a period of thousands of years, and we are not finished yet. Since the covenantal process respects humans, it means that perfecting the world happens at a human pace. Humans engage in the process of perfecting the world by trial and error, by making mistakes. The Jewish people—the pacesetter and the model—is equally likely to err and to fail regularly. One cannot force the end. One cannot have revolutions imposed from the top. If you insist on an instantly perfect world, you will end up like Stalin and Mao Zedong, with liberation systems running amok and killing the masses. Neither can you anticipate a miraculous transformation of the world by God's coming down from on high to rescue us.

One of the most profound teachings of covenant is that you cannot separate the ends from the means. The ends are human freedom, dignity, and human value. These goals cannot be realized by coercion on the part of either humans or God. Therefore, *brit* implies that God will not force us. In the beginning, God punishes and God rewards openly. As time goes on, God becomes less visible, so we are more free, more responsible. Humans who love God in their strength, in their freedom, out of their own value, truly become loving and peaceful.

The net outcome of this whole process is going to be *tikkun olam*—that is meant quite literally—the perfection and making whole of the world. The world has only now begun to grasp the profundity of the Jewish idea.

When we say that humans are going to play a central part in perfecting the world, what does this mean? There is sickness in this world. Some of it is natural sickness, caused not by human action, but by viruses or genetics, for example. The human capacity to develop medical power to cure fundamental diseases is a breathtaking expression of the human acting in the image of God. In correcting genetic defects, the human being acts as a full partner in perfecting the world. If we could measure volcano eruptions or anticipate earthquakes—these things are being worked on now—we could evacuate people in time, thus saving countless lives. In this way, we can upgrade the capacity of the world to sustain life at its fullest. Similarly, we can restructure society and its governing institutions not to oppress people, but rather to provide food and shelter for all the inhabitants. Thus, we perfect the world, making it more supportive of life. In this respect, through the covenant idea, Judaism truly understands that the Divine–human partnership opens the door to any and all possibilities.

Let me stress that the greater human role does not mean that God is not there anymore. God has *not* checked out. Rather, God acts like a responsible teacher or parent. As the child takes on more responsibility, there is less direct intervention. Of course,

God (as an eternal parent) continues to play a central role. We are helped by God. We are loved by God. We are judged by God. These Divine involvements are just as important as the original covenant services, i.e., visible intervention and redemption. As humans become even more mature, these sustaining roles become more important. God no longer simply steps in and saves us from our own mistakes. Of course, a child feels wonderful when his or her father steps in and saves the child from eating a rotten fruit or from being run over by a car. But surely that help is not equally a source of dignity as when the father does not step in to save, but rather advises and accompanies the child to make the right decision. When as a mature adult I make certain judgments, God gives me the approval I deserve, or gives me the critique I need. That is the greatest contribution—for I am strengthened in the process.

I believe that we are living in an age of breakthroughs. Humans are becoming more responsible. The sense of democracy and human equality is spreading. These developments are bringing us closer to the true covenantal goals. The ultimate outcome will be, I believe, a higher, more mature worship of God. What is described as secularization reflects the breakdown of the medieval state of human powerlessness. Medieval Jews and Christians turned to God more because they were powerless to help themselves. There were strong elements of utilitarian and even exploitative components in the relation to God. There are, after all, no atheists in foxholes. In the modern world, the minute humans did not need God, they walked away.

Now, I look for the higher, more mature faith, when freedom leads to love of God. People will turn to God not out of a desire to be cured when the doctors cannot help, but out of being loved by God even when the doctors can help.

We all know the classic type of prayer: "I am sick, cure me. I am weak, help me." But the Talmud offers us another model. In Brachot we are told that God also prays. What does it mean that God prays? After all, God can do anything! God prays: "May My quality of compassion overcome My quality of judgment." This is a different kind of prayer, not the prayer of helplessness. God's prayer is, "Let Me use My power well, constructively." I look forward to the day when the average human being will pray not the prayers of the helpless, but the prayers of the powerful. "Let me use my power well."

In medieval times, the prayer of the helpless became the dominant liturgical mode. This was wrongly generalized in the form of a belief that prayer is true action and human action is impious because "it aggressively pushes the Divine presence's legs." Therefore, in modern times, people had to reject prayer in order to assert power—because prayer stood as an obstacle in the way of taking power. Another bad consequence of the religious ethos of powerlessness was that the people who went after power acted without restraint once they achieved it. No one thought of praying once they had power. They felt that they were not accountable to God; they had sought power in defiance of or in lieu of God. Since they no longer had a partner, they acted as people without accountability. Soon, the amassed power metastasized; its use became cruel and destructive.

I look forward to the creation of unparalleled human power that will be used responsibly by a humanity that knows it is accountable to God. A humanity imbued with a sense of partnership will understand that humans must not lay waste the universe. Future generations should feel that they step up their partnership with God as they increase their power. This kind of extraordinary power would be the true expression of the covenant—for it would bring us to the stage where there could be an end to poverty and hunger. Already now, it is possible to abolish the causes of war. It will not be easy to realize this goal, but we have sufficient power to carry it out. Of course, if we use power of such great magnitude irresponsibly and selfishly, then the world can be ruined by us. But as we are confirmed in our partnership, as we feel loved and judged by God, as we use our Godlike qualities to amass this power and use it covenantally, then the goals of the final perfection will be accomplished. This is the relation between *brit* and *tikkun olam.*

4

Tikkun Olam

Shalom Freedman (Q). Rabbi, I would like to explore the concept of *Tikkun Olam* further. You have written: "God places the future of creation into our hands now because humans have infinite value now, not just when humanity is perfected. The process of *tikkun olam*—perfecting the world—and *tikkun ha-adam*—perfecting humanity, sit side by side and reinforce each other." What do you mean, Rabbi, when you speak about *tikkun ha-adam* and *tikkun olam* in this context?

Rabbi Irving Greenberg. Two core ideas in my thought are *tikkun olam* and *tzelem elokim* (the image of God). The term *tikkun ha-adam* is a play on the relationship between *tzelem elokim* and *tikkun olam.*

Being in the image of God means that each human being is born with three intrinsic dignities—infinite value, equality, and uniqueness. These dignities are mine, and yours, and everybody's. They are independent of any other factor, such as heritage, status, wealth, health. The implication of the human's infinite value is that it would be proper to spend a fortune to keep one human being alive—even for one day. That is why if you save one life it is as if you have saved a whole world. Since every human being is an image of God, there is *no* preferred image—God is neither white nor black, male nor female, Jew nor non-Jew. Then all people should be treated as if they are equal. Finally, the uniqueness of humans implies that each person should be treated as if he or she were unique. Human images can be duplicated, but the hallmark of God's creative power, God's distinctive infinite creative capacity, is that each and every image of God is absolutely unique. Even identical twins are not identical. Ideally, one should respond to the uniqueness of each person in every moment of contact.

From whence stem these intrinsic dignities that belong to every human being by the simple fact that they are human? These dignities grow out of the ground of love. When I love someone, that person is of infinite value to me. When I love someone, the person is equal to me. It does not matter whether the other is more handsome or more famous than I am. It does not matter that I am heavyweight champion of the world and this woman before me is weak. I could physically overpower her, but if I love her, I would never do it. My respect for her—out of love for her—prevents me from using force. Everyone knows that there are other caregivers or sex objects or financial supporters in the world. But once I love one person, the availability of others becomes moot. This person is uniquely precious to me precisely because love made him or her indispensable and unique to me.

Judaism proclaims the truth that God loves every human being; therefore, I am (every human being is) endowed with these three intrinsic dignities. These dignities are not dependent on whatever the world thinks of me. It does not matter whether I am born into slavery or into the class of untouchables; born into an abusive family or into a loving one; a democratic and egalitarian society or a traditional and hierarchical one. In the eyes of God I am infinitely valuable, equal, and unique.

Now a problem emerges. Despite their groundedness in the infinite Divine—beyond human control or denial—these dignities are not fully realized or even adequately sustained in this world now. In the actual experiences of existence, in the process of society, these dignities may be "increased" or "reduced." Thus, a person may have infinite value in God's eyes, but if the humans around him constantly abuse him and call him worthless, if people treat him like dirt, then after a while the person is going to believe that he is worthless. The daily experiences overwhelm the ideal.

Note that, in the course of history, there have been very few slave revolts. Why? Because the givenness of slavery, the confirmation of the slave's inferiority in the daily experiences, the attitudes of the bystanders, the corroboration by law and custom, gradually became the total reality of the slave. The living experiences lock out the external value sources that may tell the slave that he or she is really free. Out of the system of cues and rewards and punishments that surround them, the slaves learn to be slaves. Eventually, they internalize the slave status. If the conditions of the world are such that whites are superior to blacks, then blacks internalize that white superiority, and so on.

Every human being is located in this world and in the experiences of daily life. In the absence of strong religious culture and teaching, the individual does not automatically root in the eternal, in the Divine Presence. So the degradation in the earthly values and messages eventually overpowers the eternal religious culture's values, however noble. For this reason, Judaism insists that the world will not be right until the daily conditions of political, economic, social reality, confirm the ideal vision of God and Torah.

The definition of the state of *tikkun olam*—the arrival of the messianic kingdom—is when the actual legal, political, social institutions in the world will be structured so that each human being will be sustained and treated as if he or she is an image of God. The world must become rich enough to spend an unlimited amount of money to save one life. The world must be reorganized so that there cannot be systematized degradation or discrimination against people; there must be no inferiority imposed by law or by practice.

Tikkun olam, then, is the process whereby humans transform the world or improve it to the point where it truly sustains each image of God in appropriate dignity. Part of the process involves upgrading the economy. If the world is poor, it cannot support people at the needed level of dignity. Similarly, to reach the messianic stage, humans have to overcome war because wars take lives; armies kill and waste images of God. If the society, by law, opposes equality, then there will be no equality. If people are equal, then every vote should count just as much as every other. This is what democracy is all about.

This is not to imply that democracies do not have departures from the principle of true equality, but, in a democracy, the principle is clear. Despite actual or procedural deviations, equality is a principle enshrined in the law. Reaching the stage of equality in practice is the acknowledged goal of all. Those who oppose or block such a movement are on the defensive. Therefore, establishing a democratic system is an example of *tikkun olam.* In the end, the infrastructure needed to sustain the full dignity of the image of God includes law, culture, economics, and politics.

Perfecting the human being (*tikkun ha'adam*) is part of this process of making the world whole. Human beings have their own weaknesses and faults. Even if a person is given all the wealth in the world, the person might still choose to abuse others. Because a person lives in a society that is built on the principle of equal rights does not mean that, in practice, he or she is going to extend this dignity to others. Therefore, side-by-side with the task of perfecting the world is the task of perfecting the human—to bring out the best in everyone.

What does perfecting the human being involve? Part of perfection is achieving long life. Therefore, the goal is to develop a science that can cure diseases and improve human health. Part of the task is to improve the individuals' and groups' recognition of their intrinsic dignities. This requires the creation of a foundation of religious and ethical values, as well as cultural teachings that communicate the infinite value, equality, and uniqueness of every individual and the preciousness of the groups within which individuals grow. Part of the task is to get humans to want to do good. Humans are not machines; the goal is not to generate ethical robots. So *tikkun ha-adam* is not an attempt to change human nature, but rather to develop the best tendencies in people.

Society can bring out the good in people by educating them, by developing constructive options for them. If society builds up an infrastructure of dignity in every area, if the processes of life constantly communicate respect and love for the individual, then the individual is more likely to express his or her dignity and strength constructively in relation to others. Upgrading material and political conditions must go hand-in-hand with nurturing the soul of people. Judaism insists that for full human "health," there must be sound, loving relationships between humans and between humans and God. The realization of the human being involves not just self, but being in relationship and in community (as well as being grounded in the divine). This is the psychic, spiritual dimension of *tikkun olam.* Without this dimension of *tikkun ha-adam, tikkun olam* will not be realized either. This last is more difficult to accomplish than upgrading material conditions, but it must be done. One cannot simply improve the infrastructure of wealth and assume that everything will get better; one must also correct the people who are going to control that wealth.

Q. Rabbi, what about the special role of the Jews in *tikkun olam*? Is it living by *mitzvot*? And what about contradiction between the strong emphasis you give to the value of equality, and the important place the whole conception of chosenness has in Jewish thought? After all, isn't one of the great sources of hatred of Jews that we have been perceived as claiming to be closer to God, more specially loved by God than others are? And isn't this the very opposite of what you are defining as *tikkun olam*?

Greenberg. You are raising three distinct questions. (1) Does obeying *mitzvot* automatically mean that one is working for *tikkun olam*? (2) What is the role of Jews in *tikkun olam*? (3) Is there a contradiction between human equality and Jewish chosenness? Let me respond to each.

The whole system of *mitzvot* is dedicated to *tikkun ha-adam.* The *halachah* is designed to bring out the fullness of life and to bring out the best in humans. What does it mean to live a fully human life? If a person lives life routinely, this is a form of death. *Mitzvot* take the homogenized experiences of life—eating, talking, relating, making love—and turn them into distinctive, more intense moments of life. Prohibitions are designed to stop the individual from choosing death. The message of the *halachah* is that every human being must choose. You can live life wastefully, ruin your health, use your strength to hurt people—or you can live your life in *kedushah* (holiness). I take *kedushah* to mean—to be more and more like God. God is the ultimate phenomenon of holiness. God is life, the highest intensity, the plenitude of life; God is freedom, the fullness of freedom. To live a life of *kedushah* is to bring out those qualities in myself and vis-à-vis others. This is the basic purpose of every *mitzvah.* The *halachot* are actually designed to train, to bring out in the individual or in the structure of society the maximum of life, e.g., the maximum of holiness.

Here is a good exercise. Take any *mitzvah* as an example. I would undertake to show that its effect and purpose is to perfect human life.

Q. Take *Shabbat.*

Greenberg. *Shabbat* is designed to inculcate an ethic of creative, constructive work. The *halachah* defines *melachah* (work prohibited on *Shabbat*) as meeting the following criteria: (1) planned, e.g., the worker has a conception of the intended product or outcome; (2) purposeful, e.g., the work done is related to the outcome; (3) constructive, not destructive, e.g., the product upgrades the world we live in; (4) the product has intrinsic value and some permanence, e.g., it is not evanescent or an instant throwaway.

By telling us what *not* to do on the seventh day, *Shabbat* teaches us what we *should* do on the other six days of the week. The goal is to make *all* humans realize that all work—properly done—involves building a world that maximizes life, productivity, creativity, and the dignity of the laborer. In its categories of work, *Shabbat* encourages the creation of wealth, food, clothing, and shelter to raise the level of human welfare everywhere.

At the same time, involvement in work tends to grow into glorification of work. Since the unrestrained ethos of wealth creation can lead to absolutization of money and a consequent cheapening of human life in relation to property, *Shabbat* seeks to prevent that excess. Furthermore, work may expand to take up all of life and lead to neglect of self, of family, of friends. The *Shabbat* labor prohibition challenges the addiction to work; by liberating the day for personal living, it teaches that work is not everything. People must also live, i.e., be or relate. Spending time with oneself and the family restores the sense of self-worth that is not a product of net worth. *Shabbat* creates a framework encouraging the individual to experience the beauty and uniqueness of other individuals because there is free time and leisure to spend with them.

Shaping and reshaping nature to increase productivity and sustain more life is part of the mission of perfecting the world. But if one allows this utilitarian attitude toward nature to "run away," then technologists are given license to abuse nature and the environment—and society. *Shabbat* attempts to correct and enrich the attitude toward nature. On this day, the utilitarian attitude toward nature is balanced with a spirit of accepting nature and experiencing it as sacred in itself. Thus, the dialectic of using nature and respecting it (therefore, not abusing it) is sustained; simultaneously, the dialectic of humans exercising power and controlling it is upheld.

Shabbat is also the day when Jewish culture reasserts its models of perfection. Equality and justice are reaffirmed as the highest principles. No slavery is allowed on this day (although Torah compromises with slavery's existence all week). When the slave and the master experience the truth—the reality—that on this day the slave is truly a free person, then they are prevented from absolutizing the status of slavery during the rest of the week.

Shabbat is a day when one is not allowed to handle money. At the same time, one is obligated to provide the poor with food, clothing, and shelter. So, on this day, there is neither indulgence in riches nor immersion in poverty. It is as if, at least on this day, there is no poverty. Thus, *Shabbat* can be seen as a way of instilling values and structuring society to bring out *kedushah* in every aspect of life.[1]

Q. Take *kashrut.*

Greenberg. The first message of *kashrut* is that killing and eating are not to be taken for granted. In preparing to eat kosher, one is involved in a process that affirms reverence for life. Meat-eating in all its forms is restricted. In the Garden of Eden, humans and animals were instructed to be vegetarians. The message is that,

1. For a more extended articulation of the humane values in *Shabbat,* see Irving Greenberg, *The Jewish Way,* Chapter 5.

ideally, no person should live by killing another living creature. In *kashrut*, the Torah "compromises" with the real world by permitting meat-eating, but only with real limitations. There are no kosher restrictions when it comes to eating vegetables and minerals exclusively; but once people eat the meat of living creatures, then more and more kosher restrictions are applied. Eating the lower forms of life—fish—is less restricted than eating fowl; fowl regulations are less restrictive than those applying to animals. With fish, only the permitted species are restricted; with fowl, the forms of killing are also narrowed; with animals, the forms of preparation are additionally limited. Note that meat (killed animal) and milk (source and symbol of mother's life, nurturing) may not be prepared together. Then, when people are about to eat, they are required to make a *bracha* (blessing) of gratitude to God; this is an acknowledgment that the eater does not "own" this life. Thus, the process of eating is redesigned to teach reverence for life.

Q. How about remembering? Remembering the Exodus?

Greenberg. The purpose of remembering the Exodus is to teach us to free the slaves; it reminds us of God's promise to enable Jews—and, some day, every human—to have their own country, a place where they will not be strangers who can be oppressed.[2]

In sum, the *mitzvot* constitute a training ground (to bring out the best in people and thus lead to *tikkun olam*). The *halachah* is a way of life that offers a model of how to create good people. This kind of system operating over millennia has served to perfect the Jew, to make Israel more likely to live a life of holiness.

This leads to your second question. What is the Jewish role in the world? The ideal of the Torah is that Jews live their special way *in relation to the rest of the world.* The Torah does not glorify the Jews as a people unto themselves. When the Five Books of Moses tell the story of the Jewish people and its religious origins, the story

---

2. For an extended treatment of the significance of the Exodus and the role of memory in Jewish tradition, see Irving Greenberg, *The Jewish Way*, Chapters 2 and 4 *et passim.*

does not start with the first Jew, Abraham. Nor does it start with the Exodus, which is the greatest event of Jewish history. Genesis begins with the first moment of Creation. The message is that the Jews do not come into being in a vacuum. The Jews' significance and their message are to be understood in relation to the rest of the world.

The teaching of those first eleven chapters is that God wants, and intends, the perfection of the entire world. All living things—not just humans—are in covenant with God. The first covenant, Noah's covenant, is with all humans. (Noah is not a Jew.) Abraham's covenant is designed to complete the realization of the Noahide covenant. Thus, the Jews come into being as a distinctive people to help achieve the full realization of the covenant for all living things, and especially in relation to the rest of humankind.

In the biblical view (and over the course of history), Jews were meant to play three roles.

(1) Teacher: to teach this idea of perfecting the world; to preach the infinite value, equality and uniqueness of every individual; to advocate mutual, family help to enable everyone to live a full life. The teaching was needed because, throughout much of history, the very concept of full human dignity seemed to be absurd. The actual economic, political, and legal conditions broadcast the message of the cheapness of life, the lack of humanity of the other, the inferiority of women, and so on. Other colors of skin were inferior for most of human history. People were hungry. Poverty was the norm. The idea of the final perfection in history was contradicted by the facts of history, every step of the way. The Jews had to be teachers, to teach this ideal, to convince everyone not to accept the status quo.

(2) Model: the Jews are to be "a covenant nation" and "a light unto the nations" (Isaiah 42:6). To get from the existent, flawed globe populated by a suffering, miserable humanity to that end-goal perfect world is a process. There is a constant struggle along the way. Every move to improve the world has side effects and trade-offs. To increase the wealth, cultures increase technology—and cause more pollution. The effort to bring democracy and freedom may lead to anarchy and the breakdown of social systems. So the world needs models of how to go about

the perfection process. Humans learn best from other humans. The Jewish people serve as a working model. A working model is not perfect. Jews do not always do the right thing. But, with all their flaws (which show that Jews are only human), Jews can still model. (Note: If the model is perfect it is a Divine model, pure and simple. This means that most humans cannot follow it. The best personal models are people just like ourselves—only a little better. The Jews are meant to be such a model.)

The covenant with Abraham (which later became the covenant of Sinai) represents the Jewish commitment to serve as role models. People cannot serve as role models if they disappear into a faceless mass of humanity. Jews are willing to be visible. Visibility means that Jews must be willing to take on public actions—dressing, eating, or behaving differently enough for people to recognize the fact and say: That is a Jew. Then they can study and learn from the Jewish model. Jews are always on display and there is no place to hide. It is like the profession of stand-up comedy. Comedians have to put themselves on the line; every performance involves constant exposure without relief. The performer makes a joke and succeeds (or fails); in thirty seconds' time, people know how you are doing. The comedian cannot hide behind a troupe of background dancers or battle-scene crowds. As a comic, you are naked to your enemies—and to your friends. That is the Jewish role in history. (Every people has the potential to play this role.) In effect, the Jews said, "We are willing to be visible, knowing that all our flaws will be highlighted all over. We are willing to be active in *tikkun olam.*" Jews have made terrible mistakes—maybe no worse than others, but ours are visible and writ large, unsparingly related by ourselves.

One of the cruelest aspects of Jewish–Christian relations is that Christians unsparingly (even exaggeratedly) would cite passages from the Bible that depict Jewish sin and failure. Christians then insisted that Jews were the worst of people, worthy of being degraded and punished. After all, Jews were convicted by their own testimony. Their own prophets condemned the Hebrews. But Christians took the prophetic critique out of context. Claiming to speak for humanity, Christians suppressed the fact that Jews put themselves forward for the sake of humanity. To be a pioneer, one must stick out one's neck and be visible. The pioneer always makes a greater fool of himself than those who come later. Jews were willing to put themselves on display; they were willing to make the errors that are inescapable if one is the first one to try. The Jews hoped that humanity would learn from its achievements—and from their errors. Thus, they recorded their own errors and sins without softening or shading. A failure often teaches more than a success. Recall the old adage: Good judgment is the outcome of learning from exercises of bad judgment. Despite Christian caricature and anti-Semitic stereotypes, Jews have played an invaluable role as models for humanity in creating a caring society, in serving as the conscience "goading" minority, in serving as idol-smashers and prophetic critics, in exemplifying a family that crosses all boundaries in its concern for fellow humans.

(3) Co-workers: Jews have served as co-workers for *tikkun olam* in many societies. My understanding of this role has been enriched by modern culture. Modernity has brought Jews into contact with the others, who are experienced not as gentiles, not just as individuals, but as members of vital religious cultures and dignified ways of life. Such contacts evoke recognition of the important contributions that others are making and their indispensable role in the cosmic process of *tikkun olam.* In earlier times, Jews were so surrounded by enemies that they often forgot the others. The gentiles were so hostile and demeaning that Jews were threatened with physical and cultural obliteration. In response, Jews were tempted to respond that "Only Jews are beloved of God," or that "Only Jews perfect the world." In time, this turned into denial of the *tzelem elokim* of the others. Thus, Judaism developed an ethical double standard. Classic sources emerged that, in effect, rule that a Jewish life is worth everything and a gentile life is worth less. Now there are Jewish sources that rationalize: "Kill the gentiles." This is a mirror image of the gentile culture that preached, "Kill the Jews."

Q. Only we did not do it.

Greenberg. Thank God for that. We can point out with pride as Jews that we were sinned against much more than we sinned.

Nevertheless, it is important to know that these sources exist—they are a warning that Jews are as capable of anger and hatred as any other people. Therefore, we must be on guard, now that we are back in power, to check ourselves and to beware of what we can inflict on others.

Your strong reaction also suggests that you feel embarrassed and self-conscious at a public showing of this Jewish "dirty laundry." Maybe, like me, you are ashamed of what the sources are saying and wish to reduce their significance. I understand this reaction. Let me offer a word of consolation. On balance, we need not be ashamed that Jews were only human. If Jews were models who never did anything wrong, they would constitute an "inhuman," i.e., oppressive and unsustainable, model. We should be ashamed only if—now that we have freedom and power—we draw upon such sources to abuse others in the name of our tradition or history. This is what happened in the Baruch Goldstein massacre in Hebron and in the response of certain Jews supporting him. Fortunately, the positive encounter between Jews and non-Jews made possible by democracy and cultural openness and the extraordinary intercultural and intergroup communications pattern of the twentieth century are helping us come to know the others as full human beings, as being in the image of God. Knowing the other acts to break stereotypes and to disarm us (and others) from acting against the other. Thus the openness of society brings out our best behavior.

This empathetic atmosphere generated by extraordinary communication helps Jews come to see that they are co-workers in *tikkun olam.* There are many other people—organized as nations, as religions, as movements—doing good things in the world. As Jews, we should be happy to make our small contribution. In a way, it is a relief to know that we are not Atlas, having to lift the whole world by ourselves. Nor does this realization detract from our dignity or our importance in history. Jews make up less than one-third of one percent of humanity, yet we have had a totally disproportionate influence in history—on the constructive side. So, there is no reason to deny the role of others. Jews can find fulfillment enough in knowing how well we have played our three roles. There is sufficient work and dignity for the others to claim their share. Once Jews admit that others can make a central contribution to *tikkun olam* and that this area is no Jewish monopoly, we can look at this role with unjaundiced eyes. We can admit that the special role has not come easily; the effort it takes is great, and the cost is enormous. By the same token, we can conclude that the significance we have gained and the contribution that we have made makes it all worthwhile. We are freed to consider alternatives—and to confirm the value of going on with this special role. We should also be realistic enough to admit that these efforts are not made easily or "naturally." Jews are *not* genetically programmed to be good. It takes great effort—and religious training—to go on acting Jewishly. Without reinforcement, training, and memory, Jews will not automatically go on being an avant-garde.

This brings me to your third question. Chosenness. Chosenness means simply that one is singled out. The chosen one is no longer one of an anonymous mass. The chosen-people concept expresses the Jews' experience of being singled out by God's love. The experience is electrifying, inspiring, challenging, and never to be forgotten. If one has truly tasted the experience, one would be reluctant to lose that feeling by dissolving back into the mass. From this, we can deduce that the many assimilating Jews have not had the experience of being "a light unto the nations," of feeling loved infinitely by God, of being singled out.

You will note that the synonym for chosenness is to be "singled out." That means to experience being part of—in the midst of—a larger group while simultaneously undergoing a specific set of feelings and encounters that are distinctive. We lose neither connection—to God or to other humans—in the process of living the experience. Nor is the process reserved for us to the exclusion of everyone else. God's love—God's redemptive love—which is the basis of chosenness, is never the monopoly of any one people. Redemption cannot happen to one group alone. The chosenness flows from the fact that this particular redemption happened to us. Others—in the very large group of humanity (or of Jewry) of which I am part—may undergo their own experience of redemption. That cannot take away my unique experience or my feeling of uniqueness. The proper response to chosenness is to feel a sense of being uplifted; this should inspire the chosen to want to play a leadership, constructive role in bringing redemption to others—to share the wealth, so to speak.

The charge is constantly made that chosenness brings with it a feeling or message of superiority. That conclusion is a wrong application of a right principle. Chosenness is in tension with—but is also complementary to—equality. Chosenness means that in my unique way I have a special role to play. Others who are equal to me may be chosen in other ways; and even if they are not chosen, they do not forfeit their intrinsic dignity of equality. Of course, chosenness has been misunderstood by some Jews also; sometimes election leads to arrogance. The prophets constantly challenged this egotistical understanding. Jews were not chosen because they were better, or because they were more powerful. Jews are the smallest of peoples (cf. Deuteronomy 7:6 ff.). Any time Jews start to think of chosenness as genetic superiority, the tradition cracks down. This is idolatry. You are not appreciating the gift God has given you (cf. Deuteronomy 8:14 ff., 9:4 ff.; Amos 9:7 ff.).

The main point of being chosen is to know that you are not intrinsically superior, but you can respond to election in a way that makes you more worthy and a truly constructive model and teacher. Once Jews grasp the true miracle of being chosen, i.e., that we are co-workers, *loved and saved by God—not by our own merits*—then it is much easier to see the truth that others have also experienced God's love and redemption. It follows that if all goes well, everyone will experience election.

The most striking statement of plural chosenness is found in Isaiah 19:24–25. Isaiah promises that someday God will redeem Egypt—the very nation that more than once enslaved the people of Israel. The day will come, says Isaiah, when Israel will be blessed along with Assyria (another classic oppressor) and Egypt. "On that day I will bless my people, Egypt, my handiwork, Assyria, and my inheritance, Israel" (ibid., 25). The three terms—people, handiwork, inheritance—are basically synonyms; they are synonymous for a covenantal people. And why does Isaiah link Egypt and Assyria with Israel? Up to his day, these were the two most oppressive peoples, the cruelest enemies that the Jews ever had. Isaiah is saying that even the Jews' worst enemies someday will be singled out to play a role parallel to Israel's in *tikkun olam.*

Chosenness is deliberately misinterpreted by anti-Semites. Anti-Semites say that Jews are claiming superiority; that is how they justify their hatred for Jews. There is a kernel of truth behind this stereotype. Chosenness does evoke jealousy; but the resentment is not a reflection of a Jewish sin, but rather of the anti-Semite's pathology. The very fact that Jews are chosen to play this avant-garde role means that they have to be different. It is the difference that evokes hatred—particularly on the part of people who think they have the Absolute. If people believe that they have reached the ultimate perfection, they instinctively—if pathologically—challenge the Jews: "Why are you different from us? You must be denying our greatness, our absolute standing."

The Jewish role—the very fact that Jews continue to exist—*is* a denial of other people's claims to absoluteness. In witnessing to God, in trying to play a role in *tikkun olam*, Jews give testimony that the world is not yet perfect. The hatred that the difference evokes stems not from Jewish behavior—that is always the anti-Semite's excuse—but from idolatry. The essence of idolatry is to take something partial and make it absolute. A Christian who believes that Christianity is the final word of God hates Jews for being Jewish and not becoming Christian. The Jewish persistence tacitly denies the claim that a final perfection is here. The same pathology is shown by secular absolutists. Anyone who thinks that Communism is perfect will deeply resent the ongoing existence of the Jews. Stalin believed that Communism was the final redemptive system; he expected Jews to be totally loyal to it. Then the Jews greeted Golda Meir when she came to Moscow and danced wildly in the streets. Stalin turned on the Jews with a fury; he planned eventually to get rid of the Jews.

Hitler's absolute hatred of and total war on the Jews stemmed from the same world view. Hitler sought to become God; the Führer was to be the absolute ruler, the source of right and wrong. The Jews, by their existence, testified that "there is only one God" who relativizes all human claims to absolute obedience. To "destroy God," Hitler had to destroy God's witnesses, the Jewish people. Jewry's testimony has unleashed rivalry and jealousy repeatedly. Jewish willingness to stand up and deny humans' absolute claims draws upon them the wrath of the absolutists.

There are people who understand their own or their system's limitations. Such people will not need to hate Jews. There are anti-Semitic communists, but not all communists are anti-Semitic. There are anti-Semitic Catholics, but not all Catholics are anti-Semitic. The difference is not in the system; the difference is the attitude of the participants. To hate somebody who is different is really to claim that "I am perfect and no one has the right to be different from me." The persecutors would not have gone down the path of hatred had they affirmed their own limits. They should have said: "I accept my limitations even as the Jews have accepted their limitations." Instead, they clung to their idolatrous absolutes and turned to hatred and persecution of all whose difference (in their minds) denied their total claims. First and foremost, because they come out of other cultures and countries and because they insist on remaining distinctive, the Jews have drawn upon themselves the wrath of the totalitarians.

The upshot is that chosenness is not antidemocratic. Election affirms the uniqueness of each people's mission—but all are equal. In this understanding, *asher bachar banu mikol ha'amim* is interpreted to mean "chosenness in the midst of the nations." The word *mikol* expresses wonder—"Why us?"—and appreciation: One must resist interpreting these words triumphalistically. Such a tendency crops up when Jews are marginalized and under pressure, but it weakens the Jews' performance and model.

Remember that equality as a governing philosophy can pose a great danger. The only way to guarantee absolute equality is to homogenize people and cultures. Thus, equality may become the enemy of uniqueness or difference. If one group is smarter than another, we may have to make everyone "dumb" to preserve equality. The alternative to homogenization is the concept of "chosenness." Election affirms that the other is different for a good reason; the other is different because he or she is chosen for a special mission. This principle applies to blacks as well as whites, to Christians as well as Jews. Each group is called—that is, chosen. Each can become a leader for *tikkun olam*; each can share its experiences and become teachers and models for others. All peoples can avoid arrogance by recognizing that they are co-workers in this process.

There are Jews who claim that this very notion of multiple-chosenness is offensive. Such people have absolutized Jewish chosenness. They are guilty of the same kind of understanding that leads others to become anti-Semites. This is not to deny that there is a strong current in the tradition that insists that the Jews are the only chosen ones. However, one can feel much more sympathetic to the need of an embattled and degraded minority living in the midst of a hostile Christian or Muslim majority declaring that the other traditions are without religious validity. Remember that the other religions were supercessionist and had declared Judaism to be invalidated; they had demonized Jews and Judaism. Under the circumstances, Jews would be following Hillel's principle, i.e., doing unto others what the others had done unto them. But then, as Jews, we experienced only the negative behavior of those religions.

Now we have reached the twentieth century. We Jews are independent with a state of our own. We Jews live in the United States of America and other places where we are not afraid to be ourselves. We have enough margins and enough openness to see the constructive contributions that other religions and their believers make to the world. There is no need to hang onto the claim that we are the only one; under these circumstances, a monopoly is religiously narrow and ethically limited. We Jews should have enough inner security in our freedom and, out of consciousness of God's love, allow love to be exercised as universally as God wills. The fullness of the other's divine service enables us to appreciate and learn from them. We are free to truly understand chosenness—with its limitations. This limit *strengthens* the idea of chosenness. When it comes to human understandings and religious categories, the perfection is in the limits—because only God is absolute.

Q. I think that the position of Jews is different here from other groups. Jews did not like other groups trying to convert everyone to think as they thought. If anything, the Jewish sin in chosenness, if there is such a sin, might be seen as such a great preoccupation with their own role that they were really indifferent to what happened to others. Yet here I connect this with what you said about the Jewish role as teachers. I think that the Jews have succeeded in teaching certain fundamental universal values to humankind. For instance, the ideal of world peace. At least as an ideal. But this connects back with the opening question of the interview. The changes seem external; if you will, there has been a certain *tikkun olam.* But there do not seem to be really internal changes, *tikkun ha-adam.* It seems that humanity, at heart, is as evil in our generation as it has always been. In the relation between individuals, I do not see where there is *tikkun ha-adam.* Do you really see that there is *tikkun ha-adam*?

Greenberg. We can make a strong case for the decline of human nature. Given the mass murders of this century, one is tempted to react, in the words of Genesis: *Yetzer lev haadam ra m'neurav* ("The heart of man is evil from youth"). Some streams of Christianity have generalized that verse into the general category of original sin, i.e., the human is fundamentally evil. It follows that ethics and belief must be based on the need to curb and control the willful, evil nature lurking in humans that is waiting to break out.

There is a certain amount of empirical evidence for the claim of original sin. But when all that evidence is added up, I reject that claim even as I reject the moderns' counterargument that the human being has a fundamentally good nature. (This implies that faith and ethics should be based on the principle that humans innately do good unless prevented from doing it by oppressive systems. This argument, made famous by Rousseau, is a rather generous estimate of human nature given the historical experience of the past half-century.)

Ultimately, we had best stand with the rabbinic position. There is a *yetzer tov* and a *yetzer ra.* They are equally present in the individual; the ethical decision, the exercise of human will, decides whether good or evil behavior will predominate. Of course, belief in two contradictory urges can be interpreted to imply that there can be no permanent improvement of human beings. I would argue against this assumption on two levels. For one, society can bring out the best and the worst. A concentration camp is designed to degrade people; to protect themselves in that setting, people resort to defensive, self-centered, sometimes vicious behavior. The *tikkun* may not be found in a permanent change of nature, but it can be brought into being by setting up a different structure to bring out better human patterns. Thus, an improved normative structure (religious culture) or behavioral institutions, such as law and government, can improve human behavior. In my judgment, this is what Judaism accomplished. This tactic fits my criterion for *tikkun ha-adam.*

Second, through religion and through loving relationships, one can improve the psychology and behavior of people even in the present human condition. So *tikkun ha-adam* need not mean a permanent change in human nature; it can refer to other changes that can—for the lifetime of the individual—bring out the best in them.

Despite the flaws of contemporary culture, I believe that for more people than ever it has brought out the best behavior—or, at least, better behavior. Why? Opportunity is more widespread. The sense of human dignity and equality is greater because this is a society in which there is strong economic, political, and cultural upward mobility. In this modern process, the world has adopted classic Jewish norms such as human dignity, image of God, and so on. These are norms that bring out the best in people. Thus, the culture trains individuals in the idea that they are supposed to not abuse other people. The norms imply that all are equal and that they deserve respect. As a selfish or powerful individual, I am tempted to act exploitatively, but then the culture continuously broadcasts messages about the rights of others. Countless groups that were once systematically degraded in daily social intercourse are now affirmed in the cultural messages. That is one way in which *tikkun ha-adam* is going on right now. More people live in democracy than ever before. (In a way, it is sad to report this because billions are still outside this framework of dignity.)

Q. There are now more people than ever before living on a bare subsistence level without real opportunity for bettering themselves.

Greenberg. Right. But the percentages of those living in dignity have gone up.

There is an alternative possibility in the realm of *tikkun ha-adam.* The prophet said (because he felt the same tension that you feel, e.g., what is the use, we will never get there) that God will have to make a new covenant and put a new heart in us so that finally humans will *always* do the right thing (cf. Jeremiah 31:32–33). Clearly, in Jeremiah's view, *tikkun ha-adam* meant nothing less than a basic change in human nature over the long term. Rav Kook believed in this option also. He thought that evolution was bringing out the best in human behavior. By the twentieth century, people had been evolutionarily bred to go with the good (as well as to deal with bigger issues and to make more sophisticated choices). Thus, an upgrading of human nature was going on. In Kook's view, the animal or instinctual urges were weakening and the ethical, good urges were strengthening. Kook was an optimist who believed that improvement in human nature was actually happening now. In his view, the promised substitution of a new heart was happening gradually and was close to realization.

Personally, I find myself located somewhere between the two positions. Although I do not feel comfortable with the claim that a permanent improvement has occurred in human nature (given the evils perpetuated in the twentieth century), I would affirm that there has been significant development in the breadth of human consciousness. A wider group is incorporated in the universe of moral obligations of the average person.

This brings me to the heart of the issue. How can one develop love or dignity or respect for the other person? The best way is to know that person. If I do not know you, it is easy to stereotype you negatively. When I do get to know you personally or intimately, my consciousness expands to do justice to your image of God. By bringing people together across cross-cultural lines, by making people more aware of each other, by linking the world through communications and media, our society has, in a way, upgraded human consciousness. In so doing, it has strengthened human conscience—because knowledge of the other's infinite value, equality, and uniqueness evokes a response of respect (and ultimately of love) for the other.

Of course, modern culture has also increased the power for evil available to people; clearly, that power has been exercised. Nevertheless, in reading the *Einsatzgruppen* trials record in the aftermath of the Holocaust, I discovered that one major reason for the shift from shooting squads to gas chambers was that the soldier-killers were affected by the sight of the women and children that they were killing. It was determined that in a gas chamber there would be less contact and less risk of brutalizing or upsetting the soldiers. Thus the murderers recognized that consciousness of the other's humanity evokes a certain respect or awe for that other—and thus deters evil behavior. On the other hand, one should not exaggerate. Heightened consciousness did not stop several thousand soldiers from killing men, women, and children day after day for more than a year and a half before the switch in tactics was made.

On balance, I take my stand closer to Rav Kook's side of the spectrum even if I do not go all the way with his implication that evolution is "bleaching out" the evil elements in human nature. There is a wonderful passage in Rav Kook's writings on the difference between conservatives and liberals. The liberals stress the need for change because they see the ascending path of human nature through evolution. The conservatives stress caution and restraint because they see the evil in the continuing human misbehavior. Kook suggests that, instead of fighting each other, they should treat each other as dialectical partners. There can be no permanent stasis and no perfect final balance. The liberals should push for more change because they do see human improvement, but should recognize the constructive check in their opponents' positions. The conservatives should continue their fight for maintaining strong structures of control because of the ever-present danger that change will unleash negative behavior currently held in check by the status quo, but should welcome the liberals' contribution. We should all learn from Kook's pluralist vision that there is a constructive role for the two competing positions and that each should help the other avoid possible bad outcomes of their own position.

Many people believe that these utopian ideals of Jewry have been adopted by all of humanity in modern times, so that one need not be Jewish anymore. This view is a major rationale for assimilation. The biblical views of human dignity have become so widespread that many Jews feel that there is no longer a difference significant enough to justify the effort of maintaining Jewish distinctiveness. Some feel that since all humans are in the same boat and the positive values are formed in the universal culture, maintaining the differences only divides humankind and sets back the cause of *tikkun olam.* In a sense, the issue is: Are the assimilationists correct, or is this another case of premature messianism? (Declaring the arrival of the Messiah is an old Jewish tendency.) Since, in fact, there is a lot left to be improved in the world, I conclude that there is still a major role left for Jewry, as a model, as a community holding itself to a higher standard. This is not to say that there is only one standard—that would mean that everything is perfect. But until the world is perfected, we need specialists who will make the extra effort, people who will try harder. Despite the improvements in the world and despite the widespread acceptance of Jewish ideals, the Jewish role is unfinished.

Q. Rabbi, this leads me to a question to which I wanted to devote a whole other interview. The relation of *tikkun ha-adam* to *middot.* What kind of character do you feel the individual should be working toward having in this world? What is the role of traditional Jewish traits such as compassion, kindness, and humility? How do you conceive an ideal human being? Can there be such a thing as an ideal Jew?

Greenberg. By implication, you are pointing to the very rich traditional Jewish *musar* literature, which is focused on perfecting character. *Musar* is not widely studied; it is not even widely known. Yet, in the Middle Ages, many books were written in this spirit. Maimonides dealt with this topic in his Shmonah Prakim (Eight Chapters), as did many other medieval greats (Bahya Ibn Pakuda; Rabbeinu Jonah of Gerona; in later centuries, Rabbi Moshe Chaim Luzzatto—to name just a few). In the nineteenth century and continuing into the twentieth century there was the *musar* movement, founded by Rabbi Israel Salanter, which focused on the Torah's vision of the good human being rather than on just the specifics of observance. The *musarniks,* as they were called, developed Jewish educational insights into a systematic educational process for improving human beings. They placed special emphasis on developing good character, compassion, and the other qualities you mentioned. This tradition needs to be revived and brought front-and-center in Jewish education. There have been techniques developed and books written to advance the process. Nevertheless, in talking about *tikkun ha-middot,* keep in mind that there is not one model of the perfect human being. In a general way, one can hold up the image of God ideal—a human being conscious of his or her own infinite value and recognizing the same value in others, a person who feels equal and acts toward other people as equal, someone who feels unique and acts toward others as to bring out their uniqueness.

There is another possible general model for the ideal person. The tradition speaks of imitating God, *v'halachtah biderechav* (to walk in God's ways) or *lehidamot* (to make oneself more and more like God). Historically, the Talmud focused the idea on resembling God by imitating God's love: "As God is loving, so you be loving; as God is gracious, you be gracious. . . ." But Rabbi Soloveitchik taught us that *imitatio dei* can be applied to God's power, especially God's creative power. In this spirit, one should extend the principle to all of God's fundamental capacities—consciousness, power, relationship (love), will, freedom, life.

All of life is growing toward God. The human is that form of life which is most like God. Humans have more consciousness, power, relationship, freedom, and will than any other form of life. The human is called to use these God-given capacities and to develop them even more so that each person becomes more and more like God. This applies also to the Divine capacity of being alive. Humans are not the longest-living form of life, but we can act to extend life as no other creature can. To become more Godlike is a meta-*mitzvah* that guides all the other *mitzvot.* Since there is no way to develop to a level equal to God, there can be no fixed model of a perfect human being. Humans can and should develop all their capacities all the days of their lives.

Take the most fundamental divine capacity—God's capacity for love. As humans, we are commanded to develop our capacity for love—to the point of loving our neighbor or friend as we love ourselves, to the point of loving strangers, and so forth. But can there ever be an upper limit on the capacity for love? Love is like a muscle: The more you use it, the stronger it gets. The average person never gets close to developing or utilizing his or her brain's full capacity—or their heart's total capability of love.

How can one develop this quality of loving? When it comes to love of God, Maimonides suggests that love of God comes out of studying the universe and realizing its exquisite structure—and the wonderful Creator who is behind it all. Also, study of Torah leads to love of God. When it comes to love of people, I would suggest that by getting close to people, by getting to know them in their uniqueness and value, by having closer relationships—our own capacity for love is enlarged. The good person is the one who constantly exercises and develops these Godlike qualities and applies them to relationships, to behavior, to the way of life. Some people are funny and some much more solemn; some are introverts and some extroverts. Given the range of each person's talents, the model of the ideal human should not be a generic one. The model should suggest a direction in which the individuals develop themselves.

Q. Rabbi, do you have any heroes or role models? Which people have set the example for you of coming closer to God in this way?

Greenberg. Every person has models in life. No one could become human without them. Individually, I have written about some of them: my father, some of my best teachers (especially Rav Yehuda Leib Nekritz, my closest teacher in Bais Yosef, and Rabbi Soloveitchik), my brother and sisters, who are extremely kind and good people. There are also different models at different stages of one's life. I have been lucky to have good friends. Many times at turning points in my life there were good friends to inspire or help me through. My wife has been an extraordinary influence on me. Her most powerful impact has stemmed from the fact that she is extremely human. She is kind and amazingly considerate of people; she is so much aware of them. Although I am a theoretician of the image of God, in practice I am much more oblivious to the specifics and unique qualities of people than she is. Some of my models have become personal friends. Elie Wiesel and his life as a witness had a powerful impact on my thinking. David Hartman influenced and nurtured me intellectually; his work and thought have always inspired me. There are people whose life work I have admired—Aharon Lichtenstein, Adin Steinsaltz, Shlomo Riskin, Yehudah Amital—in Israel. To me they represented some of the best possibilities in modern orthodoxy. Abba Kovner was (and, after his untimely death, still is) a great hero and educational model for me. He was a secularist Jewish revolutionary with a profound appreciation for traditional values (as witnessed by his narrative schema for Beit Hatefutsot, the Museum of the Diaspora). One of the first to organize an armed revolt during the Holocaust, he came to a compassionate and wise understanding of the heroism of those who could only stand and wait. He led a group that sought to take revenge on the Nazis after the war; yet he was a pioneer in seeking reconciliation with the Arabs. His death left us bereft of a key bridge figure between the religious and secular in Israel; we will miss him even more when the Israeli Kulturkampf erupts fully.

Kovner's death was a personal body blow which summoned up the memory of the loss of my closest friend, Zev (Willy) Frank in the 1970s from multiple sclerosis. Zev was a brilliant mathematical physicist and Talmudic scholar with a remarkable creative flair and sense of humor. Like Soloveitchik, he helped me see the patterns and possibilities in halachic ideas. (I always believed that he was the person who could have and should have succeeded Rabbi Soloveitchik and carry on his unique combination of halachah [law] and aggadah [philosophy, literature, narrative].) Zev also encouraged me and opened my eyes to the possibility of growth and fresh thinking in Orthodoxy and to the human compassion that must guide it. Like my father, he proved to be irreplaceable in his influence on my life. Sadly, he was taken from us too early.

As a people, we have been fortunate to have great leaders in our lifetime, like Ben Gurion. Note that I say these are *great* leaders, not perfect leaders. No one is perfect in every area.

Some of my heroes have been non-Jews. In my childhood I was very impressed with Mahatma Gandhi. His model as national liberator, as one who renewed a dominantly Hindu civilization by infusing it with the best Western values and who used Hindu values as a source of critique of the West—inspired me. I also admired his spiritual resistance to the British and his use of religious values such as nonviolence to transform the level of politics. Years later, I became more reserved in my attitude towards Gandhi when I discovered how poor his record was on Zionism and on responses to Hitler's persecution. I came to accept George Orwell's withering critique that Gandhi's "greatness" was the reflection of his opponents' humanness rather than a personal accomplishment, considering his excessively ascetic and spiritually reactionary tendencies; yet I still retain a certain respect for him. Martin Luther King, Jr. was also a model. I always feel a special sadness that assassination cut him off just when he was needed most. His union of theology and action, of spiritual life combined with community leadership, continues to impress and inspire me. And Reverend King was right on the Jewish issues as well.

There is a wide range of public figures, people one does not know, whose models one encounters through the media or public life. One advantage of modern society is that its media are constantly broadcasting the images of models who, in a less communicative society, one would never meet. The secret is to be exposed (without coercion) to the most powerful and constructive range of models. If individual teaching is the only way of learning, then there is always a certain risk that the teacher is pushing the teacher's agenda. It may come at the wrong time for the student, and the student may be coerced into following the teacher. The advantage of learning from the media models is that the person who sees the models can take from them as little or as much as the individual wants or is ready to absorb. Of course, every good model stretches you a little.

I feel fortunate in that I have encountered thousands of models in my life, including exposure through reading, media, music, and the like. I am a patsy. I cry at movies. I like good writing. I could not begin to list all the times that I have been touched. One example: survivors. As many times as I have heard Holocaust experiences because of my wide reading and talking about the topic, still I have gone on to meet hundreds of survivors who touched me and transformed me with the power of their accounts and their personal ongoing witness. When it comes to the Holocaust, no matter how many times you think you have heard it all, you inevitably hear something new. Suddenly, you encounter depths of emotions, heroism, courage, and suffering that you never knew existed. And it makes you understand the incredible capabilities and strengths that people have. Since you are also a person, you are challenged, and you grow. It is like the line in the Talmud: Each Jew is supposed to say, "When will my actions approach those of Abraham, Isaac, and Jacob?" It sounds grandiose, but it is not. Small people have stretched and done great things.

Many times I am asked about a certain type of heroism that someone inside the Holocaust universe showed. "Would you have acted this way?" My answer is, "I hope I would." Then something analogous (although far less ultimate) comes up in my personal life, and I try to hold myself to that standard. Let me give one example of a non-Jewish model. In struggling with Holocaust questions, I was having difficulties. There was a backlash in the Orthodox community about some of my conclusions. Naturally, I felt intimidated. No one wants to rupture with one's own community. I was tempted to stop. But I met Alice and Roy Eckardt, who as profound Christian thinkers were shattered and transformed by the Holocaust. They were also going through an incredible religious odyssey that led them into extraordinary soul-searching and a soul-searing critique of their own faith, Christianity. They were so honest, so relentless, so unsparingly prophetic in their critique of Christian faith. They stuck their necks out. Although I felt that they were absolutely on target, they were close to losing all their credibility within the Christian community. I remember that several times I was close to "selling out" in terms of backing down on some of my conclusions or criticisms for fear that I would be "defrocked" in my own community. Then I would run into the Eckhardts and see what they were going through and how they persisted and were fully prepared for "martyrdom" rather than surrender to Christianity's ongoing defamation of Judaism. Once I saw that someone else could do it, my reaction was, "I can do it, too." I ended up going much farther than I ever wanted to, or maybe even should have gone. Their model was so inspiring that it lifted me far beyond the prudent. There was a heavy penalty for me. But, despite the cost, I feel it is still worthwhile.

Q. Yes, sometimes from the stories of survivors, and also in other situations, you see the tremendous capacity of the human soul, and you are awed by it. And humbled by it. You know that you could not possibly do what these people have done.

Greenberg. There are times when you discover that you do have the capacity to reach those levels! That is one of the great insights of the *halachah.* Because we live in this dialectic of the real and ideal, all behavior is imperfect and unfinished. Heroism, then, is very contextual. The obvious heroism is the ideal of heroism in battle. Or a person running into a flaming building and rescuing a child. But heroism is contextual. Take the mother who has worked all day to clean the house and make it perfect—then the child comes home and messes the floor badly. Yet the mother restrains herself and gives the child a kiss. That is an heroic gesture. It takes great spiritual energy to react this way.

This reminds me of an experience. Just after we had been married, Blu and I were at Brandeis University. We met a priest, the Catholic chaplain, Father Gouch. He was a spiritually alive and attractive liberal, full of good humor and human warmth. I was impressed by his candor. I thought of his heroism in giving up everything: Sex. Family. Accepting poverty—all for God. One Friday night he visited us, and in the flush of friendship and confidential conversation, I allowed myself to ask him that very question. What kind of hero was he? What did it feel like to have given up experiences that are at the center of most people's lives and that they treasure, for the sake of serving God and the Catholic Church and its people in extraordinary ways? He had a wonderful sense of humor. He replied with a twinkle in his eye, "In a moment of inspiration you give your life to Jesus; then you spend the rest of your life trying to get it back." We laughed. I was touched by his modesty and lack of self-pity. Nevertheless, I remained impressed by the heroism of his asceticism, denial, and searching.

I should add that over the years I have come to see that Christians have developed that side of their religion; they have become virtuosi of such sacrifice in exploration of the central image of the crucifixion. Growing out of the concept of "taking up the cross to follow Jesus," they often expect, demand—and get—a level of self-sacrificial giving that contemporary Judaism hardly asks for and that modern Jewry does not include in its expectations. I have met Christians who have spent a whole life serving the poor, the outcast, the abandoned, with total sacrifice of self. Religious Jews are much less into that kind of suffering.

Q. We have had enough suffering of other kinds.

Greenberg. Fair enough! Nonetheless, each religion develops its own kind of virtuosity. I thought a great deal about Gouch's comment and the lifestyles that he and I were leading, respectively. One day, about twenty years later, I was talking to a group of Catholic priests about our encounter with Father Gouch. By then, I had been a husband and a father for twenty years. This changed my thinking. I explained that now I think that the life I lead is much more heroic than a priest's. As a husband, one is tempted to be short, to hurt, to be annoyed, to be petulant, to be offended twenty times every day. As a parent, your patience, calm, cheer, and interest are tested tens of times a day. You cannot compare the intensity of the heroism, but, in its own way, this heroism equals or exceeds the demands on a priest!

Q. It is much greater. I know people who are relatively happy with themselves alone. Self-contained in their own world. But I think it is much more heroic, much more difficult to take responsibility for family. I think it is also true in leadership. The more the person is responsible for *tikkun olam*, the more responsibilities and burdens on all sides.

Greenberg. There you have it.

Q. In medieval Jewry, there are great examples. All the great thinkers, Saadia Gaon, the Rambam—they are not only great thinkers, they are communal leaders.

Greenberg. I like to think that that is one of the distinguishing characters of Judaism. We have, all things being equal, "moderate" images of spiritual greatness. There are Jews who give up family for the sake of humanity or Judaism. Nonetheless, the basic model is a much more democratic one. It is built on the affirmation of daily life. I often pray that humanity reach the point where the struggle is not against war, catastrophe, absolute injustice—but is just to be a kind parent. This would reflect a huge degree of *tikkun olam* achieved. For too many millennia, humanity has confronted ultimate suffering. It is a *great step up* when conditions improve to the point where the average person is middle-class and living in a law-abiding, affluent community, and the moral crises and tests are "bourgeois"—everyday, "normal."

I would affirm that in every context there is the possibility of heroism, as there is the possibility of misbehavior. Heroism is simply the intensification of normal human qualities. That is why I believe that everybody is capable of heroism all the time. Training helps to bring out this capacity. Inspiration may give people the lift to reach that level. God's commandment and God's love guide them more than anything else. But, ultimately, living an heroic life depends on individual choices made in everyday life.

5

On the Role of Women in Orthodox Jewish Life

Shalom Freedman (Q). Rabbi, you have been criticized in the Orthodox community for your views on the woman's issue. What is the basis of the *machloket* (dispute)?

Rabbi Irving Greenberg. Regretfully, I believe that current norms in the Orthodox community do not sufficiently value women, or give them their full opportunity for personal and spiritual growth. In other words, current standards fall below the line that the principle of *tzelem elokim* demands. The capacity to correct matters is there, but is not being utilized. The reasons for the lack of response are sociological and unsatisfactory, in my judgment.

I had one of two choices in this situation. To bow to the community, to the official interpreters of *halachah*—or to say "no" to the current community standard on women's issues. I feel a moral responsibility in this matter. And I feel accountable to God ultimately, and not to humans alone. I have spoken out in frank criticism of the present situation and in open admiration of some of the steps toward equality that liberals have taken in this area. I have tried to push the halachic envelope. Nevertheless, I must confess that I have not spoken out one hundred percent on these—and other—matters. In community policy issues one walks a thin line. To a certain extent, you must defer to the community. If you don't, sooner or later the community will cut you off. If you want to stay inside a community, then part of the task is to fight from within to change its position. If you constantly ignore or flout community standards, then someday the community will not listen to you anymore.

But I also reject the option that the individual can say, "This is the *psak*, and I follow it with no questions asked."

You can suppress individual judgment in a limited number of cases; if you do it all the time, then your position loses its integrity. In short, a morally mature person is constantly torn between conscience and community. Walking between the two lines is the art of moral living. Each decision involves trade-offs. Rabbi Israel Salanter once said: Life is a short tablecloth. . . . Pull to one side and the other side comes uncovered. Ethically we are constantly tugging or pulling and trying to avoid slipping off the table altogether.

Q. Again in regard to one of the most controversial issues in recent years, that of woman's position in religious life, I gather that you find yourself much farther from the community in Israel than in the United States.

Greenberg. Let me put it this way. In the United States, more is being done to correct matters than in Israel. (But not enough is being done in the United States either.) One example: Rabbi Avi Weiss in Riverdale, New York, has build a *shul* in which the sanctuary is pretty much split down the middle. As a result, women and men have equal hearing and equal sightlines. The women do not lead in the davening, but they get to hold the Torah; it is passed around the whole *shul* during *hotzaah* and *hachnassah.* In most of the *shuls* in Israel, women have second-class seating; in many *shuls,* they are "out of it." And there is almost no awareness of how bad the situation is; it is as if women do not exist. This situation is an institutional expression of a blatant and unacceptable fact: In its day-to-day practice, Israeli Orthodoxy simply treats women as "secondary" beings. Some of this behavior is unconscious, a lot of it is inherited—and Orthodoxy is, legitimately, a conservative, tradition-bound culture. But matters have become so inflamed that I consider the indignities as being in the category of intentionally inflicted degradation.

In the *Shabbat,* there is a principle of *psik rayshay v'lo yamut.* In general, if a *melachah* act is intentional it is a *Shabbat* violation; but if it is unintentional, it is not considered a violation of the biblical law of *Shabbat.* However, in certain cases, where the outcome of the act is inevitable, even if the action is unintentional, it is considered intentional and a violation of *Shabbat.* The *psik rayshay* principle suggests that you cannot say: "I am going to cut off somebody's head, yet [claim that] I did not want to kill him"—because killing follows inexorably from cutting off his head. The same principle can be invoked, especially in Israel, in Orthodox treatment of women. There comes a point where the inexorable conclusion is that women's inferiority is intended (whether intended consciously or not, and whether people are comfortable with this conclusion or not).

Of course, the community is full of apologetics. It is full of explanations that hide these facts from itself. But it is now in basic violation of the principle of *tzelem elokim.*

Let me go back for a moment in history. The ideal of *tzelem elokim* is equality. But, in actuality, you never start from an ideal situation; you start from the facts on the ground. In the time of the Exodus, the condition of women was that they were bought and sold throughout the world. They were inferior to men; they were chattels. That is where the Torah begins the process of *tikkun olam* that is to end in a state of full equality. The Torah starts by reducing the chattelage, not abolishing it. (Thus, the father's right to sell his daughter is restricted to sale for the sake of marriage only.) I have no apology for that state; I stand behind it. In the long run you can change conditions most effectively by working in the current reality, improving the situation one step at a time. This is the covenantal way of correction. But the concept that this step-at-a-time process is now frozen is not acceptable. It is a betrayal of the covenant that seeks to reach perfection. When people say, "This is the way it always has been, and we do not want to go any further," in effect, they have stopped the covenantal process in the middle and have said, "Up to here, and that's all."

The fundamental reason for the lack of halachic improvement today is that the rabbinic leadership and the lay elite are comfortable with present conditions. They act as if the Torah decrees only what they like. They give *psak* as if the *halachah* acts only in the way that they are used to, in a manner that is nonthreatening to them. But the Torah does not promise anybody peace of mind; nor does it teach that you will always behave as you are accustomed to act.

There is a real danger that Orthodoxy could turn into a community of reaction; this would be a tragedy, for it would make us not the upholders of *masoret* (heritage) and revelation, but the community that wants to not be disturbed. Many Orthodox leaders act as if they are afraid of change. Many Orthodox are afraid of the modern world. There is not a reasoned consideration of new roles for women, but a lashing out in fear against them. This is not the psychology of free, responsible, covenantal partners with God. In the Torah, Jewry starts with an adventure into the unknown. Avraham has to leave his land, his family, his homeland—in short, the familiar. He has to journey "to a land that [God] will show you." He has to deal with constant change. The Torah should not become a "front" for people who are afraid of change, afraid of new roles.

The question of women's status has now become a burning ethical, religious issue, particularly so after the Shoah. Yet the Orthodox community has not responded sufficiently. To its eternal credit, Orthodoxy has developed high levels of learning for women; it has taken some steps (in America more than in Israel) toward giving women greater dignity and equality. But in neither America nor Israel has it attained adequate current standards. So let us stop the apologies and correct the situation. The *poskim* have sufficient authority to make the changes, and the people have sufficient power to move matters. They are not using the power because the whole emphasis in Orthodoxy right now is on gaining the approval of the *haredim* or on obedience to the rabbis. Fear of condemnation by insiders is greater than outrage at injustice. That has to change.

Q. I was surprised in talking with Rabbi Chaim Brovender. He expressed the view that women should learn and progress at an equal level and pace as men. I found that surprising for an Orthodox rabbi. I am thinking of a response given by Rabbi Eliezer Berkovits, who complained that women simply have no position whatsoever in traditional Jewish worship; that, so far as prayer goes, they are nonbeings. How far would you personally go, for instance, in the question of prayer? Should women be counted as part of the *minyan*? Should they get *aliyot*? Can a woman serve as a *shaliach tsibbur*?

Greenberg. My wife has written on many of these questions, and I would stand by her positions. These include the creation of women's *tefillah* groups in which women play public leadership roles, including *aliyot* and *shaliach tzibbur*. Of course, the progress in women's learning is a breakthrough, it is a major advance for Orthodoxy, but the matter can't stop here. There can be no full dignity, if women are confined just to high-level learning. There are cases of women who went through the learning process and became outstanding talmudic scholars, and then could find no professional outlet. They could not get jobs as educators in yeshiva high schools, for example. Or, when they received jobs, they were second-rate jobs. They did not get an equal chance to teach Talmud.

In America, blacks are far from being treated equally, but by law and media policy, you cannot advocate inferior treatment. If people practice racism, there is a good deal of built-in criticism and embarrassment. Orthodoxy's problem is that there is not an intrinsic built-in embarrassment about treating women as second-class. There is a lot of denial of inferior treatment. Under the cover of God-given different roles, some blatant human discrimination is being practiced.

Eliezer Berkovits was one-of-a-kind in the whole Orthodox world. Berkovits should represent the average Orthodox rabbi's position; unfortunately, in actual fact, he was a feminist pioneer and was treated like a marginal extremist. So, until Berkovits' views are mainstream, it is a sign that Orthodoxy is still way off on the women's issue.

Let me explain my ideas about women's roles in prayer. Since religion and spirituality are essential to human dignity, my guess is that women will be admitted to equal roles in this area. I doubt that spiritual areas such as prayer will prove to be areas of essential gender differences. Prayer is an intrinsically universal human phenomenon. Women are fully capable of prayer. The famous fact is that the talmudic model for prayer is drawn from Hannah, a woman. Women are similarly able to lead and teach.

This is not to say that all roles in religion and life should be unisex. The idea that women and men have distinct roles can be one of the Torah's contributions at this time of history. When there is a rush to level all roles, then one of Orthodoxy's important insights is the legitimacy of gender differentiation. But, as Blu Greenberg has said, not all differences need to be in the form of hierarchy. And Orthodoxy will not get a fair hearing on gender differences as long as its record on dignity and equality is not up to par.

How can Orthodoxy make corrections without blowing the system out? The minimum first step is the development of women's tefillah groups. This has been started in the United States. I personally prefer the term "women's *minyanim.*" However, the Orthodox women studiously avoid the term *minyan.* If I were the *halachic* authority, the women's prayer groups would constitute themselves as *minyanim* and include *barchu, kedushah, kaddish*—all of the *devarim shebikdusha.* This is because I consider women's *tefillah* groups to be genuine spiritual communities (i.e., *tzibbur*) and I believe that all genuine communities (male or female) have the authority to act accordingly. Please note that women's *tefillah* groups do *not* say *davar shebikdusha.* I think that they have done this as a political necessity; if they acted as *minyanim,* they would be even more bitterly attacked. They have accepted the argument of the right wing that because women are not bound halachically, they cannot practice these liturgies. In my judgment, these obstacles are halachic technicalities; those who make these claims that women are ineligible are missing the substance of the issue—that any valid spiritual community can carry out these liturgies. Someday, when the psychology shifts, the *psak* will go the other way. Rabbeynu Tam's position that, since women can take on a *mitzvah* voluntarily, then they can make the *bracha* on that *mitzvah,* will prove to be correct. Once accepted, the *mitzvah* does become *chiyuv.* For that matter, one could rule that all prayer activities are permitted to women on the grounds of *ayt la'asot lashem, heferu Toratecha.* This is a needed temporary override of existing law for which action the authority exists and has always existed.

Recently I was reading excerpts from responsa by Rabbi Moshe Feinstein and Rabbi Ovadia Yosef ruling that full-time students of Torah can accept the state of being financially supported by the community. This goes directly against the Talmud, which says that you are not supposed to become dependent on others. If someone becomes dependent on others by not learning a profession in order to work, Maimonides say that this is absolutely wrong. But to live by those values today would seriously undermine the economics of *kollelim* and would delegitimize the yeshiva world. Under these circumstances, Rav Moshe Feinstein and Rav Ovadia Yosef say unequivocally that "Times have changed," that "Ours is a different situation," and permit this new social policy. Both quote the phrase *ayt la'asot lashem, heferu Toratecha.* This is right. But the same principle should be applied even more urgently to improve women's condition, and to resolve other matters of high priority.

Ayt la'asot means there is a time when you can override the customary law to deal with emergency situations—which women's condition certainly is—for God's sake. This legitimates special time-bound *takkanot* (rabbinical legislated enactments). *Ayt la'asot* enactments are to be labeled "temporary." Then let that be the rubric to solve an issue. (You know that Rabbeynu Gershom's *takkanah* prohibiting polygamy was to expire in the year 5000. It is now more than 757 years later—and it still has not expired!) From my point of view, the issue is not what is the halachic category that covers the needed outcome, but what is the outcome. The demand for conventional traditional justification for needed changes is partly a stalling process based on lack of appreciation of the urgency of the issues. This position makes process an end in itself and dismisses the outcome. This is a wrongful interpretation of the halachic system. Process is essential, but it must be guided by goals.

The *halachah* has goals. The goals are *tikkun olam*, upholding *tzelem elokim*, and so on. If you employ the *halachah* correctly, it will get you to those goals. Declaring that a needed matter is not in our capability to address is an abdication of responsibility of the first order. Wringing hands and claiming that this generation has no authority to act simply puts an unconscious substitution of traditional values ahead of a conscious teleological use of the system to achieve true goals. The *halachah* will be far better served when it admits that its goals are *tzelem elokim* and *tikkun olam*, and when *poskim* rule accordingly. In other words, the *halachah* must use whatever authority it has, or needs, or wants, to achieve its own goals.

Q. But if the situation is so bad, why are so many Orthodox women happy with it? And why do certain modern women leave their secular "liberated" backgrounds and become *ba'alot teshuvah*?

Greenberg. That is an excellent point, and I appreciate your raising it. I do not wish to imply for a moment that women are miserable or degraded within Orthodoxy. On the contrary. The strengths of Orthodoxy uphold and give dignity to the lives of women as well as men. The sustaining power of community, the rich family life infused with tradition and observance, the high level of learning and the sense of mission and religious commandment, the spirit of obedience to God that make Orthodoxy a great way of life inspire Orthodox women as well. Moreover, the stability, the clear role models, and the removal of some of the negative pressures of modernity are also appealing to many women. (I think of Lynn Davidman's study of Orthodox *ba'alot teshuvah.* She describes the revulsion that many felt at the sexual exploitation or pressures on single women that are found in the general American culture.) Moreover, most Orthodox women feel that the present situation is the will of God, or the only possibility sanctioned by sacred *halachah,* so they must accept it—and they do. In order to avoid conflict and cognitive dissonance, women learn not to see, not to hear, not to feel certain situations as slights or devaluations. Still others feel that the disadvantages are part of the package that must be taken whole or given up. Rather than lose it, they accept the composite condition and adjust. They feel—as I do—that the rewards far outweigh the costs.

Now when I say that the rewards far outweigh the costs, I speak from a different condition. Let me make it clear that I personally am delighted and in love with the Orthodox way of life, and my argument stems from no frustration or personal deprivation. After all I happen to be a man, a rabbi, and a *kohen*! Every privilege in the system is mine!

But, over the years, thanks to feminism and its message that women are *tzelem elokim* (that was Rabbi Soloveitchik's message, also), and to my exposure to women's roles in the liberal communities, I have attained new insight. Most of all, thanks to the removal of the protective blinders that I, too, wore in order not to come in conflict with my community and its inherited conventions, I have come to see that current practices in the Orthodox community fall below an ideal standard of *tzelem elokim.*

For instance: Let us accept the fact that women are exempt from fixed *tefillah* in its congregational forum, so they cannot lead services and thereby fulfill obligations on behalf of the men, who are legally bound. Let us stipulate that there must be separate seating. But what excuse is there for building a *shul* where women have no sight lines or adequate ability to hear and see the Torah? Since, contrary to superstition (and unconscious sexism), a *niddah* cannot make a Torah impure, what excuse is there for unyielding, sometimes violent, opposition to providing women with *hakafot* on Simchat Torah and even the opportunity to kiss the Torah whenever it is taken out? Why cannot women address the congregation at least after services or serve as officers and board members (as they are excluded in many congregations)? What excuse is there that, at Orthodox organizations' annual dinners, no women are on the dais? What excuse is there that conferences—including those dealing with women's issues—are staffed and addressed solely by men? This is not to mention the outright suffering and abuses in the process of *get* and inheritance.

I have come to see that the halachic distinctions have been extended and distorted by folk and outside cultural influences (albeit, often inherited from past centuries and now mistakenly covered with pious glaze) and endowed with *kedushah* of *minhag* when they should be dismissed as *minhag srak* or *emunah tefeylah.* The process of upgrading women's condition, started by the Torah and given over to Torah *she b'al peh,* has been prematurely stopped along the way. Much of the resistance grows out of fear of change and yearning for authoritarianism rather than pure halachic reasoning and principle. Also, the excessive influence of the right wing, which is living in a different social reality in which women are less educated and have less of a sense of self, is crippling modern Orthodoxy's response. As the defensiveness wears off, as the urgency to dignify *tzelem elokim* in the generation after the Shoah grows, now as more and more Orthodox become educated in Jewish learning and in American culture, the time comes for a halachic and communal upgrade of women's condition in Orthodoxy. For me personally, that time is now. This will strengthen Torah and observance, as well as lift all of us toward greater fulfillment of the Torah's norms of *kavod habriyot.* Only this upgrade will restore the credibility of Orthodoxy's just claim that men and women are different and that role differentiation is legitimate and enriching. As Rabbi Soloveitchik put it:

> The foremost distinguishing characteristic bestowed upon man is his Divine image, his *tzelem Elohim,* which denotes particular qualitative endowments, such as a moral sense, free will, and intellect. Man partakes of these attributes within human limitations, while God's representation of these qualities is absolute. Maimonides embodied man's likeness to God primarily in terms of his intellect (Guide 1:1). This Divine gift was given to both men and women. . . . In their spiritual natures, they were equally worthy.
>
> Two humans were created who differ from each other metaphysically, not only physiologically, even as they both partake of Divine qualities. This contradicts the perverse notion that Judaism regards women as being inferior to man. It also cuts away another false notion that there is no distinction between them in terms of their spiritual personalities.

Q. And do you see the Orthodox community making progress in this direction on the women's issue?

Greenberg. The record is erratic, very spotty—but there has been progress. The irony is that, unlike Blu's and my own critics, we truly believe that the *halachah* can deal with all the moral and cultural challenges adequately. The *halachah* that incorporates God's word can rise to every occasion. It can transform itself and the world to achieve great goals. The real problem is the lack of will on the part of leadership and community.

Q. I think that the problem in relation to the Orthodox conception of the woman's role also relates to the central place

Judaism gives to family life. There is no doubt that increasing educational advancement for women in the Western world has been accompanied by serious problems for the family. I think that many would say, for instance, that women are freed from time-bound positive *mitzvot* because of the central role they have in the home.

Greenberg. Saul Berman has made this point very eloquently. The concern for family is real. Judaism is built on the family; one's personal self, one's *tzelem elokim* can only be nurtured adequately in a healthy, loving family situation. But, in essence, the traditionalists are saying that the only way to protect the family is by keeping the woman *exclusively* in her traditional role. Since most women perceive that there is room to improve women's status and that a greater degree of choice is a key to such improvement, restricting women's career and personal choices is unlikely to be a winning strategy to save the family. Rather, this is another example of the claim that a classic human institution (in this case, marriage and family) cannot compete in an open society without a "protective tariff" (in this case, women's secondary status). The argument is that however inefficient it is to exercise such a tariff, society cannot afford to lose the institution at risk.

The counterargument is that a *tzelem elokim* has a fundamental need for family, e.g., love, commitment, companionship, mutual help, and guidance, to sustain it and realize it. Therefore, our strategy should be to build up women and the family simultaneously; the full realization of women's image of God will create a greater need for family. Such a family, as an institution built on more ethical relationships and women's fuller dignity, ultimately will compete better in an open society. The traditional *halachists'* instinctive reaction to uphold the familiar and to prohibit new or expanded roles for women is, therefore, an error. I believe that this generation is called upon halachically to prove just the opposite; it is supposed to show how to achieve equality and strengthen family side-by-side. This is much harder to do, but in the long run this way yields more human dignity for women and men. And more of the children of such families will grow up to be true *tzelem elokim.*

To return to an earlier image: The salt-water sea of modernity is growing, is overflowing its banks. The salt water is flowing into the fresh-water lake. There are two possibilities. One can build a seawall and keep out some part of the water. Possibly one can shelter a small fresh-water pond with dikes—but most of the lake will be lost because the sea overflow is becoming ever more powerful. (In the case of the family, only a small percentage of women can be persuaded to stick to the traditional roles exclusively in order to save the family.) Or one can conclude, as I do, that the sea of modernity is overflowing because it is meeting fundamental human needs successfully, and that—if properly channeled and directed—it brings with it the promise of potential world redemption. Then God wants us all to learn to live in salt water. I do believe that.

Contemporary culture offers us unprecedented possibilities of power, dignity, freedom—all the goals of redemption that we have always held. Modernity also has brought with it this sting in its tail—significant erosion of values, loss of community, breakdown of family, exaggerated materialism and consumerism. Our task is to learn to live in the presence of alternative values, to develop an internalized value system. Then we will be able to live on this ocean of modernity instead of desperately seeking to build walls to keep out the salt water—which will be an unsuccessful task. Just as we can breed fish that swim, live, and breed in salt water, so can we raise up religious generations that maximize the output of *tzelem elokim* in modernity without being undermined by its negative phenomena.

The bad news for unchanging traditionalists is that the future of the family cannot be built on male supremacy; the good news is that chauvinism can be separated from role differentiation and traditional observances. To save the family, it is necessary to raise women who are fully educated, and even career-oriented, who have a real appreciation for and dedication to the family. I believe that in the new culture most women will choose that family-nurturing role as their primary goal. But they should not have to choose it by dint of not being allowed access to career opportunities or because they have been socialized to accept secondary status and enabling roles exclusively.

Remember that social and communal phenomena never

operate precisely within the ideal parameters. They spread everywhere; they develop side or "halo" effects. In certain settings, the traditional role spells acceptance of "abuse" of all kinds. It is not just that women do not lead in the Orthodox synagogue service; it is that the *shul* is built so they are excluded with poor or nonexistent sight lines and little ability to hear what is happening. Thus, starting from the point of different roles, the system ends up moving toward devaluation.

Freezing women in enabling roles is the wrong solution to the problem of creating distinctive sex roles and preserving the family. The better answer to the question of how to strengthen family is to get women more help in raising children. Then some will stay home, some will combine career and family, and the smallest group will give career the priority. Thus, overall, the best mix of women's roles and family will be upheld. Currently, five percent of Jewish women—socialized to concentrate exclusively on mothering and family—are having six to nine children each. Simultaneously, another eighty percent—socialized in American career values and believing that traditional values are reactionary and associated with restricting women's standing—are having an average of 1.2 children. My goal would be to raise all the women to understand the dialectic of family and profession and then motivate the average woman to have 3.1 children. (This is not meant literally; some will have five and some will have two.) This would mean that, overall, more Jewish children would be born. Apply these policies universally, and there would also be many additional social gains: elimination of various forms of exploitation and degradation of women—including slavery and female infanticide in the Third World. The classic traditional women's roles do not maximize women's dignity, healthy populations, or maximum social growth.

When a society is committed to nurture the *tzelem elokim* of each inhabitant and to *tikkun olam*, then life wins out overall. If you build the right kind of society respecting *tzelem elokim*, then life wins out quantitatively *and* qualitatively. Women have a twenty-five percent higher death rate in traditional societies than men do. Since their lives are worth less, the parents feed them less. If there is a shortage of food, then they feed the boy first; sometimes the girl is not fed at all. There are over 100 million women unaccounted for in India, China, and southeast Asia, in comparison to the birthrate (not to mention the much higher rate of abortion of female embryos). Apparently, if parents can have only one child, they work to ensure that it is a boy, of course. We do not have that gross a phenomenon in the Orthodox community; but women's minds are less tended, and their lives and choices are less developed in that community.

The path of dignity and of new roles of women points toward the long run, in which we try to maximize the *tzelem elokim* of everyone. If we learn to do it right, we can support the family through various religious forms, teachings and values, through daycare, *and* through husband help, *and* in a hundred other ways. Then women can have decent-sized families and professional training and full standing.

Q. Is there any present community within the Jewish world that comes close to this ideal? I have the sense that, after the Second World War, many Jewish families did have three or four children, but not, of course, with the women working outside the home.

Greenberg. There has been some slippage during the past twenty years. This is reflective of the growing polarization in Jewry. But I have lived in modern Orthodox communities that live by these values and have been able to create striking examples of combining dialectical standards—family and career, tradition and full dignity. Modern Orthodoxy offers the most promise from this point of view, because, in principle, it is committed to integrating both tradition and modernity. Unfortunately, in the past twenty years, modern Orthodoxy has not enjoyed full exposure to both cultures. It has had more double exposure than most Jewish communities, but there has been a trend to second-rate access in both cultures. That is not healthy. Also, as modern Orthodoxy lost its way and its leadership defaulted, it turned to the right in its own institutions and in its educational philosophy. Polarization rather than synthesis was strengthened. Nevertheless, the matter can be corrected. Modern Orthodoxy can still play a very promising role in the future. However, I should add the caveat that no one group all by itself can save Jewry. All the groups have to strike a better balance between family and new women's roles, between tradition and modernity.

I am especially worried about the secular Jewish family in the Diaspora, precisely because the people in it are so exposed to modern practices. Modernity—when not taken dialectically—is poisonous. When it comes to medicine, some people think that if taking two pills is a good cure, then taking ten pills is even better. Only it turns out that when you take ten pills, you die of an overdose. That is what we know about modernity. It has very good qualities; but, taken "pure," it is like heroin. High-purity heroin kills on the spot because the system cannot handle it. Making the new mix, learning to absorb modernity dialectically, with sufficient limits, is a major cultural task that still lies ahead of us. That is one of my main areas of interest.

All Jews have to work on this task, and no one group can create the needed culture. This is what led me to CLAL. This is why I remain convinced that Orthodox Jews must reach out beyond the Orthodox community. More than thirty years ago, feeling the impact of the Shoah and Israel and seeing the coming impact of a fully open society, I concluded that the Orthodox community could not accomplish this monumental cultural task alone. It needed the critique of the others and their alternative models in order to create its own synthesis. Furthermore, it needed to influence other Jews so that it could be part of a stable Jewish community. Orthodoxy is no longer, and will not be for some time to come, the majority of the Jewish people. Rather than write off the majority, Orthodoxy should hold itself up as a model and try to share its values and ideas with them. Thus, Orthodoxy could function as the vital center for Jewry.

I once had this argument with Rabbi Norman Lamm, President of Yeshiva University. He had been using the term "centrist Orthodoxy," which I felt was a way of trying to distance himself from the left wing of modern Orthodoxy, i.e., people like me. I said, "What does the term 'centrist' mean? If you mean that the center is located in the middle of the Jewish people, with fifty percent to its right and fifty to its left, then that is where Orthodoxy would be. If you mean by 'centrist' that modern Orthodoxy should station itself halfway between Yitz Greenberg and the Satmar Rebbe, then you turn Orthodoxy into some lunatic fringe—because more than ninety percent of the Jewish people is to my left."

This is what has gone wrong with modern Orthodoxy. Instead of being at the center of the Jewish people, responsible for the secularists' fate, offering solutions and living models usable by the entire Jewish people, it has been maneuvered to the fringe. Modern Orthodoxy acts as if its primary loyalty is to those who keep the lifestyle of the mitzvot exclusively. Sometimes it ends up supporting the *haredim* when they exploit the Jewish people unfairly; as for example, when the traditionalists leave the defense of Israel to Zionists and they abuse their exemption from the Israeli army. The modern Orthodox have gone along when *haredim* seek to impose public religious observance on others and when they act to delegitimate all liberal religious alternatives. As it drifts to the right, modern Orthodoxy becomes defensive, insular, and sectarian. Therefore, it cannot meet its true responsibility to the entire Jewish people. To justify this abandonment of other groups, it is tempted to caricature or write off the rest of the Jewish people as a lost cause.

The women's issue is a classic expression of this problem. Instead of reasserting its distinctive values, which include upholding the fullest dignity of women and broadening their roles, instead of glorifying role models and improved opportunities for its more autonomous, more highly educated females, modern Orthodoxy has gone along with the halachic status quo. It has been maneuvered into supporting the expansion of separatist, less-than-equal interaction between men and women. (The notable exceptions are some marginal improvements in dealing with *igun* [women anchored without a *get*] and some breakthroughs in higher-level traditional learning for women. Even these improvements have not been matched by provision for women's leadership roles or by developing a model of a more partnership oriented, more coeducational, more egalitarian lifestyle). The result is that modern Orthodoxy is not sufficiently improving its women's opportunities or correcting disabilities as it should; instead, it is driven to apologetics and evasions. These are much more dangerous tactics, when practiced in its circles, because the women are getting powerful feminist messages in their other exposures. People who tried to correct these trends, such as

Eliezer Berkovits, of blessed memory, and Blu Greenberg, *tibadel l'chayim*, are too often marginalized—instead of being defended—by their modern Orthodox colleagues.

Nothing could be more affirmative of renewed vitality for modern Orthodoxy than to stand up and lead the way to fuller halachic affirmation of women's possibilities and then creating community structures and personal lifestyles to exemplify these values. This would make women's issues a force to bring the modern Orthodox closer to the role of the community instead of a trigger for moral exclusion and ethical conflict between Orthodox and non-Orthodox. As of now, the principle of women's equality and fulfillment is the battering ram breaking down remaining areas of cooperation between modern Orthodox and liberal Jews. This polarization encourages excesses of unthinking egalitarianism (such as unisex ideas) among liberals, and justification of status quo and continuation of unnecessary or unjustified suffering by women among modern Orthodox. It is a pity—and it is particularly regrettable in this generation, when great advances in human dignity are possible and necessary.

A renewal of the commitment to respect and realize the *tzelem elokim* of men and women, of observant and non-observant, of Jew and gentiles alike is the key to revitalization of Judaism and Jewry. This is the generation that must be *machmir* in (treat with extra seriousness) the principle of *tzelem elokim*. This emphasis will guide us to the right policies in every area. Coming after the Shoah, such a stress would constitute a great *tikkun*.

6

The Jewish Family in the Modern World

Shalom Freedman (Q). Rabbi, you see the modern world in primarily positive terms—the greater opportunity for freedom, for *tikkun olam.* But isn't it true that in one area especially, the family, the effect of modernity has been distinctly negative? The Jewish people, which is traditionally known for its close and warm family life, is plagued by family breakdown, divorce, a high rate of intermarriage. The great value the Jewish tradition has placed on education is, in part, responsible for the fact that Jewish women as a social class are the most highly educated women in history. But, consequently, the Jewish people has one of the lowest birthrates in the world. The price of greater individual freedom and development is seemingly the loss of the value of giving to and sharing with others. Is this not leading to the breakdown of the traditional family? In this sense, isn't our world in decline?

Rabbi Irving Greenberg. In the flagship countries of modern culture, the family is under siege. We are seeing significant pathological phenomena in human relations. Nevertheless, one must first give credit to modern culture for upgrading the family. Furthermore, I would argue that the pathologies are not caused by modern culture per se, but by the excess of modernity. This diagnosis suggests a different approach to defining and curing the problem.

Despite the haze of nostalgia and glory that surrounds the

traditional family, one dare not simply romanticize it. The Torah, which places family at the center of religious life and makes it the vehicle of the covenant, also unsparingly portrays the Patriarchal families with all their dysfunctional phenomena. There was jealousy between wives and hatred between brothers, sexual rivalry and lack of communication. In every generation, there was conflict over succession which, in Jacob's family, even led to an attempt to kill a brother.

One can point to three key weaknesses in traditional families over the centuries. Owing to the prevalence of severe poverty, parents could not care for children adequately. There is even some evidence that the high rate of child mortality made it difficult for parents to invest full love and care in each child—for fear of the emotional cost of losing the child. Second, women were generally not equal. This made female children less highly valued, or even "dispensable"—which raised the death rate among girls. Finally, the absence of individuation in women also made for less love between spouses—or, at least, love played a lesser role in establishing families. Considerations of inheritance, family continuity, and values transmission took precedence over love as well as over individual satisfaction. Today, we would describe such marriages as marriages of convenience. While many arranged marriages developed into stable and even loving relationships, one senses that the deepest levels of love and individual bonding were rarely sought (or achieved) in most families. Of course, the pressures of deprivation and the needs of survival also made the family a bastion of mutual help and solidarity that countered some of these weaknesses.

Modern culture led to increased wealth in society; the margins of security within the family widened. Improvements in public health, science, and medicine brought down the death rate; in turn, this gave parents the confidence to have a lesser number of children while relating to each child with greater attention and emotional investment. In conjunction with the overall rise in education, this led to greater individuation and self-expression in personal relationship and in childrearing. Some scholars believe that these new circumstances gave rise to the nuclear family, which built stronger emotional bonds between family members and created a space within which children could have genuine childhoods for a longer span. In the twentieth century, particularly, the rise of economic opportunity for women combined with the development of ideologies of equality gave women greater independence. As a result, more and more families were built on love relationships rather than on inheritance or economic security concerns. Thus, in many ways, modern culture initially strengthened the infrastructure of love and personal development that is the most humanly nurturing basis of family.

Q. With all due respect to your exposition of the positive input of modernity on the traditional family, can you deny the obvious breakdown of the family even in Jewish circles? The divorce rate is soaring in America. While the Jewish rate is lower than the general rate, it is generally thought to be around 30 percent. The Jewish birthrate is so low that Jews have not ZPG (zero population growth), but NPG (negative population growth). Yet the statistics show that Jews *can* afford to have families. We read about rising numbers of wife-beating and child abuse, alcoholism, and drugs in the Jewish community. Need I say more? Can you deny that these are the negative effects of modern society and values on the Jewish family?

Greenberg. These negative phenomena are real. We cannot solve any problem if we evade the facts. Modern society does not deserve to be romanticized by us any more than traditional society does. If these negative trends remain unchanged, they will jeopardize the family. This would be a catastrophe, because the family is the basis of humanization as well as being central to the inculcation and transmission of Jewish values. However, I question whether modernity, plain and simple, is the source of the problems. And the critical question remains: What, if anything, can be done to shore up the family?

I contend that the trends in modern culture that have increased the dignity of the individual, upgraded the family morally and humanly, and opened the door to universal *tikkun olam* are the very trends that, *taken too far*, are the source of the growing pathologies. Cultures and people do not always make fine distinctions. Trends turn into self-fulfilling prophecies; self-sustaining feedback cycles develop into irreversible social movements. Then one extreme leads to extreme countertrends. Thus, in the case of modernity unchecked, affluence tends to turn into materialism, individualism into narcissism, and rationalism into skepticism and the inability to believe. Self-interest too often leads to selfishness and neglect of community. The Jewish people is a major beneficiary of modernity; therefore, Jews tend to identify strongly with modern culture. This puts the Jewish people on the cutting edge of the exaggerations and the growing pathologies. Jews are concentrated in the sectors of the population with the highest percentages of participation in higher education, so the total impact of the modern experience on Jewry is exaggerated. The Jewish situation is more intense, but it foreshadows the coming effects of modernity on all cultures.

The Jews have served as the "canaries" of world history in that the pathologies that are implicit in the culture show themselves first vis-à-vis the Jews. The unrestrained power, the dangerous absolutization of the human, which was building up steadily within the framework of modern culture, took one of its most total and "pathological" forms in the war against the Jews, i.e., the Holocaust. The deification of the human—which was an exaggeration of the trends for human empowerment—turned various constructive liberation processes into new forms of totalitarian control. It turns out that when humans try to become God, they become the devil—because they tend to set their own worth at infinity and reduce and degrade the dignity of others to give plausibility to their own master role (self-divinization). In this extreme form, scientific and technological power and bureaucracy (which make modern culture function well) combine to create an unchecked force; this generated the very power that carried out unrestrained mass murder.

Take, for example, the destruction process in the Shoah. The system could not have functioned for years on the basis of pure personal spite and anger. The genocide was successfully pursued because it took the form of an impersonal process. The same universal ("nothing personal") value system that modern culture has elevated to the highest degree operated in the killing process. Thus bureaucracy, "law," and institutions combined to use the affective neutrality and universal categories of the modern culture to classify, pursue, and eliminate the Jews. (Unfortunately the universalist categories, which are the glory of modern culture, compounded the evil by creating a psychology of leaving no exceptions. In the end, there were no legal, political, institutional, or philosophical bulwarks to buffer [or reduce] the application of unlimited force on the Jews.)

When there is a pathological excess of modernity, the ethical universalism (which incorporates everyone in the same categories and makes everyone equal) metastasizes into a total universalism that "equalizes" by homogenization. The outcome is totalitarianism—the annihilation of all variety, the destruction of the different. One of the profound truths underlying the concept of covenant is that limits are the key to life. Even the Divine, if unlimited, would leave no room for finite existence. By self-limitation (entering into covenant), God makes room for humans. The subtler implication is that all ideas, values and structures are valid and good only over a certain range and within certain limitations. (This is the case for pluralism!) When good ideas are taken beyond these limits, they become pathological. Modernity itself is "good" up to a certain point; when it spreads out of control, when it becomes all-dominant, then even its good tendencies become forces for evil.

The idea of limitation is central to Judaism. (Note that this principle applies to Judaism itself.) In Judaism, the ultimate evil is idolatry. The definition of idolatry is taking something partial (a force, a value, an authority) and absolutizing it—by calling it God, by worshiping it unreservedly. The partial value, before it is divinized, may be very good in its limited form; once absolutized, it becomes idolatrous and pathological, a source of death. Human power and dignity are good Jewish values. But when they are totally unleashed, they become idolatry, the culture of death. Work-creativity (*melachah*) is a *mitzvah* all week long; it is modeled on the sacred service in the Temple and on God's work in Creation. But if no restraint is put on it—if there is no prohibition of labor on *Shabbat*—then the work expands and humans break the limits. That is why to violate the Sabbath is the equivalent of idolatry. Unchecked, the work will consume your personal life. Uncontrolled power is cancerous. If unchecked by society's norms, work and productivity will eventually consume all life. Uncontrolled modernity is deadly to the very good people, institutions, and values that it nurtures in its controlled forms.

Rootedness in land is a good (Jewish) value. But if the culture absolutizes that condition and demands the sacrifice of the firstborn to Baal in order to "ensure" the productivity of the land, then it is guilty of idolatry. The message of Sukkot (which celebrates Israel's journey through the desert and asks Jews to dwell in "mobile" homes) and the message of *shmittah* (the sabbatical year in which ownership rights in the land of Israel are renounced for the year) are designed to check those who would "absolutize" land and rootedness—and thereby absolutize the gods of space.

In short, one of Judaism's central teachings is that only God is absolute and only God's image is infinite. All other existence, and all human creations, are of finite and relative value. This is the framework of meaning that limits the good and thereby prevents it from becoming uncontrolled and turning pathological.

This principle applies to the problems of the family. The breakdown of the family is the "canary"—the Jewish family even more so—signaling the poisonous gas leaks being generated even as we mine the positive effects of modernity. "Individualism" is a fulfillment of Jewish dreams; it is an expression of the infinite value, equality, and uniqueness of the human being that for too long were shortchanged in other cultures. The growth of the sense of self, the flowering of the individual, the restructuring of society to allow for greater self-expression and individual differences—all are part of the glory of modern culture. The greater individualism and equality initially led to more relationships based on love rather than on power or utilitarian need. But as the value of self-expression becomes more prevalent, it is increasingly glorified as an end in itself. As self-fulfillment is recognized and encouraged, the countervailing claims of community, relationship, and obligation are neglected. When the rewards and even the training for reaching out beyond oneself disappear, the individual becomes like a solipsistic atom, seeking only self-fulfillment. The individual becomes impatient with any demand for self-control; limitation is perceived as deprivation. Yet the ability to postpone gratification and to recognize the value and needs of the other is the foundation of family living and the key to all relationships. One cannot be a responsible member of a family unless one is willing to defer to or help someone else.

The sense of being part of a collective group historically has been healthy; it is a source of values, meaning, and continuity. On the other hand, this was inculcated and preached in a one-sided way. Thus, individualism was discouraged, and the individual often sacrificed for the (perceived) collective good. Now the pendulum has swung so far to the other side that the individual becomes all. The interests of the group are denied as of no account. (This is a major factor in the rise of intermarriage. Individual love is valued above all; the fact that intermarriage may threaten group survival is dismissed.)

In the past, society often treated wives as chattels because families wanted to ensure the continuity of family and inheritance. The woman was "bought" and "sold" in conjunction with the land and could marry only the person who would preserve the land for the tribe or the family. That subsidiary rating and use of woman is being undermined by the growing belief in and a legal structure upholding the equality of women. In the next step, this concept leads to women's right to full education (which I also affirm). But educated people are, in general, more self-centered; this feeds into consumerist tendencies in which pleasure and fun become all-consuming. Suddenly, the idea of having children is perceived as onerous. Then the educated public, in particular, becomes aware of the ecological dangers posed by a large population. Suddenly, educated women are practicing birth control to a fault. I contend that this negative development for Jewry represents the side effects of a good value being absolutized.

Similarly, careers and constructive work for women are an expression of *tikkun olam.* Earning power bestows new dignity on women. This is a major modern breakthrough for women. But when the value of work and success are absolutized, women become driven by their work as pathologically as men are. When career becomes all-consuming, there is precious little patience for family or love or responsibility.

In all these cases, the breakdown of family represents not the triumph of bad values, but rather the domination of good values, which, taken to an extreme, become corrosive and destructive. In the early stages of modernity, these trends (affluence, self-expression, individuation) have a good effect because they are correcting the imbalances of the past. The spread of material welfare corrects inherited poverty. The upsurge of individualism corrects the excess of collectivism. The growth of hope and the attitude that humans can change the world for the better overthrows the fatalism engendered by traditional norms (God has assigned my place in life). Upward mobility erodes the fixity of the world that encourages resignation to suffering. But the same impulses keep getting stronger; amplified and reinforced, they begin to become self-evident and all-powerful. It is very difficult to keep cultural values in balance. Instead of each person or group keeping a dynamic balance between power and restraint, between utilitarianism and romanticism, between tradition and change, typically one of these polarities triumphs in one group while another is enshrined in the countercultural groups. This polarization reinforces the tendency for a value to be taken "all the way." If the group that upholds a particular pole wins out, the group tends to push these values as far as possible. Thus, human technology, productivity, and feelings of mastery over nature spill over into soulless exploitation of the land, into pollution and destructiveness. Affluence turns into consumerism and materialism. The bonds of family fray, and the search for freedom turns into fear of commitment.

The correct response to these phenomena is to become critics of modernity—from within. We now understand that modernity's values, taken too far, yield social pathologies. We see that there is a built-in tendency to take these values too far, i.e., to the level of social pathology. (This phenomenon is found in every society, but is exaggerated by the seductiveness of modern culture and the power of the media and intense forms of communications incorporated into modernity.) The first step back toward health is to demythologize the absolute claims of modernity and to liberate ourselves from excessive worship of its achievements and norms—no matter how impressive and constructive they have been.

All this applies *a fortiori* to Jews and modernity. I consider myself a post-Holocaust Jewish thinker. Jewish thought was dominated by the desire to become one with modernity up until the Shoah. Think of Mordecai Kaplan, a giant in the American Jewish community. In retrospect, we can see that he was overimpressed by the contemporary culture; as a result, he made too many concessions to modern values. His thinking is too secular, too naturalistic. These words are not meant to dismiss him; nor are they said with any sense of superiority—as if I were smarter. My "advantage" over Kaplan is that I live after this great tragedy. I am able to see much more clearly how the excesses of modernity led to the Holocaust. This event is a signal of fundamental tendencies that must be checked.

In effect, I am calling for Jews to help move the world toward postmodernity. "Post" implies that one must go through modernity, but not be totally circumscribed by it. Judaism should play its classic role as a critic from within. The Jewish people should offer, through its personal example and community witness, a form of contact with the Absolute (God, Torah) that relativizes all peoples, powers, and cultures. Instead of surrendering to this absolutism of modernity, Jews should critique and demythologize. The current flood of assimilation is an outgrowth of excessive Jewish internalization of modern values swallowed whole. Intermarriage grows out of the belief that all humans are the same, so that there are no legitimate group differences that would demand continuing diversity. Low birthrates exist when education and self-fulfillment become the enemy of enabling and creating life. But those tendencies represent the further extension of the pathology of modernity.

Jews cannot save modern culture from its own worst tendencies by acting alone. However, they can make a major contribution to the emerging critique of modernity's excesses. Personal rediscovery of Judaism and Jewish values enables the individual to become skeptical of modernity. Thus, Jews can affirm universalism but recognize that it must be checked by pluralism and by the concrete affirmation of our people's (and every other people's) distinctive life and culture. By dispersing cultural power among many religions, one can prevent the dominance of one value system.

Judaism must teach correctives for modernity's excesses on every front. Jewish culture must offer alternatives to the runaway individualism that leads to the breakdown of community and the rise of crime. Judaism can proclaim the need to restore the dialectic between individualism and collectivism that makes for a true cultural balance. The tradition helps the individual in the image of God to be fulfilled. But the Torah also teaches that no human can be completely fulfilled without becoming part of a larger unit—such as family and community. (Of course, it must be clear that we are preaching both–and, not either–or.) A fundamental of covenantal thinking is that my life is not an atom of existence; it is part of a horizontal molecular chain of life—friendship, family, community, nation, humanity. My life is also a link in a vertical chain of life. The current level of human life was made possible by the growth of life's capacities. That development was realized over the course of eons, thanks to the individuals who never allowed the chain to be broken. The level of my individual life is the outgrowth of the achievements of all the generations before me.

The covenantal chain assures that the generations before enrich the generations after; this means that all generations are partners working toward the final *tikkun olam.* It would be selfish—and an act of folly—for the individual to throw all that away out of the demand to be accountable only to oneself. It is folly to care nothing for the future and feel no obligation to the inheritance from the past—because the selfishness jeopardizes the gains of the past and gives a lower yield of value in the present. In a balanced, dialectical lifestyle, the individual becomes fulfilled in a way that cannot be achieved by one-sided, self-centered living. By offering a critique and a living model of such a balanced community, Judaism can offer a very important corrective to the excesses of modernity. This is one of the ways in which Jews can become "a light unto the nations."

This model calls for rebalancing our values. The goal is not to teach the world to reject modernity but to critique the culture from within. Rejectionism is the fallacy of those who resist modernity and nostalgically long for the restoration of the past. Similarly, fundamentalism (and *haredi* values) stipulate the rejection of human power. We need to offer a model of how to use and limit power. By remaining different and distinctive, Jewry helps break up the tendency to homogeneity which leads to the concentration of moral and spiritual power in the dominant culture. This redistribution and division of cultural power is a check-and-balance necessary for the health of the mainstream as well as for Jewry.

Through its *halachah* and historical testimony, Judaism offers a paradigm. The *halachah* shows how to give the individual a proper place, while balancing the family needs. The Torah puts tremendous emphasis on family. The family is the carrier of the covenant. Family is the biological matrix in which you are born into being a Jew; it is the context in which you create life (which is a human's primary task in *tikkun olam*); it is the optimal ground to nurture life in the image of God. By affirming all these values and creating a culture in which they can grow, traditional learning and halachic living practices strengthen the family.

The family is at the heart of much Jewish observance. This simultaneously gives the family a dignified cultural role and strengthens its actual performance. The classic example is *Shabbat. Shabbat* provides ideal family time and rituals that bind the members to each other. This day provides a natural frame for teaching the value of family and friendship. Shabbat is Judaism's way of invigorating an alternative culture and putting limits on modernity. Our community should show the way to postmodernity by building alternative social and cultural structures. These balance factors can help modernity be a constructive force while checking its pathologies.

Q. Aren't you really suggesting that the way for the Jewish people in the United States and other places outside Israel to strengthen the family is through returning to traditional religious practice? Do not the breakdown of the family and its secularization go hand-in-hand? Isn't it clear that, by and large, it is the religious Jews who have done best at preserving the Jewish family?

Greenberg. Your first point, which I fully affirm, is that Jewish tradition and heritage is a tremendously rich resource for renewal and strengthening the family. *Shabbat* and the holidays are family-centered. They provide free, undisturbed time to spend with loved ones; they provide encounters between children and parents, and so on. Equally important, the tradition inculcates the *mitzvot* of helping, the pleasures and values of *gemilut hasadim* (sharing bounty, visiting the sick, comforting the afflicted). These experiences certainly represent a tremendous force for strengthening the family even as these values offset the negative trends in the general culture. An example: The dominance of secularization has undermined the sense of reverence, of obligation to anything beyond oneself (this includes people, not only God). The triumph of secularism turns material well-being into consumerism; the only pleasure one has is to have more pleasure and more gratification. The consequent lifestyle erodes the sense of limits. People lose the norms and models of wanting to share. People grow up without a sense of obligation. There is little or no sense of accountability before God for how one creates wealth, whether one is exploiting others, and so on. Traditional Judaism counters these excesses and restores the sense of community, transcendence, and the value of connecting to others beyond oneself. In all those ways, one cannot separate the renewal of religious practice and tradition and the family's renewal.

Nevertheless, I must insist that traditionalism removed from modern culture is not the answer. Why has the family been so eroded? Part of the problem lies in the fact that people on both sides have made errors. The religious have not been able to separate some of the past distortions from the intrinsic eternal message of Judaism. For their part, the secular have not been able to separate some of the present distortions from the essential message of modernity. Many people believe that if you put any check on consumerism or individualism then you will be undermining modernity's key message: freedom. This is a grave mistake. Without checks and balances, individualism will turn into narcissism; that will lead beyond the breakdown of the family to the breakdown of society. Self-fulfillment and self-indulgence become so linked that one leads inexorably to the other.

The most striking expression of this trend has shown up in American society. The people who do not have the ease and pleasures of middle- and upper-class life are nevertheless saturated with messages of self-indulgence, pleasure without limit, and immediate gratification. This frustration leads to openness to drugs and other forms of instant pleasure that provide an "escape" from the contradictions of daily life but also lead to an ever-intensifying spiral of self-destruction, family erosion, and despair. People who are better off also lose their sense of self and purpose. Life becomes a search for pure pleasure, which becomes self-destructive. We can recognize these ailments all around us.

Nevertheless, we must also confront the need for corrections of the past. If we do not, then we will underestimate the pull of modernity and why people are drawn to it even when the outcomes are dangerous. We have to eliminate the excesses of the past to make purification of the present possible. The inherited evil is that women have been unequal; many opportunities for women were denied. (I do not say that they were always actively denied; the process and the assumptions made for denial.) We cannot rebuild family without overcoming this regrettable inheritance.

In spite of the fact that I affirm that Judaism gave women importance, dignity, and roles that were different yet valuable, still the women were not given full value in Jewish society and way of life. One cannot honestly claim that, in Judaism, women are genuinely separate but equal. After people make this discovery and undergo the shock of recognition that the tradition itself has some distortions, there is a double reaction. Some pull to the "secular" side (the side of equality); then the record of exclusion becomes a weapon against tradition. On the other side, some people who want to withdraw from modernity withdraw from equality. Both responses do not do justice to the dialectic of the covenant. The covenantal way is to correct the balance internally rather than to retreat into either–or. The *haredi* alternative seeks to create a situation where the traditional Jewish woman is not so well educated, but will bear a larger family. This is held up as the only solution to the ZPG being practiced on the other side. But if we abandon the secularists, then those people will continue to have fewer children than replacement-level—which means that the culture of modernity will continue to devour Jewish identity and will itself deteriorate.

I would work for an alternative model for women: the Jewish woman well-educated but simultaneously fully educated Jewishly, given the fullest support by tradition and values. The Jewish woman can mother, enable, and create life, with the back-up of a community that is willing to help her combine the strength she has in the public sector with fulfillment in the private world. This challenges the inherited model that the man goes off to work and to *shul* while the woman stays behind and does all the house work. We seek a tradition willing to make adjustments that can lead to a much healthier synthesis of family and work, of the public and private sectors.

By contrast to the present situation, if we create the right blend of modernity and tradition, then 90 percent of Jews would have families of three to four children. The community with 90 percent having three children per family would have a much healthier demographic balance than in the present situation, where 5 percent of the families have ten children and 80 percent have one.

The current polarization is creating a vicious circle. The modern Orthodox and the moderate secularists have declined. This has left us with two extremes. The smaller fringe (i.e., the traditional sector) is not big enough to handle modern culture. The Orthodox right also loses its credibility because it is reaping the benefits of modern culture without doing its fair share to meet the challenges that modernity poses to the Jewish people. The secularists are swept up in the clichés and the excesses of modern culture without an anchor in tradition to guard them from being overwhelmed. Each side is increasingly impatient with and disrespectful of the other.

The only solution is to build bridges between them and then to raise people in each community who are willing to make these connections. This way is admittedly more difficult. It involves entering into a more complex relationship to modern culture. It is always more difficult to juggle career and family. It is particularly difficult for a man to make the shift, owing to inherited cultural patterns and expectations. But such a path would lead to a better-balanced world. There would be more constructive successful careers and fewer excesses. There would be fewer heart attacks and ulcers for men (and now, increasingly, career women). That is my solution to the family crisis. The goal is to correct modernity, and not to give up on tradition in order to do so.

Q. Rabbi, your wife, Blu Greenberg, has written about the special intensity and joy of the large family. And you and she do represent, I think, the rare case of two people who are known for their work, and yet have managed to raise a large family. What's the magic secret?

Greenberg. In our family my wife is the magic secret, for a number of reasons. For one, she subordinated her career to the family. To a certain extent, that enabled me to do more in my career. Blu sacrificed opportunities in her career for my sake and the children's. Part of the reason she acted that way is that we were brought up in the traditional models, and new ideas took time to evolve. She also loved these traditional roles. Blu also recognized that a very important extension of life was occurring among women. Owing to their longer life expectancy, women can afford to think sequentially. This enables them to concentrate on family or career at different times of their lives. Blu argued that, in the past, a twenty- to thirty-year childrearing period preempted most of a woman's productive career life. Now, the years of childrearing often leave twenty-five to forty productive years ahead for a strong career track. The woman can be a full-time or primary mother and make up career ground after the children are grown. This is not to mention the possibilities of husbands sharing significantly in childrearing or the family getting domestic help (both occurred in our family) so that women's careers can be pursued even during childrearing years.

Blu has loved her career. Early on, she grasped the idea of the dialectic and the need to pursue it as part of one's total life. Blu felt that the work time made her a better mother during the other hours. She also felt that the rewards of mothering made the career delay or sacrifices more than worth it. Her insight that sequencing is a new model for women's lives is an important contribution to breaking out of the present polarization. It also made her a patient, farsighted parent—not a frustrated homebody.

The other contribution that Blu made to our family life concerns her remarkable capacity as a mother and as a wife. I participated intensely in childrearing. We did not follow simple traditional models; still, her gift for parenting made the experience of childbearing and bringing up the children easier and more fulfilling for all of us. She stayed cooler and calmer in a crisis. She is very giving and has a patient sense of how people can grow. She understands that one need not fight at every step; one can allow room for people's errors and people's needs. That was very helpful to me, since I tend to be more anxious and more uptight about matters.

Despite my own strong career involvement, I did not cut out family to follow that career. I felt the desire to be part of the child-rearing, and I was involved. However, I must say that in light of my workaholism, *Shabbat* was a major factor in keeping me involved in family life. We also set up a pattern of family vacations every summer in Gloucester, Massachusetts. I give Blu all the credit for this idea. In the beginning, we would go away for the entire two months of the summer; as I moved forward in my career, I eventually had to cut back to one month. We took a home on the ocean and spent the time away from every involvement, exploring our family's life together. There was a very small Jewish community in Gloucester that held occasional services during the summer. We could not go to *shul* on *Shabbat* anyway, because the building was too far away from our home to be able to walk there. This intensified our *Shabbat* experience. In Gloucester, we had, in effect, a two-month *Shabbat*—undisturbed time to catch up with ourselves and our family. We could intensify our life together, have pleasure as a family, face the challenges and reap the rewards of family. During those summers, we stored reserves of communication, sharing, love, and discussions, which we drew upon the rest of the year.

Blu made another contribution with her approach to feminism, exploring her own insights as to the dialectic of feminism and Judaism, family and career. Blu has always had wonderful ideas. I have been repeatedly impressed by her judgment. Feeling fulfilled in family, she felt no need to throw out the baby (of family) with the bathwater (of women's secondary status). Finding genuine pleasure in creativity and career, she would not let herself be limited by traditional roles exclusively. She worked on the ideological and the practical—a balance of family and career, feminism and tradition, which I think she represents at its best. Hers is not a simple feminism that dismisses or destroys Judaism; nor is it a traditionalism that fears or fights feminism. She uses each side's insights and strengths to help the other side grow and avoid excesses. She incarnates and stimulates a dialogue. From early on, I felt that she represented the true avant-garde—the reconciliation and harnessing of the two positions rather than a one-sided following of the extremes. I strongly supported the development of her career and her need to write and to think. We had our priorities straight.

Let me give a trivial but crucial example. In the very beginning we invested our money not so much in savings or stocks, but rather in getting domestic help. Many times, this help provided the margin for her ability to have energy sufficient to do career and family, rather than just family or just career. The standard joke Blu uses in her talks is a true story. At an early stage, I was not making enough money for us to afford household help. By the time we had a second child, we realized that we would need someone full-time. We went to the bank and requested a loan. When asked the reason for the loan, we naively explained that it was to hire help to take care of the children. The bank rejected our application, saying that we did not have enough earnings to justify the loan. Since the money would be spent on consumption (not on starting a business or investing), they did not think that we would be able to repay the loan. Then we asked what banks would consider a valid reason for borrowing. We were told, "To fix up the house, to improve the value of a property." Once we understood this, we considered further what our real needs were. We still felt that getting help was the key to the fullest measure of achievement in career and family. After a decent interval of time had passed, we went to the bank, and applied for the same loan. When the loan officer asked what the purpose of the loan was, we said, "It is a home-improvement loan." And it was.

Another insight that Blu taught me was the reality of "trade-offs." No one can accomplish everything in career or family; the same is true in policy. Every step in a certain direction has consequences. These consequences mean that you must give up some other value or possibility for the sake of accomplishing the chosen goal. Sometimes the side effects overwhelm the original goal; at the least, one may miss out on some constructive alternatives. The correct response is not to be paralyzed by the trade-offs and not to resort to frenzied activity in the hope of preserving all choices. Rather, one must decide what is the true priority and, at every step, take responsibility for whatever the costs or trade-offs are.

This analysis implies that there may be good on the other side; the road not taken may also be worthwhile. It was just that one was precluded from taking it by the weight and needs of the priority choice that one made. This approach helps prevent absolutization of one's own cause and alerts one to the complexity of every policy choice. It offers a guide to inner calm while recognizing the range of shading on both sides of policy choices. It offers a way to live with one's options. It encourages the individual to do the best in general and to try to mix the best in all the options into one's personal choice—insofar as is possible. Then, in the end, you live with your choices.

This is called living with finitude—a very covenantal lifestyle. Living with finitude means that one cannot have everything, certainly not at once and at all times. One must sacrifice. And one does pay a price. I am sure that our children paid a price for the conflicts in our careers. They may have had less attention than is ideal—certainly from me. Blu decided very early that she would teach part-time in Hebrew school. Part-time work did not pay very well; however, she realized that life was not just a matter of mothering. Teaching was a source of sanity. It gave her a certain openness to life and a perspective. It made her more calm and more fulfilled; she was happier when she was with the children in the house. This was a trade-off in which the side effects were positive. Yet the financial cost and burden of not having a full-time, higher-paid job put extra pressure on me. This, too, was part of the trade-off.

Incidentally, I do not offer our lives as a model of success in an easy sense of the word. I believe that we had enough failures to prove us human and enough satisfaction to make life worthwhile. In retrospect, maybe we could have had a family of ten. Maybe we could have had a career that would have been more effective had there been less conflict about goals, or the time needed, or the money. On balance, with all the trade-offs, our lives have been worth it.

Q. Rabbi, do you think that there are any specific practical actions the Jewish community worldwide can take to move toward the kind of balanced family model we have been speaking about?

Greenberg. Family and childrearing, parental roles, and career choices are fundamental personal decisions. These decisions cannot be dictated by tradition or easily guided by community. However, communal values shape decisions, and culture can give parameters to personal conclusions. Blu and I have talked about this many times. We were lucky, in a way, that the full acceptance of birth control and abortion came after we had already had our children. Not each one of Blu's pregnancies came at the right time. Had we lived in a community in which abortion was taken for granted, it would have been easy to have an abortion and go on. We are very grateful that we never lived in an environment that denigrated large families. Casual abortion never crossed our horizon because we were brought up and raised in Orthodox communities where having children was the greatest blessing and abortion was just about off-limits. I know many women who, having grown up in this later culture, either did not have children or had abortions. Afterwards, these women deeply regretted it. Some missed out altogether on one of the greatest life experiences.

One of the most powerful reasons that Blu and I could combine career and family was that we both found tremendous fulfillment in family. In other words, one of the reasons that people go all-out in career is that they get gratification and rewards. I felt that whatever thrills or chills I received by recognition in career were more than matched by the joy and fulfillment that came from the children, from family experiences, and from my relationship with Blu. Certainly our Orthodox community's values played a very big role in our life's constellation. I conclude that the Jewish community must articulate a strong framework of values that sustain, respond to, and respect positive decisions for family life.

The community also must provide some of the technical help that families need. There is a shortage of childcare programs at reasonable prices within the Jewish community. Surveys show that even unaffiliated Jews mostly would prefer to send their children to Jewish childcare settings. The community is only now beginning to wake up to the need to provide this service. If we want career women to have children, we need to move in the area of childcare. I speak often about the ideal of having families with three to four children. Many of those mothers will need daycare programs. One also has to work for equal pay for women; this will help out the woman who has the strength to become a mother. Equal pay will begin to overcome the problems of deprivation (and even poverty) that appear in single-parent homes. Some women become single parents because of divorce or death; some women decide to become single parents because of their family values. (They cannot find a man; they are not prepared to marry because mutual love or mutual respect is not there, and they are not willing to have a man at all costs.) Given that kind of reality, the community has to think in terms of concrete help, social introductions, marriage counseling, and so on.

Blu has written that each rabbi should find the time and the commitment to counsel couples. Before two people marry, rabbis should spend time with them; then there should be rabbinic recall—a counseling session six months or a year later. Couples should feel that the community wants to help them with their difficulties. Extended families are a tremendous reinforcement for nuclear families. The community and the extended family can be of great help in sustaining the family.

Those are areas where the community can help. What communities cannot do is to dictate family policies. Even the governments of Russia and France, which tried to build up birthrates by making serial payments for each child, failed. Nevertheless, the community can create a more positive, supportive atmosphere conducive to the creation of somewhat larger families. For example, Jewish organizations should press for family-support policies in taxation and for increased personal exemptions for children. American Jewry should support government aid to private (parochial) education. Right now, the community considers the separation of church and state as one of the ten commandments (which is why American Jewry overwhelmingly opposed vouchers to aid parochial education). Yet attendance at day school is a strong nurturer of Jewish identity and gives strength to the family. In the absence of sufficient government or community aid for day schools, tuitions are set so high as to weaken attendance. My brother-in-law jokes that the most powerful form of birth control in the Orthodox Jewish community is day-school tuition.

There were years in Blu's and my life when the single largest item in our budget (by a factor of two or three) was not food or shelter, but tuition. We just gritted our teeth and did it because we were committed to our children's Jewish education. It was very hard financially and physically. I had to work hard; I took on extra teaching and extra lectures in order to raise the money. Less committed parents would reduce the number of children or skip day school. It is in the community's interest to help lower tuition.

In sum, exhortations are of little help. Concrete policies of the right kind can help. The most important contribution that the community can make is to create a nurturing and sustaining background, to offer countervalues that uphold the value of family and the (ethical) authority of parents. A strong Jewish cultural model can compete with the one-sided excesses of modern culture and strengthen family—for the benefit of the family, the Jewish community, and American society.

Q. But is it clear that one model of modern Western culture, of Protestant culture, of the individual seeking fulfillment in and by himself even in relation to God, is not the Jewish model? That is, in Judaism, the family is not just an "option"; it is essential to the true religious life.

Greenberg. It is. But there are certain ways of achieving the goal of family that are no longer available, and that is for the good. In the past, if you were a woman without a family, you had no standing, no dignity, no value. (This statement is exaggerated, but not by much.) That value system is gone except in *haredi* society. In other words, the goal of family and children cannot be achieved by ruthlessly suppressing the alternative models at all costs. The cost for women is too high.

What is the cultural alternative? The alternative is to create an environment (not just in religion, but in society) in which the individual sees his or her own self as part of a larger whole.

In Victor Frankl's metaphor, the human being is a meaning-seeking creature. The human being is not just someone who is looking for gratification; the search for meaning, not the pursuit of happiness, brings happiness. Those who seek happiness directly generally find the path very frustrating. Such people are often very unhappy, because the more you pursue happiness, the harder it is to catch it. Happiness is typically a by-product of meaningful action, such as creative work; or, it grows out of fulfillment in relationships. Happiness is sustained by intellectual, emotional, and sexual adult relationships; it is also obtained through caring, loving, concerned relationships with children. The confusion of enjoyment and recreation with happiness has wreaked emotional havoc on many people. The difference has to be articulated.

In general, truths have to be spoken to power and to society. These truths, in particular, have to be modeled as living experiences. The Jewish community itself has to model its way of life for others. It has to offer a clear paradigm so that people can choose to live within its framework of meaning, instead of chasing every possibility and everybody else's conception of happiness.

Q. Rabbi, I want to ask you: In regard to living a full Jewish family life, do you think that it is possible to do that outside of Israel?

Greenberg. It is a lot easier to live Jewishly in Israel. The Jewish majority in Israel makes Jewish living the path of least resistance. The banks—indeed, most businesses—are closed on *Shabbat* and Jewish holidays. In a typical supermarket—at least in Jerusalem—you would have to search hard to find a nonkosher product. The media focus on forthcoming holidays, on special moments in Jewish history, on what is happening in the Jewish world. . . . Israeli culture is marked by the presence of Jewish religion formally, and by Jewish tradition informally. Many secularists keep Jewish holidays and *Shabbat* as the time for families to be together. Israeli culture includes an influential residue of the traditional culture (including some less attractive aspects, such as superstition, wonder-workers, and machismo). But, overall, the residue helps create an environment in support of the family. It is easier to raise children in Israel. The temptations, the radicalism, the violence, is twenty-five years behind America—and, if we are lucky, it will stay that way.

However, do not draw from this response the conclusion that raising a Jewish family is impossible in the Diaspora. It is just much harder. Diaspora Jews have to come to grips with the fact that living as a Jew is easier in Israel; one is more supported by the culture, by the economy, by the values, by the school system. On the other hand, there are no guarantees in Israel. There is no absolute guard against erosion of Jewish identity in Israel. There are challenges on both sides. Those Jews who choose to stay in the Diaspora have to consider that they are lowering the percentages in favor of Jewish family vitality and survival in the future. That is a realistic statement of the choice that Diaspora Jews are making. It is also true that the Diaspora is hard to give up for many Jews. One can have an easier life there.

Nevertheless, we should not write off the Diaspora. Some Jews who decide to stay in the Diaspora will look in the mirror one day and say, "Losing out Jewishly is a real cost. Let's make *aliyah* now." On the other hand, many Jews will conclude that the comfort of Diaspora life is so great that they will find it hard to move. When the Jews came back from the first destruction in Babylonia, the majority stayed in the Diaspora because they were doing well. Instead of attacking the Diaspora, one should do everything possible to strengthen it. I cannot say it often enough: Israel has a major stake in strengthening the Diaspora.

Q. Rabbi, aside from the Hasidic communities, are there American Jewish communities that are internally strong as Jewish communities?

Greenberg. The American Jewish Committee once commissioned a study on (what they called) "points of vitality"—communities or groups that seem to have a vital force of their own. Lincoln Square Synagogue was one of the communities that they studied. There are modern Orthodox congregations that have managed to keep a high degree of social cohesion and positive religious atmosphere. The Lincoln Square and, more recently, Ohab Zedek synagogues were examples. (By the way, their achievements are particularly striking because they are located on the Upper

West Side of Manhattan, where there is a lot of population turnover. There are also a lot of singles in the area, which creates a less stable base population.) The Riverdale Jewish Center (where I served as a rabbi and lived afterwards) has such an effective community. There was a school linked to the synagogue and a social nexus that, together, were able to communicate real values. Blu once did a study of The Riverdale Jewish Center. It was striking to see the very low rate of divorce and intermarriage. (I do not know whether the rates are as low now as they were then.)

There are other such communities, although I am less familiar with the grassroots in the liberal Jewish community. B'nai Jeshurun Congregation in New York City has drawn wide attention for creating a vital liturgical community in which thousands gather weekly, and for backing this with a strong social-action and mutual-help community. Many of the *chavurot* (which are heavily non-Orthodox) have played a similar kind of role—combining community, learning, and religious experience. Rabbi Harold Schulweis' synagogue has a strong component of community and *chavurot.* Living in such a context makes a strong impact on family life and values transmission.

There have been friendship groups centered around youth experiences. Groups like NFTY (Reform), USY (Conservative), and NCSY (Orthodox) generate strong peer groups. The Ramah camp (Conservative), NFTY camps (Reform), and the Bnai Akiva Moshava camps and Y.U.'s Morasha camp (Orthodox) have had life-transforming effects because they generate strong follow-through and lifelong commitments. Those are the "points of light," so to speak. These provide a classic Jewish form, the holy community that serves as a model for Jews and for the world.

Do these models need to be further developed? Yes. Are there enough of them in the Diaspora? No. It is very hard to create internal communities, particularly in an environment so open and attractive. Nonetheless, the alternative of being closed off culturally is not a plausible model. In the long run, ghettoization does not give us a real, workable model. Even in Israel, when peace comes (and, God willing, peace *will* come), we will see a lot of the same problems that we see in the Diaspora. The central need remains to develop communities that are not simply sheltered, but are voluntarily constituted within the larger environment. This is hard to accomplish, but it is doable. Creating such communities would prove that Judaism and the Jewish people are adaptable, as they have been in the past. Judaism must adapt to the ecology of modern culture, including finding and maintaining its distinctive niche and values. Then Jewish values must shape and reshape modern culture and absorb it in the form of assimilation *to* Jewish culture, instead of the present assimilation away from Jewish culture.

Gerson Cohen argued in a classic essay that Judaism has flourished in the past, in part, by assimilating the outside culture to its own. That kind of assimilation is healthy. It is like a body absorbing food and digesting it into itself. The other kind of assimilation weakens the body. Instead of Judaism absorbing only that which can strengthen it, the outside culture is so powerful that it sucks out Jewish loyalty, values, and allegiance, and replaces them with foreign qualities. This is the heart of the challenge in Jewish culture: Can it become dynamic enough to absorb and flourish within the outside culture? Or will it lose its ability to hold people so that Jews will drift into the general culture? That challenge is easier to meet in Israel, but it is not yet resolved in Israel, either.

Q. Rabbi, how did you get your values across to your own children? Where were they educated?

Greenberg. They all went to SAR elementary school, which is the school that Blu and I founded. We shaped the conception of the school, so, not surprisingly, we found its educational process very compatible with our views. SAR teaches some wonderful values, including a strong sense of both self and group. The teachers cultivate individuality even as they communicate a social ethos of *gemilut hasadim.* SAR is an open school, so the children can work at their own pace. There is individual instruction and the freedom to move around. At the same time, that emphasis on individuality is matched by a stress on community responsibility. The students visit the nearby old-age home to help the people, to entertain and talk with them, to help take care of them where appropriate. The school features openness to non-observant Jews and a powerful sense of Jewish mission. There is a strong commitment to Zionism and Israel. Both principals who shaped the school eventually made *aliyah.*

After graduation from SAR, half of our children attended high schools run by Rabbi Shlomo Riskin; the other half went to Ramaz, which is one of the best modern Orthodox schools in New York. Then our children went to study in Israel. That option is one of the great revolutions in modern Orthodox education over the past thirty years. Each child spent a minimum of one year learning intensively in Israel. This has become a norm in the modern Orthodox world.

When I graduated from high school, it did not occur to me to go study in Israel. At that time, it just was not done. When Blu was already in college, she heard about a new six-month institute for Jewish study in Israel. When we met on our first date, she had just heard about it and was very excited. However, she feared that her parents would never agree to let her go. Girls were sheltered. . . . Israel was far away. . . . It seemed a bit risky for Orthodox parents. So I volunteered to go home with her and talk them into it. (The truth is that I was trying to put her on ice to remove her from other social opportunities—but that is another story!)

By the time our children were of age, going to study in Israel was an accepted principle, practically a norm. I would guess that almost 90 percent of their class did the same. Moshe went to Kerem B'Yavneh Hesder Yeshiva on its special American program. David went to study at Rabbi Aharon Lichtenstein's Gush Etzion Yeshiva in Alon Shvut. Deborah went to Machon Gold. J.J. went to Beit Midrash Latorah—a Y.U.-sponsored institute that was less Talmud-intensive than a standard yeshiva. Goody also went to Machon Gold. As it turned out, each child continued for a second year (and even third year, in some cases). Deborah returned to Hebrew University. Goody returned for further study at Brovender's Yeshiva; then she ended up studying on her own; then she worked in Sherut Leumi/Volunteer service at Shaare Zedek Hospital. Each child developed a very deep attachment to Israel. One proof of that love is that two of them have made *aliyah.* The other three are strongly connected. They go regularly to spend time (especially *chagim*) in Israel. In my judgment, two of the three others will likely end up making *aliyah* eventually.

The main result of their Israel study years was that they came out with a higher degree of learning, a higher degree of attachment to Israel, and a religious experience that is incomparable. (It is incomparable in the sense that they experience a fusion of intensity of learning and community spirit, combined with the electrifying historical and Jewish background of Israel. Walk the streets of Jerusalem and you absorb the past. These are certainly features impossible to replicate.)

One of the projects that looms larger and larger in my mind is to provide study opportunities for *all* American Jewish youth in Israel. Of course, many groups are advocating the Israel experience. But I propose to create networks of study opportunities in Israel to deepen the experience—out of the belief that every American Jew (not just children from Orthodox homes) study in Israel for a month or six months to a year. Institutions offering a wide variety of learning and experiences should be created in every form and fashion. This experience would revolutionize American Jewish life—as it did modern Orthodox Jewish life in America. Israel-based study will strengthen American Jewry; it will make it more likely that American youth will stay Jewish in America. But it also raises the probabilities of *aliyah*, as it did with my children.

Let me restate my favorite paradox in this area. The single best way to increase *aliyah* from North America (short of catastrophe, which would be bad for Israel also) would be to increase and intensify Jewish life in America. The richer, the more fulfilling, the more total Jewish life in America, the more *aliyah* there will be. It is also true that the more magnetic, the more outstanding, Israeli society is, the more inspiring it will be for more American Jews. Then they will want to stay more Jewish in America (although some higher percentage will also make *aliyah*). So, the more Israel does for American Jewry, both by upgrading its own life and model and by helping American Jewry directly, the more *olim* there will be. This is the dialectic in the relationship of Israel and the Diaspora.

7

The Situation of Modern Orthodoxy

Shalom Freedman (Q). How would you describe the situation of modern Orthodoxy today?

Rabbi Irving Greenberg. When I consider the state of modern Orthodoxy, I often think of a visit to England in 1987. CLAL had been asked to send staff to start a parallel program in Great Britain. Our leadership felt that we could not provide sufficient resources or supervision to run a genuine branch of CLAL. Instead, a colleague and I went for a three-week trip to tell about our work and meet with people who wanted to start some interdenominational activities. The goal was to talk with leaders of Orthodoxy and the other religious groups. However, it was the official policy of the Orthodox not to participate in meetings or programs that legitimated Reform. Since the Orthodox would not meet with liberals on an official basis in a setting that tacitly conceded that the two sides were speaking as equals, I was informed that I should not address liberal forums publicly. That would undercut the Orthodox policy. The information came with a warning attached: Should I speak at any official Reform meeting, I would *not* be invited to address any Orthodox group thereafter—for I would have breached the Orthodox line. Hoping to get some leeway, seeking to make clear my good intentions and to explain why I believed that the Orthodox should take a more positive approach to non-Orthodox movements, I went to see the then Chief Rabbi, Sir Immanuel Jakobovits.

Personally, I thought that the Orthodox policy was scandalous in light of the threatening crisis of assimilation. I was particularly bothered by the contrast between the treatment of non-Orthodox Jews and of Christians. Sir Immanuel was then the head of the Interfaith group that carried on dialogues and cooperative programs among the various faiths in England. In his role as head of the Interfaith group, the Chief Rabbi met regularly and talked respectfully and publicly with various Christian groups. That he could and would do—because the average Jew, especially the average Orthodox Jew, is still afraid of the gentiles. In religious theory, most Orthodox rabbis look askance at Christianity and cite Maimonides' view that (unlike Islam) certain Christian teachings can be classified as *avodah zarah* (idolatry). But the community leadership—including the ultra-Orthodox, whose pressure against any respectful conversation with non-Orthodox is writ large in the Orthodox non-dialogue policy—acceded to Jakobovits' interfaith work as necessary politically. After all, Jews cannot afford to make the gentiles angry; Jews have to win acceptance. Jakobovits himself had a very distinguished role in public life. The Chief Rabbi of England could not be perceived as disrespectful (or as bound not to deal) with other faiths.

Q. In fact, he is a very close friend of then Prime Minister Margaret Thatcher.

Greenberg. Exactly. If it ever got out that the Chief Rabbi of England would not deal with other religions, he would be "finished," pilloried as a benighted bigot. The very standing of the British Jewish community could be hurt by such a revelation. So the interfaith policy had the touch of duplicity about it. He was dealing with gentiles without engaging them theologically. He was being nice to them and saying nice things to them. Ironically, he sat with Reform rabbis when he talked with Christians because it would be too blatant and obvious if the Reform were not there. But, as Chief Rabbi of the Jewish community, he refused to talk directly with the Reform in any public forum because that would legitimate them.

Jakobovits was unmoved by my arguments. He was upset, therefore, that I was planning to address Reform groups. He reiterated that no other Orthodox rabbi would do such an act. He stressed that I was breaching official policy and that no Orthodox synagogue or body would invite me to address them publicly once I spoke to Reform. As it turned out, two more open-minded Orthodox rabbis with large, liberal-minded congregations did invite me to speak, but for the most part I was boycotted by Orthodox groups.

In my conversations with Rabbi Jakobovits and other members of the Orthodox leadership (as to why they were pursuing these policies), I concluded that the logic of their position was very understandable, but was disastrous for modern Orthodoxy and for *clal yisrael.* (Unfortunately, their logic is being followed by the Orthodox in Israel as well.)

The average English Jew is religiously and Jewishly uninvolved; therefore, Jewry is increasingly exposed to assimilative forces. But the average English citizen has respect for tradition. Combined with the fact that the United Synagogue controls the cemeteries and that most people want to be buried in Jewish burial grounds when their time comes, the result is that 80 percent of Anglo-Jewry join the United Synagogue (the modern Orthodox synagogue network), though they are not religiously committed to Orthodoxy. That cultural presumption (of the special sanctity of tradition) was the main barrier to the growth of liberal and Reform movements. These groups are trying to reach out to people by offering shorter services, by being more forthcoming on cultural and value changes, by making greater room for women, by welcoming converts and the intermarried, and so on. Unfortunately, Anglo-Jewry, as represented in the United Synagogue, became modernized in a "hollow" way. Religious fervor cooled to indifference. Jews' College became modern in that it brought Jewish studies into the curriculum. But, in a typically shallow move, the course of study cut back on Talmud but stressed etiquette and proper speech. In the process, Jews' College lost much of the fervor and most of the learning of traditional *yeshivot* without injecting any new spirit or depth in

Judaism. The typical synagogue turned into a gentleman's club. Jewish education in that network is shallow and weak. The net result has been that the United Synagogue as an institution still possesses the social leadership of English Jewry and some financial strength. But its congregations are bored, restless, slowly dwindling; it is gradually losing people to the Reform and to assimilation.

This void created an opening for the right-wing Orthodox. Their base started with postwar immigrants. As they built *yeshivot* and developed a missionary approach, they began to build their own institutions and to eat into the United Synagogue constituency. The numbers have not been large; they make up maybe 5 percent of Anglo-Jewry. However, they increasingly began to set the tone of the United Synagogue and the parameters of its policy choices, as well. The most striking infiltration was their taking over of the London *Beit Din* owing to the monopoly of *lomdus* (halachic scholarship), which their *yeshivot* possessed. Jews' College (which was dying) could not or would not contest this course. (If men were sent to Israel to study in *yeshivot*, there, too, the values being communicated were increasingly *haredi*.)

Instead of trying to revitalize the modern Orthodox rabbinate and educational system, Rabbi Jakobovits was with the ultra-Orthodox psychologically. His children had moved to the right, and his grandchildren had moved even further! At one point, he boasted that they would not eat in his home—and he was proud of the fact.

Two deadly results flowed from this void. The United Synagogue was led increasingly by a spiritual leadership that did not believe in its foundational values. This made it likely that if a young person caught fire religiously, he would move to the right. Second, the *haredi* influence dictated policy more and more. Through the *Beit Din*, policies were imposed on constituents for whom such guidelines were irrelevant or alienating. The *Beit Din, de facto*, made conversion so difficult as to be almost impossible—this, at a time when the society was opening up and intermarriage was growing. This policy foreclosed any positive tack that the United Synagogue might have taken to help families deal with the problem; i.e., in those cases where the gentiles could be persuaded to become Jewish, this treatment closed the door. Of course, this policy fit the *haredi* social situation perfectly. Intermarriage was rare because social contact was almost nonexistent; the best policy to further discourage it might well be to erect higher walls, to treat the gentile potential partner with social exclusion and hostility. But for Jewish families living in a society where children were inevitably going to meet gentiles, a policy of welcoming and converting receptive gentiles would be the most likely to sustain the positive Jewish commitment of the Jewish partner.

Jakobovits moved to strengthen Jewish education, but he did not raise enough money to stop the erosion substantially. Not only did he stay locked to the right, he refused to work with or to consider how to cooperate with liberals to face the common growing challenge of assimilation. The United Synagogue laity (with some exceptions in the leadership) were similar in profile to the Reform groups, but he felt that the residual traditionalism would keep them from joining liberal groups. The Chief Rabbi rationalized the refusal to even recognize liberals on the grounds that: (a) the right demanded it, and (b) if he took a positive tack, this might erode a traditional respect barrier that kept people in the United Synagogue even if they did not believe in or practice *halachah.* He drew the analogy of Israel, where Orthodoxy is established; most people are alienated, but consider liberal religious alternatives beyond the pale. By using the monopoly and pulling a modest amount of legal and institutional levers, the liberals would be kept at bay.

I pleaded for a reconsideration. The surrender of policy control and of norm-setting to the right-wing Orthodox was foreclosing the ability of the United Synagogue to respond to its own constituency's needs. Some of the pressures—further separation of girls and women in education—were bound to alienate modern Orthodox women who would want more, not less, equality and access to learning and leadership. Moreover, as the new values soaked in, the spiritual leadership was increasingly unwilling to uphold the moves toward modernity that were the essence of modern Orthodoxy. Despite their Zionism, they were unwilling to say clearly that they were in conflict with *haredi* anti-Zionist values. Behind the Zionist issue was the fundamental one on which Zionism was based: the affirmation that God wanted people (Jews, in particular) to take power and exercise it to carry out the Jewish mission. Acceptance of Zionism also implied an alliance with the whole Jewish people for the sake of renewal rather than withdrawal into a sectarian ghetto.

I also argued that the swing to the right detached Orthodoxy from the rest of the Jews, thus removing an anchor that was holding the other Jews back from assimilation. At that time, Jakobovits and the United Synagogue leaders were still living with the illusion that Anglo-Jewry was insulated from assimilation owing to the strong traditionalism of English society. Since then, more and more studies indicate that in England—as throughout the developed world—increasing communication leads to an open society with greater social contact and the inevitable rise in assimilation and intermarriage.

Modern Orthodoxy had to develop an alternative policy, I argued. At that time, the United Synagogue was living off its institutional strength, its establishment, its resources, its monopoly. These tactics were based on the assumption that lay people would continue to drift in the Jewish orbit, held there by inertia and traditionalism. This policy might hold off the liberal denominations for another generation, but it could not stave off the inroads of modernity. Society is becoming more and more open. This is the worldwide crisis for all cultures that are losing their shelter and monopoly.

There are two serious choices in an open society. Either you withdraw—the policy that the right-wing Orthodox were trying to accomplish—or you recognize that the lot of your community is decisively cast to live with modernity. Then you develop the full range of approaches and institutions needed to maintain a viable Jewish loyalty and lifestyle in the contemporary culture. It is the choice between building a dam to keep out the ocean or learning how to swim, eat, and live in a new ocean. Choosing this second direction meant that modern Orthodoxy would have to become more modern—to deal with some issues it had hitherto avoided. The challenge of historicism and biblical criticism could not be swept under the rug. Full exposure to the sophistication of higher education also demanded upgrading of the learning levels and complexity of traditional learning in order to compete for attention. The learning would have to yield guidelines for dealing with an advanced culture; positive values such as freedom, pluralism, and new roles for women would have to be incorporated or addressed with some positive alternative. It would take high-level training and rethinking to raise a cadre of rabbis and educators who could handle the questions, address the issues, and display the openness essential to being heard in a multivoiced environment.

Therefore, the policy of dialogue with Christians but not with non-Orthodox was pernicious. It made the Christian activity into a charade; a social front, not a genuine encounter. At the same time, it deprived Jewry of a needed, serious exploration of its own values and beliefs. If the Orthodox and Reform would enter into a deep theological dialogue or debate, each community would get the benefits of responding to an alternative set of views. The rabbis would grow intellectually and spiritually. The people might well be excited by the exchange, and be stimulated into religious deepening. Of course, this proposed policy involved risks. What if the Reform impressed people? What if the Orthodox could not deal with serious questions? However, this approach would be based on the assumption that the tradition had the strength to grow and compete. In the process of carrying out this policy, the Orthodox would become deeper, and more able to deal with the open society. This would represent a major upgrading of Orthodox skills.

The present policy, *de facto*, was writing off the bulk of Anglo-Jewry. It came close to a philosophy of *après moi, le deluge.* The drift and inherent passivity of the lay people might keep Orthodoxy dominant for another generation. The collapse would come later and would likely drag most of the community with it. Thus, the modern Orthodox would have betrayed their historic role of synthesizing the best of the two worlds and of opening the door for Judaism to flourish in the new culture. The present policy was comfortable for the modern Orthodox spiritual leadership because it reduced attacks from the right. But this policy bought protection for a handful of leaders while it threw the bulk of English Jewry to the wolves of assimilation.

I predicted to Jakobovits that the United Synagogue would suffer increasing losses to continuing assimilation, and to the slowly growing liberal movements on the left as well as to the *haredi* movement on the right. This erosion would eat away at the United Synagogue; it would become less and less effective. To sit down with the liberal and Reform would be more challenging and more "risky." However, CLAL had considerable experience in this area. Our work showed that all the sides would gain but Orthodoxy would do especially well. This meant that taking this risk would constitute choosing the correct risk, as against the "safe" policy, which was a prescription for a slow but accelerating landslide.

Rabbi Jakobovits rejected my proposals out of hand. After Rabbi Jonathan Sacks was elected Chief Rabbi, he commissioned a study of the United Synagogue. The study came to the same conclusions: that the rate of assimilation was high and rising, that the United Synagogue was losing ground to its right and its left. The sad part is that the decline of modern Orthodoxy is a tragedy for the total community, which loses its buffer and its potential cutting edge in generating a vital Jewish lifestyle inside the modern culture. (Of course, Reform, liberal, and conservative are exploring these issues also. But they are more hamstrung by their constituents' weaknesses, whereas the Orthodox were more hobbled by the critique from the right.)

On my 1987 trip, Jonathan Sacks, who has been a good friend, invited me to speak at Marble Arch Synagogue (his community). This took some guts, since Rabbi Jakobovits had decided that no chief rabbinate institutions should give me a public forum. (I do not exaggerate the courage. The rabbi is given that kind of freedom to invite guest speakers; he knew that I would bend over backward not to embarrass him.) Yet, there was some disapproval and some public expressions of displeasure with the fact that I was going to speak to the Reform. Two years later, Rabbi Sacks organized a conference on the future of Orthodoxy. He invited people from a broad spectrum (including, from the right, Rabbi J. David Bleich of Yeshiva University). Bleich told him that he would not come if I participated. He cited my work with the Reform and liberal groups, and Sacks caved in. I was not invited.

Afterwards, Sacks was somewhat apologetic because he realized that he was collaborating with those who were delegitimating me. I felt that he should have not let Bleich set the rules. Sacks should have said, "I want to have you (Rabbi Bleich), but I do not allow people to delegitimate other people." The fact that the right-wing could exclude *from modern Orthodox forums* people engaged in the frontier exploration that modern Orthodoxy had to undertake, symbolized the crippling of modern Orthodoxy and its loss of self-respect. Unfortunately, Sacks was under political pressure. He was running for the Chief Rabbi's post. He was less liberal than some of the other candidates, and he wanted the right-wing to lean against his opponents. He probably feared an incident that could harm his electoral support or standing with the right.

It is not that I do not understand his behavior. I myself have always defended the talmudic rabbis and their prudential halachic compromises as against the prophets' unyielding standard. After all, Sacks had to look to himself first. As an individual, he could not carry out his plans and hopes for Orthodoxy and the total Jewish community unless he reached the chief rabbinate first. I have also made decisions affected by concerns for my own political safety. So I accepted his decision, and it did not rupture our friendship. However, over the years, too many of these kinds of decisions have been made by too many modern Orthodox leaders. The cumulative effect of all those choices has contributed substantially to the disintegration of modern Orthodoxy. For this reason, I have become more hard-nosed in making judgments. I now believe that my peers and my friends who were the leaders of modern Orthodoxy during these two decades have to take serious responsibility for this collapse.

One of the truly shocking aspects of the National Jewish Population Study in 1990 was its portrait of Orthodoxy. The general impression was that Orthodoxy has been flourishing over the past two decades. In fact, the Orthodox percentage dropped from 14.4 percent in 1970 to 7.7 percent of American Jewry in 1990. Notwithstanding the greater visibility and influence of Orthodoxy and the greater respect for it, and notwithstanding the greater power and presence of the *haredim* in America and Israel, Orthodoxy had undergone a severe numerical decline. In retrospect, the right *was* getting stronger—by cannibalizing modern Orthodoxy.

Institutionally, Orthodoxy was giving the impression of becoming stronger, but it was losing people in droves. With the benefit of hindsight, we now know that the turn to the right has devastated modern Orthodoxy's numbers. As they swung to the right, they talked more and more about *halachah*—and halachic conformity. As the Union of Orthodox Jewish Congregations of America started the drive to reestablish *mechitzah* in Orthodox *shuls* that had removed them (or never had them), as they went further and kowtowed to the right, they were communicating to the non-observant Orthodox: *You are not wanted.* The non-observant or semi-observant Orthodox had made up 50 percent of the Orthodox membership. They were driven out; their children moved and joined non-Orthodox synagogues or were undermined by the gap between their home life and synagogue–school expectations—and drifted off into assimilation.

Despite the decline, modern Orthodox Jews probably still constitute the majority of the Orthodox community; indeed, there is still a significant (albeit shrinking) non-observant element in Orthodoxy. But the policies being followed will inexorably complete the erosion of those two groups. Thus, this policy overall spread polarization in the total Jewish community and caused a continuing decline in Orthodoxy; the shrinkage was a product and a cause of its growing sectarianism.

Take the case of Yeshiva University, which is the flagship institution of American modern Orthodoxy. Historically, its faculty has provided the leadership for this community. Rabbi Joseph B. Soloveitchik, *zt'l*, and Rabbi Emanuel Rackman come to mind as classic models. For the past two decades, Y.U. has been under the leadership of Dr. Norman Lamm, whom I consider to be a friend and a man of genuine capacity. Until the last half-decade, Lamm was not ready to fight for modern Orthodoxy. As he went along with the trend, the Yeshiva (of Yeshiva University) slipped into the orbit of the *roshei hayeshiva.* They defined themselves by right-wing standards and desperately sought legitimacy and approval from them. As talmudic and halachic mastery became defined as the only relevant criterion of spiritual leadership (disregarding the relationship to the secular, the importance of philosophy and history, the ability to cope with reality), Dr. Lamm himself became marginalized inside the yeshiva. He would give *sheurim* to validate (implicitly) his bona fides as a talmudist. He used the title of *rosh hayeshiva*, but everyone knew that he did not know as much Talmud as the *roshei yeshiva.* No one—including Lamm—pointed out that sheer familiarity with *halachah* was not enough of a qualification for leadership.

Dr. Lamm tried to check some excesses. Typically, he could stop certain extremist policies at some point, but he could hardly roll them back; nor could he introduce strong modern Orthodox policies, either. There was never an analysis or a strategic plan to reverse this trend—to identify younger scholars and cultivate them to be more open; to reward forward thinking; and to nurture a new modern type of Orthodox talmudic scholars, rabbis, educators, or even lay leadership. Five years ago, Lamm finally decided to fight back. At that point, he received a lot of abuse for daring to articulate the case for modern Orthodoxy and for offering a critique of the right way. I was shocked at the extent to which his own colleagues and peers let him hang out there to dry for fear of being abused themselves if they stood by him. Their cowardice stunned me, but his fate is, in part, self-imposed—it summed up modern Orthodoxy's catastrophe.

Over the years, I came to visit Dr. Lamm especially in relation to CLAL and Yeshiva University. There is a senior rabbinical student interns program at CLAL, in which one or two students from each denomination study together at CLAL for a year. As the years went on, the Y.U./CLAL interns felt more and more isolated. Y.U. was afraid to openly and publicly cooperate with CLAL in interdenominational activity. Thank God, privately they did not stop it altogether. In some cases, students were not told not to go, but they were told that a year with CLAL would not help them professionally. Truth to tell, CLAL was opening up important new fields for rabbis—especially as CLAL was helping to persuade federations to invest in Jewish education. The federations were beginning to create jobs and were quite receptive to hiring open-minded or pluralist Orthodox rabbis. Instead of meeting this need, Y.U. was raising a generation of rabbis that were so *frum*, they were afraid to mix. Many Y.U. rabbinical graduates would not or could not work at Hillel, also, because they had been taught that it was forbidden to work in pluralist settings. This abdication of opportunity occurred simultaneously with a sharp decline in the number of Orthodox *shuls.*

Another example of the retreat before right-wing pressure was Y.U.'s handling of traditional synagogues. In the Midwest, these were Orthodox *shuls* without *mechitzahs* that had been set up in the last generation by graduates of Chicago's Hebrew Theological College. Many of these congregations were large institutions. With the decline of Hebrew Theological (also a mirror of modern Orthodoxy's fate), Y.U. began to service them. But as it played to the right in these past two decades, Y.U. stopped sending rabbis to these synagogues. The original rabbis had been sent out to hold the fort—almost like scouts sent to hold a distant frontier post where conditions were less civilized. Then Y.U., to protect itself, cut them off, leaving the rabbis there to twist slowly in the wind. The message—"Serve there, and you are delegitimated"—frightened off any young rabbis who were tempted to serve those congregations. Gradually the institutions drifted off; either they disintegrated or the positions were taken by Conservative rabbis if no Orthodox replacement could be found.

If, on the other hand, such synagogues remained traditional and did not want to accept the egalitarian trend in services, the congregations could find no rabbinic replacement. Sometimes they would turn to CLAL (or to me personally) to help them find an Orthodox rabbi. Mind you, these were important institutional-size congregations, often found in cities where the rest of the Orthodox presence had shrunk to a small *shtiebel* or two. However, when I spoke to Y.U. administrators, they were afraid to serve the *shuls*. When I asked students directly, they replied that they could not go because Y.U. told them that if they went to those congregations, they would be "finished for life"; they would never receive a rabbinic post in any mainstream Orthodox congregation. A generation earlier, Y.U. had sent in rabbis to reclaim marginal congregations; now they were abandoning whole cities and shrinking Orthodoxy into safe areas—only this was hailed as establishing "strict halachic standards." To me, it looked like retreat into sectarianism.

Nevertheless, I was stunned by NJPS' implication that Orthodoxy had declined during this period, although I'd had an inkling that there was slippage. In the 1970s and early 1980s, I had made extensive trips to the South and was struck by the erosion of the classic Orthodox *shuls*, which had been built on the coalition of the observant and non-observant who came because their grandfathers had built the *shuls*. Such people were now being driven out. For every *shul* that put in a *mechitzah*, a few others were lost because of the pressure to become more *frum*. But, somehow, I practiced denial; I did not see the side effects. Because I was struggling to establish CLAL, I guess, I did not want to know too much that would put me further outside the Orthodox consensus. The modern Orthodox were convinced that the policy of walking in the footsteps of the right wing was leading to an Orthodox renaissance. It was a classic self-delusion. To the extent that Orthodoxy was gaining at all, it was the right wing that was growing in numbers and power—mostly at the expense of the modern Orthodox.

Another shocking example of false public impression leading to bad policy choices is the *baal teshuvah* movement. In many ways, the *baal teshuvah* movement became the flagship of Orthodoxy. The returnees were said to represent the magnetism of Orthodoxy and its avant-garde status. Hundreds of millions of dollars were raised for this work. Lubavitch rose to world class on the back of the movement. The modern Orthodox gave substantially to the *baal teshuvah* institutions, not infrequently at the expense of their own institutions. The *baalei teshuvah* were held up as a magic talisman, "proving" with their choices the superiority of Orthodoxy. Now, the 1990 NJPS study revealed that *baalei teshuvah* were barely 10 percent of Orthodoxy, i.e., less than 1 percent of the total Jewish population. Ironically, Orthodoxy had the *lowest* number of people in its ranks who were born in a different kind of home. Reform had the highest percentage of people in its ranks who were born in a different religious background than the movement they joined. By the measuring rod of *baalei teshuvah*, i.e., shifting affiliations, the Reform was clearly the "superior," more magnetic movement.

My retrospective analysis suggests the following. The *baal teshuvah* movement always was far more marginal in actual numbers. The return for the staggering amount of dollars spent was very low. The reason is that the gap between the lifestyle offered to non-observant Jews and their current lifestyle was so vast that very few could make the jump. Had modern Orthodox (or even liberal groups) been the leaders in *baal teshuvah* work, the yield might have been higher. But most people could not make a total shift; among the few who did make the change, the drastic nature of the shift led to great instability. Many dropped out within a few years. I also suspect that many *baalei teshuvah* were Orthodox Jews by birth who dropped out in their teenage years and then were drawn back by outreach. In other words, for people with no Orthodox background, the message of right-wing Orthodoxy was almost impossible to hear. As a result, most of the money spent and most of the institutions in outreach were concentrated in the zone of lowest return. One of the unfortunate side effects was that the highly publicized *baal teshuvah* accomplishments brought a strong backlash from the secular sector, which felt (correctly) put down by the *baal teshuvahs'* extreme rejection of their previous lifestyle (i.e., the secular sector). By contrast, leadership in Orthodoxy moved toward the *baal teshuvah* groups, further weakening support for the modern Orthodox.

When I first grasped the stunning implications of the Orthodox census, I went to see Norman Lamm. To me, this evidence suggested that the modern Orthodox had driven away important constituencies while failing to pick up new people. That was another result of writing off the large marginal congregations when Y.U. should have been serving them. The people there were more receptive and more accessible to Orthodoxy; then the process of not sending rabbis out there had been a mistake. Dr. Lamm said to me, "Yes. We miscalculated."

I have brooded on that answer for years, as I have about the overall results of the National Jewish Population Study. If this happened to a government, if there was a national disaster and they realized that they had lost 50 percent of the country—even if it was not a direct outgrowth of their ineptitude—then the leaders would have to resign. Then perhaps anyone who has represented American Jewry spiritually in the past ten years, anyone who had claimed to be upgrading Jewry in the past ten years (including me), should be resigning.

As you can see, I am in the process of putting myself back together—so I allow myself to criticize myself and others; admittedly I felt harsher, more judgmental initially than I do now. Since the forces of openness, increased social contact, and economic advance were broadscale and beyond the ability of the Jewish community to contain, the leadership cannot be blamed totally for the surge in assimilation and the loss of affiliation. However, the leadership of modern Orthodoxy chose to shift toward a policy of authoritarianism and withdrawal just as the general society was opening up and preaching individual empowerment and responsibility. The leadership passed on the authority to an often reactionary, sexist group of authority figures (including [some] *roshei yeshiva*) just as the women's movement was transforming society. These were disastrous decisions, complicated by the failure to point out the utter flight from reality in *haredi* behavior. The leaders also did not speak their conscience when they knew that things were going wrong. As a result, they created an Orthodox community with a strong conformist tone. The exercise of conscience was discouraged or punished. Thus, they forfeited moral stature and turned numerical erosion into a collapse. The leadership has not, as they say in Israel, "drawn conclusions," but it will be accountable at the bar of history.

The price of this diversion will be paid by the entire Jewish people. *Clal Yisrael* needed (and still needs) help in developing a lifestyle governed by Jewish models and memories that can function in current society and culture—even with full exposure to contemporary values and experiences. Not only did the Orthodox swing to the right cut off *clal Yisrael* from a natural source of positive integrating models, but the negative examples offered (Lubavitch offers the tacit message that they must "return" to a Hasidic way of life) have driven them further toward unrestrained immersion in modernity. This tendency has spelled greater assimilation.

The saddest truth is that, whatever the gains of right-wing Orthodoxy, they will clearly turn out to be transient. *Haredim* have created temporary shelters in a culture in which there is no permanent shelter. They are dependent on the very Jews whose disappearance they predict and whose pace of assimilation they are intensifying. Once—and if—that outer ring disappears, the ultra-Orthodox will be exposed to the full force of contemporary culture. I daresay that they will then undergo the same processes that other Jews have undergone. They will have the advantage of greater learning and some insulation, but I believe that this will be not enough to stop the process. Thus, they will have the same problems as the other Jews—only they will have a much smaller base of Jews to cooperate with in the process of developing the responses that can stand up to the presence of the full culture. Then they will rue the day that they abandoned or pushed away the others instead of learning from them and working with them.

In the end, there are only two choices before Jewry.

One is to try to live Torah in this culture. Historically, the Jewish people has lived its distinctive way of life within the context of the historical culture. The Torah's goal, *tikkun olam*, transcends every local, historical civilization and will do so until the messianic age is achieved. No culture, short of that final accomplishment, deserves our ultimate loyalty. On the other hand, the Torah affirms this world, and the covenant affirms human creativity and life. Therefore, Jews have entered into each local (historical) culture, lived within it and revised it to move it toward the values that the Torah upholds. Even in the Middle Ages, when Jews were outcasts—indeed a pariah people—Jews worked within the parameters and took on many of the features of the host civilization. Thus, Jews relate dialectically to every host culture; they are in it, but not totally of it. They resist being absorbed fully, for no partial culture deserves absolute loyalty. Also, were Judaism totally integrated, this would mean that Judaism would be dragged down when the local culture comes to its inevitable end. We are committed to outlast each civilization and to be reborn as often as necessary to reach the kingdom of God.

In modern times, Jews have overidentified with the host civilization because it has been both intrinsically attractive and particularly welcoming to Jews. As a result, many Jews have been completely absorbed into the emerging new "universal" culture. Our first option, then, is to further develop Judaism so that its practitioners can participate and its inner spirit can be immersed in modern culture without being totally absorbed. The goal is to successfully synthesize modernity and Judaism; this means preserving Judaism's millennial vision and direction and ensuring that it is the active shaping force in this new civilization. Achieving this goal would demand new constellations of values, experiences, new (and renewed) institutions to communicate Judaism's messages, and continuing and additional (halachic) models of memory and values. Not enough has been done in this direction in part because those most rooted in learning and tradition have leaned toward the second option (withdrawal) and have conceived of their role as *preserving* the tradition rather than applying and developing it.

The second long-term survival strategy available to Jewry is to provide a strong, almost hermetically sealed counterculture that would insulate itself from the contemporary scene. This might have been possible if a major geographic enclave was developed within which traditional Jews would be the majority—this would be the equivalent of the Mormons' achievement in settling Utah. However, the right wing opposed Zionism, so that geographic option was forfeited. The actual *haredi* culture is deeply implicated in the current society and technology; therefore, it will prove to be not really insulated (I predict). Thus, its short-term achievements (and its mini-enclaves like Boro Park and B'nei Brak) will prove to be vulnerable to further exposure—and erosion—by the general culture. At the same time, the *haredi* community has cannibalized modern Orthodoxy, removing some of the insulation it needs to protect itself. Also, its spiritual aggressiveness has paralyzed or closed off modern Orthodoxy's capacity to respond adequately to the issues of historicism, biblical criticism, women's condition, freedom and conscience, and so on. All in all, Orthodoxy has massively overestimated its own strength and underestimated the continuing pull and staying power of the contemporary culture.

Q. Rabbi, I have the impression, mainly from what I see in Israel, that there is an intense, vibrant Orthodox Jewish community that is, in a sense, open to the modern world. Are you sure that you are not missing it? You and I both know that a large number of the people who thirty or forty years ago were statistically classified as Orthodox were nominally Orthodox, not really observant. And maybe what has happened is that these people have drifted away while the Orthodox core has remained, intensified, grown both in its Jewishness and its participation in modern life. One group that Samuel Heilman has written about is those Holocaust survivors who came to the United States after the war and helped to revive Orthodox life. So I am wondering whether you are not underestimating the strength of the modern Orthodox. For instance, in communities such as Jerusalem's Har Nof, I do see a strength.

Greenberg. Har Nof is a model of *haredi*—not modern Orthodox—growth. You could also describe Har Nof as a place where the children of modern Orthodox parents are living a quasi-*haredi* lifestyle. The growth of Har Nof expresses a certain strength of the *haredim* in Israel. But this path is a cul-de-sac in the long run. In Har Nof, for example, a high percentage of the population is supported by parents. In other words, this is basically a learning, welfare-supported community. This means that, of necessity, the group must remain small, e.g., not so large that the working population cannot support the learning population and its dependents. As there is a population explosion in places like Har Nof, they may already be creating families so large that they outstrip the parents' capacity to support them. When the elder generation that works and earns big money (thanks to their modern work ethic and values) passes on, Har Nof parents raising large families will not have the capacity to support their (much larger number) of progeny in the manner to which they are accustomed (including purchase of apartments, and the like). This running up against the limits has already begun, but it has been softened and offset by an increase of government support for the *haredi* institutions and social network. However, the general population's willingness to support the *haredim* has reached its maximum. Indeed, there has been erosion of the goodwill of the general population, which senses the belittling and exploitative attitude that *haredim* take toward them.

The revival of the right-wing is part of a needed dialectical movement within Judaism and could have been a totally constructive development. Modernity had to be challenged. Jews had committed too deeply to universalist liberalism. The modern Orthodox had to be challenged to deepen their Torah learning and their observance. By their intense demands on themselves for higher learning standards and more rigorous observance, the *haredim* set a positive model for all Orthodox Jews. Their refusal to simply submit to modernist standards helped check the social conformity and one-sided accommodation to modernizing, which was undermining distinctive Jewish values. They made their contribution to a backlash against modernity's excesses that was growing in many quarters. This helped open the door to post-modernity, a more creative and promising environment.

The *haredim* also built strong communities, marked by a network of *gemilut hasadim* (lovingkindness) and mutuality to be envied and emulated by all groups. The sheer proliferation of mutual help groups in the *frum* community is a wonder, worthy of applause and imitation—free-loan societies, volunteer rescue (*hatzolah*), clothing and food distribution for the poor, medical home help, *bikur cholim, hachnassat kalah* (bridal or dowry aid), and more. The *haredi* community is an oasis of personal care and help in a bureaucratized Welfare society. In rebuilding their numbers, institutions, and leadership ranks after the decimation of the Holocaust, the *haredim* showed a remarkable vitality that exemplified the Jewish will to live, and snatched classic Jewish ways of life from the jaws of oblivion. All in all, an astonishing, praiseworthy accomplishment.

The right-wing development would have been most constructive had it seen itself as part of a corrective process to help Jewry move away from the overimmersion in modern culture and values that had begun to show pathological excesses. As such, this is a precious group that we want to conserve. This community—which is between 3 to 5 percent of the Jewish people—could have tested and strengthened all the others. Unfortunately, because this group is unable to cope with pluralism, i.e., the presence of alternative viewpoints with independent dignity and values, it defines itself as the only valid religious position. The *haredim* are trapped in the premodern ethos in which their culture grew; it is a world of insulated values with limited interaction between cultures. In a world in which tradition is strong and "self-evident," the "Other" is marginal and, often, illegitimate. When exposed to modernity, the presence of alternatives *in itself* is threatening to the authority structure of their beliefs. If you will, it is their weakness, not their strength, that drives them to insist on a monopolistic control of Orthodox policies, to reject the legitimacy of the non-Orthodox, and to fight for political exclusion of different religious options in the state of Israel.

To protect themselves in their self-defense exclusivity, the ultra-Orthodox have blocked experiments and developments necessary for the other groups to flourish, or, at least, to persist in modern culture. Far from allowing liberal options to be explored (and to learn from them even in the process of critiquing them), the *haredim* have gone on to swamp modern Orthodoxy and take over many of its institutions. This victory was not achieved on the merits of the *haredi weltanschauung* or vitality alone, but also by use of the *kesafim yichudim*, the special Israeli government budget allocations totaling hundreds of millions of dollars a year. Broad fundraising and aggressive outreach—using the *baal teshuvah* flag—yielded them equivalent funding in the Diaspora, especially the Lubavitch (Chabad). Since Orthodoxy is a relatively small world to begin with, pouring hundreds of millions of dollars into backing such small groups had a totally disproportionate impact. The money supplied by secular and liberal religious Jews (who had no such intention in mind) destroyed the balance of power and even determined the outcome: the short-term victory of the right-wing and the ruinous decline of modern Orthodoxy.

Nevertheless, your initial comment shows that you have detected an important fact. Smaller, outstanding local concentrations of modern Orthodoxy have grown. People have shown the ability to handle modern culture and synthesize it with a vital religious life. There has arisen a new generation of integrated Jews, deeply rooted in tradition and observance, who play leadership roles in the general society. The most striking example is the knitted-*kippah*-officer cadre of the Israeli army, reaching 40 percent in a field that religious Jews once shunned or were shunned by. Showing a dedication to country and cause second to none, the modern Orthodox have flowed to the "fighting" brigades that carry the burden in battle. In recent years, up to 50 percent of the army's fighting casualties have been religious. This cohort reflects the remarkable creation in Israel of a network of yeshiva high schools that have elevated academic and Torah learning standards, as well as *yeshivot hesder* (which combine army service and learning). In America modern Orthodox win Nobel prizes, serve as leading political figures, writers, and business-people, and have attained academic presence and leadership.

American modern Orthodoxy plays a disproportionate role in communal activism, in providing professional leaders to Jewish organizations, and in creating community educational institutions. The incredible network of Israeli study opportunities that Orthodoxy has created for its young is a measure of what standard the rest of American Jewry has to reach. The creation of a popular literature for Torah study and Jewish living in both Israel and America is another historic achievement. This sector of Jewry also has created strong communities and vital centers of living.

Unfortunately, the numbers overall are small, and modern Orthodoxy is not a closely knit community. *Haredim* tend to cluster tightly to create neighborhoods and institutions that provide shelter; in turn, their concentration provides critical mass for stores, institutions, and the like to meet their needs. The modern Orthodox do not feel the same need for shelter. But, as a result, sometimes their percentage of concentration is so small that their cause loses out. Take the case of the Meimad (modern, peace-oriented religious Zionist) party in the 1992 Israeli elections. The group was so small that many electors feared to vote for it lest their vote be wasted. And many modern Orthodox were swept up in the dreams of territorial grandeur. As a result, despite widespread support for its views and admiration for its model, Meimad was unable to win even one seat in the Knesset. The actual significant level of agreement with its views was lost in the shuffle. The *haredim*, who concentrated their votes, used their Knesset seats as leverage to win extensive government support.

Meimad's failure also dramatizes another breakdown of modern Orthodoxy. Abandoning their historic role as moderates and mediators (the outgrowth of wrestling with and integrating two cultures), the modern Zionist religious population had been drawn into the political messianism and extremism of Gush Emunim. Important elements in the political and religious leadership have made a fundamental error in becoming so fixated on the land. The definition of Orthodoxy's primary loyalty has become possession of the land rather than cultural synthesis and responsibility for the whole Jewish people. This tendency was strengthened by the *haredi* influence and the waning of the belief (and weakening of the will) to synthesize modernity and Judaism in a constructive, dialectical fashion.

The resultant extremism led to other regressions. In an unspoken "deal," the settlers' lifestyles went *haredi* instead of staying modern. That was a trade-off: halachic respectability for political radicalism. The trade-off went the wrong way. The modern Orthodox need to move more into the secular world, more into learning secular studies, more into building the state. This misdirection is a major error of fundamental proportions. The result is a missed historical task. There is a real risk that peace will be made without mainstream modern Orthodox support. This will leave a moral stigma on modern Orthodoxy; it will be translated into a message that Zionist Orthodoxy is aggressive and undervalues human life—Arab and Jewish alike.

Another tragic outcome of this development is that the tremendous energies that went into Gush Emunim were not available to fight the historic cultural battles for the Jewish character of the state or the ethical struggle for Jews to take power without becoming brutalized or corrupted in the process. There is a direct link between political extremism (the insistence on not giving back one inch of land) and ethical insensitivity to Arabs. If people felt the Arabs' pain or need for dignity, they would have to moderate their political demands. This would lead to a compromise that made room for both sides. (Obviously, if the Arabs would not offer genuine peace, then there would be no territorial compromise. But if the Orthodox were flexible, they would be part of the peace process and in position to guard against utopian and dangerous decisions.) Overall the policy of cultural and social isolationism—fueled by and made necessary by withdrawal into premodern lifestyles—increasingly disconnected Orthodoxy from gentiles and non-observant Jews; inevitably, they were likely to be morally uninterested in the others. The tradition could have been so much a source for ethical sensitivity and concern for the "other." Instead, it has been used to proclaim expansionist and even racist policies that show little tolerance for other Jews, or, *a fortiori*, for gentiles. From the perspective of the next century, this path taken by modern Orthodoxy will be seen as a cul-de-sac, as a road taken that distracted Orthodoxy from its central tasks.

By initiating and by applying themselves with dedication to the work of outreach and by aggressively asking for support, armed with the full conviction that they alone deserved help, the *haredi* right-wing gathered a great deal of money for their community. This money underwrote much of their institutional world (including the institutions that serviced *haredim* only). Thus, outreach became a very important ultra-Orthodox patronage machine. These jobs were particularly critical for a group teaching its young men that they should *not* go to work in the secular world and should not get a secular education. The ultra-Orthodox set up 80 to 90 percent of the outreach organizations; a combination of zeal and financing gave them dominance in the field. This dominance was counterproductive for the Jewish community because the contacts being offered to the unaffiliated represented a religiously withdrawn counterculture—intrinsically a not very appealing choice in the eyes of most marginal Jews. Not surprisingly, many of the successes—*baalei teshuvah*—were drawn from people who were in *extremis*, e.g., drug culture, dropouts, psychologically deeply alienated. Stories of the successes gave a veneer of effectiveness, but the overall returns were small. As the modern Orthodox moved to the right, in part due to the pressure and influence of the right wing, they lost many institutions and jobs. Thus, the right-wing became the ideological, sociological, and institutional leaders of Orthodoxy.

Ironically, the great growth and dominance of the right was not all that good for them, either. They had little sense of their own limits because they were growing rapidly—off a very small base. Instead of defining themselves as fillers of a specialized niche and making themselves available to those who were seeking a stark alternative to the dominant general lifestyle, they presented themselves as the mainstream, indeed as the only true representatives of the only true form of Judaism. Ultimately, this led to internal excesses as well. In the mood of euphoria and expansion, no one raised real questions. The right—in its yeshiva and Hasidic forms—was lionized by Orthodox and non-Orthodox alike.

Take the case of Habad. Habad is a constructive organization as a Jewish alternative, especially for spiritual seekers and for people who are in search of authority and looking to find a place in a total community. This lifestyle is appealing to 3 to 5 percent of the population; it should be a specialty offering. Instead,

Habad has become the dominant Jewish outreach organization in the world. On campus, for example, it is almost as widespread as Hillel. Habad attracted support particularly because Hillel was weak in the 1970s and 1980s (in fact, Hillel was almost moribund). But, as the primary Jewish offering to the unaffiliated, Habad does not work. To jump from campus life to becoming a Lubavitcher *hasid* involves climbing over such a huge hump that, at most, 5 percent of the people who go through that encounter are able to live with the new lifestyle in a stable, permanent way. Even the returnees typically stay with that way of life only if they marry and move into the *baal teshuvah* world. Often they must be supported permanently in that new location. The result is that money invested in Lubavitch gives a low yield. (Of course, few records are kept in this world; Lubavitch is secretive and not accountable financially, let alone open to assessment in terms of efficiency.) No one stopped to ask how much it cost (and what further decline in yield occurred) when Lubavitch went off on the Rebbe-as-Messiah tack. Again let me stress that, as an alternative, Lubavitch is a positive option. As the main Jewish outreach offering, it cannot be effective; however, those who should have provided the mainstream option have been swamped by Lubavitch in the process. The net effect—to borrow a term famous in American history—when a narrow group (the Free Silver populists) hijacked the Democratic party and distracted mainstream political reform is that Lubavitch is the "cuckoo bird" of the outreach field. Like the cuckoo bird, they left their eggs in the mainstream nests, whose givers end up raising and supporting a handful of Lubavitchers instead of their own children.

To restore the balance of my words, let me say that Lubavitchers are attractive, good people who show dedication and love to Jews everywhere. For this, I greatly admire them. But there are perhaps three thousand *shluchim* of the Rebbe in the world. The results beyond the lives of three thousand and their families are constructive, but limited. (I believe that this judgment is accurate despite the fact that Lubavitch runs synagogues and schools around the world; in places like Morocco, they are the mainstream.) Still, the cultural gap is great; they cannot deal constructively with the steady encroachment of modern values all over the world. And they preach and support hard-line antipeace policies as well as runaway messianism. Overall, the outreach movement has widened the breach between Orthodox and non-Orthodox despite its goal of doing the opposite. The fruits of this setback will come when there is a peace settlement. When peace arrives in Israel, there will be an explosion of pent-up resentments.

Let me give another example of the side effects of *haredi* dominance. Orthodoxy has become synonymous with fundamentalism; views egregiously in conflict with science and scholarship are universal in the talmudic–halachic leadership. In the early months of the Rabin administration, Shulamit Aloni served as Minister of Education. In one of her appearances, she spoke about evolution and the age of the earth. She mockingly dismissed traditional views of the Torah's Creation story. Shulamit Aloni must take responsibility for the deliberately provocative nature of her comments; in any event, she evoked hysterical outbursts from leading Israeli rabbis, who upheld the story of a world shaped in six 24-hour days and in existence for only 5,750-plus years as the Orthodox, exclusive, divinely revealed, literal truth. Such is *haredi* influence and the cultural isolation of the Israeli rabbinate that this view is the only legitimate view; it was the only one offered by spiritual leadership.

So when *haredim* set the tone, think of the cultural impact. Think of the most devastating message the *haredim* are giving: You cannot be a serious modern person. You cannot go to college. You cannot study science and still be an halachic Jew because Orthodox Jews must believe that the world is less than six thousand years old. You have to take a child's version of Genesis as the norm—ignoring the fact that, from Midrash to Maimonides, from Kabbalah to Kook, a long list of great religious figures did not take the Creation account, or the six days, literally. The very calendar that dates the age of Earth as thousands of years since Creation was not developed until the tenth century under Moslem influence. But, in their invincible ignorance of history and denial of historicity, the citizens of the *haredim*–yeshiva world do not know that.

The modern Orthodox rabbis (those who went to university and know geology) did not speak out of fear of being attacked by right-wing. With the present mood of conformist, simple-minded obedience, any rabbi who implied that the text was not to be read literally would be hurt. Norman Lamm once said to me, "If you do not want the heat, become a professor." Were I to take my stands on pluralism or on women's issues as a professor, I would not be bitterly attacked and delegitimated. Lamm understood that *roshei yeshivas'* monopoly on who is acceptable to serve as an Orthodox rabbi is what gives the strength to the right. I would not be so much a target to the right-wing if I were content to be an academic. By serving as a rabbi, by building community, and by serving as a spiritual authority, my provision of an alternative Orthodox approach is particularly dangerous in the eyes of the right. In Israel, no such option as CLAL exists. That is one reason that Rabbi Joseph B. Soloveitchik feared to go there and serve as Chief Rabbi. The real victims of this whole situation are the Sephardi children and the Ashkenazi *kippot srugot* teenagers. When they go to college and study science, they are going to be convinced that the world is not five thousand years old. Based on the belief that to be Orthodox one has to take literally the words of Genesis, their religious faith and practice will be undermined.

Q. A whole strain of Orthodox thinkers have dealt with this issue.

Greenberg. They have made no dent on the mainstream of the yeshiva world, for whom they are *treyf.* Of course, the Rambam is also *"treyf."* If I were to read whole sections of Maimonides' *Guide to the Perplexed* or even *Mishneh Torah* without identifying the author, the bulk of *roshei yeshiva* and *yeshiva bochurim* would cry out that this is *apikorsus.* Take Maimonides' views on the age of the Earth; that many stories in the Torah are parables or dreams, not actual events; that *midrashim* are not always to be taken literally; that aggadic views, especially on science, are not binding; that science and astronomy are religious callings, that there are *mitzvot* given as concessions to human weakness and the dominant values of ancient cultures, and so on—these Maimonidean positions (if read without attribution) would be judged as *apikorsus,* according to the official right-wing views. Of course, whole sections of Maimonides and other great figures (especially Bible studies) are "off limits" culturally and psychologically in the *frum* world. The tradition has been impoverished, censored, and truncated, in the same way as the Artscroll translation has removed women's breasts and navels and men's firm thighs from the Song of Songs.

Ultimately, I have no quarrel with right-wing Orthodoxy for taking these positions for themselves. They only know how to maintain themselves in a culturally sheltered environment. But their seizure of leadership of the total Orthodox community, and, through that leverage, their disproportionate role in the total Jewish community, have had a destructive side effect. The tradition is hamstrung, incapable of responding adequately to the cultural crisis. Modern Orthodoxy has many more answers to offer than it is currently allowed (or equipping itself) to offer. Furthermore, instead of learning new skills—such as how to live in a pluralistic world, how to use social scientific and literary analysis to deepen insights into Torah, and so on—modern Orthodoxy has been led to surrender some of its existing skills and best insights. This crippling, in turn, has pushed modern Orthodoxy increasingly into policies of sectarian withdrawal—just when it is desperately needed to help the mainstream of the Jewish people learn how to cope with and live successfully inside contemporary culture.

There are two main weaknesses in this scenario. The Jewish people ends up marginalized in the world. Judaism becomes a sectarian minor faith, an "Amish" type of spirituality. This is an abandonment of the central role in Creation that the Torah projects for Jewry and for itself. The other weakness is that it is doubtful that any cultural dike or set of dikes can keep modernity from infiltrating the cracks of the sheltered culture. In the long run, the *haredi* strategy is a delaying action that eventually will leave the shrunken number of Jewish survivors of these culture wars vulnerable to the same dominant cultural forces.

The alternative strategy is to make up our minds that Jews are called to live *and lead* in whatever main civilization develops. Judaism, all the more so, should be involved in modernity, a culture that incorporates many blessings that bring humanity closer to *tikkun olam*, and whose excesses cry out for the checks and critiques that the Torah can supply. But to play this alternative role successfully, we must reposition the Jewish people. We must learn how to "feed" on native food supplies in the civilization; we must learn how to communicate in the modern medium (e.g., a medium with higher levels of communication; open to all culture; influenced by science, universal principles, the presence of the other, and the like).

The challenge of modernity is that it gives a much wider range of people access to power and freedom. Science and reason lead to productivity, affluence, and ease on an unprecedented level. We need to "breed" a "Jew fish" who can swim, breathe, feed, reproduce, and serve as an inspiring model and an influence on this new culture. The strength of this second model is that it keeps Judaism at the center of the world's cultural and religious arena. Jewry becomes—again—teacher and model (a "light" to the nations). Furthermore, Jewish continuity is no longer totally tied to a shrinking, dying (premodern) culture; nor does it demand that we become a small sect on the sidelines of history. The weakness of this approach is that we do not know for sure how to make the transition successfully. We will have to develop many new cultural and religious skills if we are to succeed at all.

In the interim, the costs—in terms of assimilation and loss of Jews, in terms of debilitation of tradition and Jewish culture, in terms of loss of memory and distinctiveness—are quite heavy. There is a danger that we may never succeed in breeding a cohort of culturally successful fertile Jews who can renew the tradition and the covenant. (For this reason, in part, I support putting a "side bet" of 5 percent on the Jews—the *haredim*—who are prepared to create a ghetto and remain immersed in insulated Judaism. However, more than a 5 to 10 percent investment would be a serious error because the mainstream strategy is the main chance for producing a vital Jewry living a world-redeeming Jewish way of life.)

Here let me make clear my own commitments and assumptions. The Torah is the tree of life of the Jewish people; the covenant remains the mission and glory of Jewry. The transformation that I call for will bring with it much—if not all—of the classic Jewish tradition. However, there will be new definitions: shifts of meaning, different priorities, different applications of established principles. This is entirely consistent with past Jewish experience.

The task of every covenantal generation includes living out the covenant and doing whatever is necessary to apply it and to communicate its values and wisdom in the cultural terms of the "local" civilization. It is no accident that the Holy Temple strongly resembles the central sanctuaries of Canaanite and Mesopotamian civilization, even as sacrifices were the dominant form of religious behavior in that era. It is no accident that the Talmud is saturated with Hellenistic cultural tools, including modes of rhetoric and analysis. Of course, in each civilization, Jews asserted their distinctive values and long-range overarching vision. They lived their distinctive way of life; if they had not, they would have disappeared into the local culture. We have the same task before us, except that we are encountering the most dynamic, the most magnetic, the most productive and welcoming host civilization ever.

Each generation preserves the Jewish tradition, renews it, and expands it as one. Each leadership has the necessary authority to do so—how else can it meet its responsibilities? "Jephthah in his generation is as authoritative as Samuel in his generation." The claim that leadership does not have the authority is a decision to uphold certain practices or policies rather than to change them. That, too, is a legitimate choice; but, in a time of drastic change, it may not be the right choice. In any event, it would be better to make clear that this choice, too, is an exercise of authority rather than inaction owing to lack of authority (as claimed).

This analysis leads me to return continually to the importance of rebuilding modern Orthodoxy. Since I believe that Torah and *halachah* are the key to the future of the Jewish people, I am particularly concerned that we invest heavily in those groups that keep Torah central in their lives, even as they grapple with the challenge of living it in the contemporary culture. Some of the grappling is done by liberal Jews (in Conservative, Reform, and Reconstructionist denominations), especially by Conservative Jews whose traditionalists live observant lives and who, as a movement, acknowledge the ongoing authority of the *halachah*. The modern Orthodox remain the largest group numerically who center their lives around Torah and *halachah*. In principle, they remain the key group (or at least one of the key groups) that can mediate between Jewry and the tradition. Using the credibility they have earned (by dint of sharing the contemporary way of life with the rest of *clal Yisrael*), they can enrich the lifestyles of other Jews, as well as inspire them to study and take seriously the options of halachic living. They can also play a role in critiquing the contemporary civilization's excesses because criticism from within is generally taken more seriously than criticism from without.

It is all the more troubling, therefore, that modern Orthodoxy has lost its way vis-à-vis modernity and vis-à-vis the ultra-Orthodox. This failure of nerve (withdrawal in the face of the radicalization of modern culture) combined with the success and growing aggressiveness of the ultra-Orthodox has led to surrender to the right. The ideological retrenchment led modern Orthodox leadership to back away from its own accomplishments. Instead of stepping up its investment in mastering modern culture in Israel, it retreated, allowing rabbis to be excluded from attending university. The yeshiva world was turned over to the right, and the *yeshivot hesder* accommodated their religious standards to those of the ultra-Orthodox. While Zionism and army service were not repudiated, the cultural context and values base on which these practices were built were, so that Zionism and *hesder* increasingly became "concessions." Their practitioners were no longer nurtured by the underlying religious messages. (Some evasion of military service and a significant withdrawal from attending university have made their appearance in some *yeshivot hesder.*)

In the United States, Yeshiva University's yeshiva was hijacked by *roshei yeshiva* who no longer believed in (or who marginalized) *Torah u'madda. Torah Umesorah* was taken over by the *roshei yeshiva* of the other *yeshivot*; this translated into local day-school policies that separated boys and girls, distanced non-observant Jews, and weakened community links. Thus, at a time when the Jewish people was awakening to the need for Jewish renewal through more intensive Jewish education, disproportionate growth in day-school enrollment went to Conservative (Solomon Schechter) and community-based day schools. The *frum* atmosphere that marked Torah *u'mesorah* schools made them unable to serve broader groups and meet community-wide concerns.

This is another very troubling aspect of the collapse of

modern Orthodoxy. This rollback has had negative effects on Orthodoxy overall, in terms of loss of membership and decline of synagogues. But the greatest loss, in my judgment, is that the rest of the Jewish people was abandoned just as a great wave of assimilation swept over it. As the representatives of Orthodoxy-Torah-*halachah* are reimagined to be people living outside the main culture (or living parasitically and self-centeredly off of it), then the unaffiliated and the assimilating are confirmed in their belief that there is nothing in the tradition for them. If anything, they feel cynical about *haredi* political behavior. (There is a double standard here, but the effects are deleterious nevertheless.) When the exemption of *yeshiva bocherim* from the army is exploited by the *haredim* for mass draft-dodging, the general population is offended. When it turns out that the modern Orthodox leadership (persuaded by the growing inside Orthodox psychology that it is us [Orthodox] against them [liberals and seculars]) is silent in the face of this abuse, then the secular Israelis are outraged. This confirms their feeling that Torah values add up to an in-group morality that justifies allowing other people's children to fight and die to protect you. They are left with the feeling that Torah means that you shirk your duties to your fellow human beings and feel superior as you do so.

The equivalent deterioration in America is that when Orthodox rabbis preach pluralism and are active in joint projects with Conservative and Reform, they are aggressively delegitimized. Again, the leadership of modern Orthodoxy is silent. Instead of developing and asserting the active links between Orthodoxy and the rest of the community, they stand by or actively acquiesce in the delegitimation and boycotts that follow. The message that the average Jew out there grasps is that, in modern Orthodoxy, positive attitudes and respect for non-Orthodox Jews is a "punishable" crime. Not surprisingly, the conclusion is that the Orthodox have a tribal morality and are not *menschen*.

Last year, my son J. J. and I sat in on a series of focus groups with unaffiliated Jews. We were stunned by the near-unanimity of their conviction (too often based on personal experience, but based equally on their reading of media stories) that the Orthodox were tightly knit together against all the other Jews. It was their consensus that the Orthodox believed in a "God-given" right to exploit gentiles and to use other (non-Orthodox) Jews. The resultant distancing from Torah and tradition leaves these Jews feeling closer to the non-Jewish world and pushes them farther into the maelstrom of assimilation.

In Israel, the full force of these trends is not yet clear because of the great advantage of a Jewish majority. Because the Arabs of the Middle East, representing the gentile majority in the world, are still trying to destroy Israel, the Israelis are spared the full attraction impact of Western culture. I shudder to think of how the many secular Israelis, who have imbibed these images of the traditional Jews and are very vulnerable to the same kind of blandishments of Western civilization, will fare when peace comes. The "Americanization" of Israel is proceeding apace. With Orthodoxy pulled to the right, there is a void in the center that legitimates a growing radical, materialist secularism. This, in turn, paves the way for the assimilation of Western values. Admittedly, there probably is not the same risk of high intermarriage rates in Israel simply because the Jewish majority will remain a majority in the near future. Propinquity is still the main factor in finding a mate. Still, Israel will be running many of the same risks of assimilation in values and in cultural and personal life during the coming century.

Q. No doubt about it. I think you see it when you see many Western people who, on coming to Israel, become less religious. They feel, "Here I am simply Jewish. I don't have to prove it. I don't have to do something distinctive or to be attached to a synagogue to preserve my Jewish identity. My language is Hebrew; all around me is Jewish life."

Greenberg. On balance, I do not believe that being either a withdrawn minority or an apathetic majority is the way the Jewish people are going to survive for the next thousand years. This brings us back to the main point. Since the Jewish people is at risk and since they will not give up modern culture, then the task is to live Judaism as a dynamic option within the contemporary civilization. If all this is true, then many of the efforts of the right-wing (and the attempts of modern Orthodoxy to accommodate the right) are wasted energy. Many of the successes of withdrawal Orthodoxy are temporary; they are not of much help to the bulk of the Jewish people. At a time when we are bleeding away many Jews, this is not fruitful; a people that is suffering blood loss should not be wasting energy.

I have hard feelings about the decline of modern Orthodoxy because we are going to have to redo a lot of Orthodox policies of the past two decades. Much of that work—coming to grips with modernity, finding and inserting holiness into the secular realm—we will have to do by operating from a smaller base of modern Orthodoxy and of Jewry. Since numbers provide critical mass for many needed experiments and margins for error, the losses of the past two decades and the lost years weaken our capacity to win this battle. What a tragic waste that a policy hailed by Orthodoxy as a triumph has actually weakened both Orthodoxy and *clal Yisrael*.

Having said all this, I still believe that modern Orthodoxy can and must be restored. There are no short cuts in history. There is no escape from the task of reconciling the contemporary culture and the tradition. Jakobovits once said to me that the modern Orthodox position would disintegrate. Then, when the *haredim* would be in full command, they would be exposed to modernity; then, the cycle of renewal would come from them. I reject that view, and believe that there is no choice but to rebuild modern Orthodoxy. Now, if you believe that the Jewish people can live without the Torah (behaviorally, perhaps 70 to 80 percent of Jewry is living this way), then we need not rebuild modern Orthodoxy. If you think that the Torah can live without the bulk of the Jewish people (behaviorally, this is the assumption underlying *haredi* psychology), then you can stay exclusively with the *haredim*. If you believe, as I do, that the Jewish people cannot live without the Torah, and that the Torah cannot survive without the Jewish people, then we need a group to mediate the two. So we have no choice but to rebuild modern Orthodoxy—and we will.

Q. I agree with you. I think that the only way for the modern Orthodox, for the halachic Jew, to operate in this society is to persuade, to set an example. In other words, to hope to move others closer to God through their own free choice; providing that is the most convincing alternative for living a meaningful life in Jewish society.

Greenberg. My greatest hope was that modern Orthodoxy would supply leadership to meet this challenge. But it cannot do so by retreating into the yeshiva world. On the contrary, it has got to open up even more to the culture and to others. This will take a *deepening* of inherited positions.

In a sense, this was the key failure of the past two decades. The first modern Orthodox positions were approximations. That is nothing to be ashamed of. These views should have been offered as first attempts that could be deepened and further explored. Instead, when the state of Israel was born, the Zionist Orthodox realized that the halachic responses needed and the ideological transformation that must come would demand much more growth—and significant further distancing from the *haredim.* This was implicit in the covenant between Orthodox and secularists that made possible the creation of the state of Israel.

In embracing Zionism, modern Orthodox leadership made one of the most successful and high-return religious decisions of all time. Yet, rather than following through and taking up the task that would lead to a more comprehensive broader-gauge Torah, they panicked and backed away. A Torah that took the state of Israel seriously as a religious phenomenon would admit women to new roles and central theaters of action. Managing a society would involve applying *halachah* in a host of areas where it had not yet penetrated. To do this, the traditional categories would have to be widened and expanded beyond the capacity of the inherited rabbinic learning leadership. *De facto,* the religious Zionists had done the equivalent—in defiance of the halachic scholars' consensus—by creating the Zionist movement and the state of Israel. However, they now lost their nerve. They were tempted to move to the right.

The same policy failure showed up in dealing with intellectual challenges. Instead of dealing with biblical criticism or Darwin and evolution, Tanach was cut out of yeshiva studies. The same ostrich-head-in-the-sand position has been assumed on women's questions. There has been some indirect recognition of the problems, mostly by "refutation." Still, most Orthodox response has been hostile, condemnatory, and totally unsympathetic. One typical response is the five RIETS' *rosh yeshivahs'* responsum declaring that "women's *tefillah* is prohibited," a responsum full of hostility, false generalizations, and ignorant fear of what the women were doing. These are all the wrong responses. (Not that everything the feminists do is right.)

Q. What about the work David Hartman has done in Israel?

Greenberg. I remain a long-standing admirer of his work, as well as the work of Aharon Lichtenstein, Shlomo Riskin, Adin Steinsaltz, Jonathan Sacks, Norman Lamm, and others. These are people whose activities I have supported. They run programs I have benefited from and that I have publicly praised. I feel especially warmly about David Hartman's work and despite our differences over the concept of redemption, intellectually, I am considerably closer to him than I am to the others. He, too, has preached and practiced pluralism; he too has affirmed Israel as the Jewish people's act of coming back into making history. He has taken risks as he has gone further in dealing with these issues—and I enormously admire his accomplishments. Hartman's penalty (in that this is Israel) is parallel to mine in the United States. There has been a lot of delegitimation of him in the Orthodox community. He has also paid a price in that people sought to block his views from the Orthodox community. I give him great credit for standing his ground. He decided that he would carve out an area of work and stick to it. He chose a more academic, more philosophical area than I did. His work has been very constructive—and it is not yet done.

Q. Rabbi, is the primary challenge before modern Orthodoxy intellectual or ethical? Many people have spoken with concern about various scandals and signs of corruption in the Orthodox camp. Is the main problem ethical, then?

Greenberg. In terms of modern Orthodoxy, there is an intellectual *and* spiritual *and* ethical challenge. When a group seeks to mediate two powerful forces like modernity and Jewish tradition, there is a real danger of ending up *pareve*, neither here nor there. Sometimes, this endless conflict leads to a stalemate. Sometimes these outcomes lead to ethical fatigue. Because the emotional struggle is so great, it is very tempting to lower the guard ethically; embattled movements tell their people that if they toe the party line, they will not be held to too-demanding ethical standards. If Orthodoxy ends up fighting the whole structure of modernity, the energy needed is so all-consuming that people become too exhausted to fight for the fundamental principles, including the ethical battle. I think that modern Orthodoxy has been so besieged that the community decided not to press the ethical issues; yet these issues should be at the top of the list.

Generally, I believe that when two value systems are exposed to each other, the ferment and the mutual criticism evokes a more vigorous, more principled response. So, modern Orthodoxy at its best generates very high-level ethical models. However, when it (or any other religion) becomes established, or when it becomes fixated on detail, if not trivia, then there is a tendency to corruption and moral exhaustion. Modern Orthodoxy in Israel must start by addressing corruption, especially in the rabbinate and its procedures.

Then there is the intellectual challenge. Currently, a censored or filtered version of Rabbi Joseph B. Soloveitchik's views are about as far left as you can go in modern Orthodoxy and still be respectable. (In truth, many of his more progressive insights are not being pursued or taught.) Some of his closest students evade his emphasis on the centrality of creativity in the *halachah* and on the almost untrammeled authority of the *talmid chacham* to rule on the law. They ignore his teaching that the highest calling of the rabbi–*posek* is to protect the downtrodden and to fight for the rights of the oppressed; they suppress his insight that the practice of science, medicine, and technology constitutes *imitatio dei.* They fail to act on his teaching of the full human dignity of the gentile—and of women. The list is endless.

I honor Rabbi Soloveitchik's extraordinary contribution and model. He opened up many cultural areas with his insights. But there were many areas he did not want to, or could not, deal with—that must be confronted. Item: Historical criticism, especially the history of *halachah.* Item: biblical criticism. The Rav officially dismissed it, although he used it and learned from it. (See his comparison of the two accounts of Creation in his essay, "The Lonely Man of Faith.") Modern Orthodoxy must be deepened intellectually. But the effort must go beyond any one area.

When the synthesis of modernity and Orthodoxy does work, the result is very effective. Hartman, Riskin, and Steinsaltz are among the most attractive people in Jewish life today. At best (as in Soloveitchik), one sees how deep modern Orthodoxy can be. Yet, in other situations, one sees how shallow it can be. An example: One of the most powerful effects of modernity is that it communicates the existence of multiple values, standards, and cultures. Inevitably, when people experience the wide range of alternatives, they are forced to develop a certain internal, coherent standard to reconcile their conflicting claims. That is what conscience is all about. Modern culture has raised the phenomenon and the impact of conscience to new heights. However, when the norm is conforming to a monolithic culture, there is much less of the phenomenon of conscience. People may do the right actions, but often they are simply conforming.

Conscience starts when people have conflicts and have to make choices. By contrast, over the last twenty years, the modern Orthodox community has said: "Face modernity—but you cannot express certain new concepts." But to face modernity means that you are bound to say certain things that were not said before. The community has not begun to understand or integrate the challenge of conscience. The community must go through a whole series of what I call deepenings, culturally and ethically; it must mature before it can grasp the nature and centrality of conscience. The Torah is profound enough to yield the needed responses. Rav Soloveitchik showed us how much deeper we can go into Torah to meet such challenges. This is not just an intellectual exercise or a political question; this is a maturation process. The result must be a deepening of thought and spiritual upgrading.

When I first went to college and was challenged, my Orthodoxy was shaken. It was broken open, but it grew whole again in a much richer form. In those days, science and religion and the challenge of the outside culture were the irritating sand grains that produced my pearls. In that first round, I did not have answers. In the first stage of awareness, I was sustained by neo-Orthodox Christians because they had faced these questions as orthodox religionists. Most of all, this very wonderful *musar* yeshiva kept me going. Of course, the Bais Yosef people were not *haredim*; they were survivors of the war. This "*frum*" flight direction had not yet made its appearance. The religious experience was deeper at Bais Yosef. I was able to hang on, even though I had no answers. From my own experience, I am highly confident that modern Orthodoxy, if its votaries are given profound religious experiences instead of conformity in their education, can handle any challenge. This process of deepening religious experience, broadening the intellectual, intensifying the ethical responsibility, is the main front for rebuilding modern Orthodoxy.

In truth, I remain deeply optimistic that modern Orthodoxy will be rebuilt. Living organisms regenerate themselves. The Torah and the community are still alive. Moreover, I believe that the Torah and the tradition have the depth to grow, that Judaism is able to match up to the most dynamic culture of all times. Modernity needs the purifying critique and the covenantal reshaping by which Judaism can make a great contribution. Retreat to the right is the counsel of despair; the *haredim*, deep down, believe that Torah is so fragile that it cannot face up. One is reminded of the chilling image of R. Eliyah Kretinger, a disciple of R. Israel Salanter, that the Torah is in the category of *gosays* (the human in his death rattle). Halachically, since the situation is hopeless, one is not allowed to move the *gosays*—even an attempt to genuinely improve the patient's condition can only hasten his death.

I believe the opposite. The same greatness of mind and spirit that empowered the people to go from powerlessness to power and from near death to renaissance, will now climax in a religious ethical renewal that perfects the world. Modern Orthodoxy cannot do it all—certainly not alone. But it can make a major contribution. When modern Orthodoxy recreates itself, it will help the ultra-Orthodox rediscover and go with their own best qualities. And it will help heal the whole Jewish people. This will be an important signal that Jewry has moved beyond modernity into a holistic, dialectical synthesizing postmodernity. In this process, modern Orthodoxy will integrate into itself the best insights of the *haredim* and of the liberal groups. In postmodernity, this will all be possible. This is why I often say that I consider myself to be a postmodern Orthodox Jew.

8

Of Land, Peace, and Faith

Shalom Freedman (Q). Rabbi, if you and I have one major difference, I think it relates to the question of *eretz yisrael*, of what the Jews are doing in Judea and Samaria. I view these people as pioneers, idealists who are striving to realize the biblical promise of God to the Jewish people. I know that you see this somewhat differently. Would you explain what your position is on this?

Rabbi Irving Greenberg. Mine is a complex position.

When I was a *chaneech*, just a teenager in Hashomer Hadati, one of my *madrichim* (guides) and the *rosh ken* (the head of the branch) in Boro Park was Moshe Perlman, *zichrono livracha*. He was one of the thirty-five men sent as reinforcements to Gush Etzion when it was under its final siege at Arab hands. The thirty-five were spotted by an Arab shepherd. They could have killed the shepherd to protect themselves, but they would not put to death someone who had not tried to attack them. They released him. He then alerted the Arab countryside; the thirty-five were caught by the Arabs and killed.

That incident always haunted me. First of all, as an individual, Moshe was a wonderful person. Then there was his family—two unmarried sisters and elderly parents; their lives were totally devoted to his. The family lived in Boro Park not far from my home. I remember that the incident devastated them. In fact, they never recovered. The whole story of Gush Etzion's heroic last stand remained vivid in my mind. Blu had a cousin who was among the survivors because he was evacuated just before the end. These memories brought Blu and me to visit Gush Etzion when we took a trip to Israel in 1970.

To our surprise and astonishment, we discovered that a whole group of young people, the children of those who had evacuated Gush Etzion, had stayed together during the intervening years. There was no plausible belief in anybody's mind that they were going to get back to that land. Yet they continued to meet from 1948 to 1967 to remember the "old country" and to talk about return. This was the contemporary analogue of the Jews who, for two thousand years, chanted: "Next year in Jerusalem," although there was no chance that the prayer would come true. Miraculously, in 1967, Israel went from threat of destruction to national redemption, and the area of Gush Etzion fell to the Israelis. The youth group came together, went back in, and reestablished Jewish settlement there.

Blu and I visited the area and were deeply moved. Who would not be? They had kept the faith; now they had come back to their Jewish roots, to the place from which Jews had been driven out. The head of Gesher, Danny Tropper, was a former student of mine. I had helped him develop Gesher and was involved with the organization. Together, we had this inspiration. We would get the Riverdale Jewish Center community to raise some money to build a Beit Sefer Sadeh (field school) in Gush Etzion. We made an appeal and raised the money. Remember that at that time Israel was ready to give the territories back. Most Israelis could not wait to give all the territories back for the sake of peace. People at the Riverdale Jewish Center asked me: "Rabbi, what is the point of building schools and settlements on land that is likely to go back to the Arabs within years?" My response was twofold. The story of Gush was so moving, so resonant with the total spirit of Jewish faith and history, that I did not believe that the Israelis would ever again give up this spot. Then, too, Jerusalem itself was at stake. Jewish Jerusalem had been so isolated in 1948 that it almost fell. Although Gush Etzion was lost to the Jordanians, it held out for a while. The extended siege played a valuable role in saving Jerusalem. Had Gush fallen more quickly, the full might of the Arab Legion might have tilted the outcome against the Jewish defenders of Jerusalem. I was convinced that, whatever territories were returned for the sake of peace, no Israeli government would give back Gush because that would endanger Jerusalem again. All in all, I was confident that we were not throwing out our money.

Obviously, I had a great deal of sympathy for the people who resettled Gush Etzion. Initially, I felt a similar sympathy for the people of Gush Emunim when they settled in places further out. I recognized the elements of *halutziut* (Zionist pioneering) and historical renewal that the settlers represented. In an ideal world, I would love for modern Israel to settle and incorporate the biblical heartland of the Jewish people.

However, we are not living in an ideal world where our wishes are unchecked by reality. When we returned to Israel, it turned out that there were Arabs here. Similarly, when we returned to the West Bank, there was a large Arab population there. Hundreds of thousands of them were refugees from the earlier wars with Israel. True, their refugee status is their fault. They tried to throw the Jews into the sea; they started the wars. But Jews must take some responsibility for the outcome. I cannot say that I know how to measure the correct degree of responsibility. But regardless of what the Jewish share is in causing the Arab misery, the bottom line is that hundreds of thousands of Arabs were turned into refugees. They lost their original homes. Whether they brought it on themselves or not is, in some sense, of limited relevance. This development was a double tragedy—for them and for us.

I—indeed, most Jews—did not want our dream; the fulfillment of our historical wishes; our return; our recapture of special closeness to God to cause suffering, necessary or unnecessary, to other human beings. Given that that happened, I regret the outcome in terms of Arab pain and suffering. Now I—we—have no intention of pulling out of Israel despite Arab anger at our presence. We have a moral right to be here. Our ethical right to survive has evoked their hatred; that is their problem. Sometimes historical events lead to tragedy; in history, one has to take the good with the bad. I do not want to minimize Arab suffering, but I do not feel that Israel was born in "original sin," i.e., Arab displacement. There was room for two peoples on this land. We were more needy than they were. Our dignity and our very existence were under greater assault than theirs were.

However, since 1967, as the peace opportunity dragged, as the settlement movement became more messianic, the expansion became a problem for me. The danger arose that there would not be any flexibility to trade territory for peace. Note, however, that I do not believe that giving back territory wins peace. Fundamentally, the decision to make peace and to put aside war is what makes peace. But I also believe that there are times that people need psychological breakthroughs when one can "prove" the true desire for peace by making territorial concessions. This applies to the Arabs, too, and I believe that, without some reciprocal concession on their part, there will never be peace. (Although I remain deeply grateful to Anwar Sadat for the key breakthrough to peace, I felt that Begin should have held out for one city, one area of territorial concession in the Sinai. Begin was convinced that he would have to give back 100 percent to get this landmark breakthrough. If his judgment was correct, then I accept that outcome. In the final analysis, peace is more important than any one piece of land. But the suspicion has never left me that Begin thought that by giving back the whole Sinai, he would be freed to keep the whole West Bank. This was a mistaken calculation that continues to cost us as peace is negotiated.) In any event, the location of settlements increasingly looked to me like an attempt to forestall any exchange of territory for peace, which I felt would be a serious error.

A reality factor also began to affect my judgments. Annexing a million and a half Arabs on the West Bank—adding them to the 800,000 Arabs living inside Israel—would raise the prospect of an Arab demographic majority in Israel within a century (given the higher Arab birthrates). I am convinced that, without a democracy, neither Israel nor any country can flourish. Assuming that Israel will remain a democracy, then a demographic Arab majority would decisively change the Jewish character of Israel—an outcome that would be disastrous for Jewish history and religion. The other alternative—as many religious people began to tell me—was to suppress or even expel the Arabs. Such behavior violates the fundamental norms of Judaism as I understand them. The ethical loss would be a permanent stain on our historical record; it would evoke continuing rage and hostility in the Arabs surrounding Israel; it would turn off and alienate many Diaspora Jews from Israel. These costs were unacceptable to me.

One can argue that this policy, which leads to expulsion, is no different than the actual effects of past policies that ended with hundreds of thousands of Arabs fleeing the boundaries of Israel. Admittedly, some of the Arabs were actually driven out, so is the difference only one of degree? My answer is: No. Morally speaking, a policy to deliberately drive out Arabs is of a totally different kind. Such a strategy is particularly troubling in a situation where (I perceive) the driving force is not security, but the yearning to regain the full dimensions of biblical Israel. There is a big difference between an inescapable evil and initiating evil for the sake of a grand vision. When the sense of grandeur makes you feel that you must rule over these people, that begins to border on idolatry—of land, of political strength, of lording it over someone. That perspective is morally and historically skewed.

In the interim, Arab-Palestinian nationalism has been awakened (a compliment to Israel's impact). There are now two needs for self-determination. By their persistence in the Intifada (admittedly helped by Israel's moral self-restraint), the Palestinians have proven their devotion to achieving national existence. As I assess the two needs, I conclude that the Palestinian Arabs are entitled to full self-determination if they are ready to live in peace with us. At this moment, we do not trust them fully—for a very good reason. But as the chance for autonomy or a process evolves whereby they could earn the trust, I am convinced that the peace possibility should not be foreclosed—not even by good people with good intentions, who only want to live on the land.

Now, I believe that the settlers are morally and historically entitled to live in Hebron and the West Bank. But this does not mean that the Jews have to be sovereign over those areas. Rav Aharon Lichtenstein or Rav Yehuda Amital (I am not sure which one) of Gush Etzion Yeshiva said that for the sake of peace and saving lives, he would be willing to show a passport when traveling to Gush Etzion daily. I feel the same way. I remain convinced that if the Arabs truly want to make peace with Israel, then the settlements can stay all over the West Bank. Tragically, even as they negotiate the peace, Palestinian Arabs have not turned their backs on the hatred and resentment that led them in the past to deny Israel's right to exist. Therefore, I increasingly fear that those areas under Palestinian control will prove to be untenable for Jewish settlements to continue. That is a loss for all sides. For its part, the government will not give back Gush and other areas of concentrated Jewish settlement.

In the beginning, the settlements were a contribution to peace because they put pressure on the Arabs to make a deal before the settlers' population reached an irreversible density. As it turned out, the main pressure for making peace came from the collapse of the Communist empire, hitherto the key Arab ally in their intransigence. This was reinforced by the weakness of the PLO after its support for Iraq in the Gulf War. In the end, the fantasies and nightmares of neither group were fulfilled. The settlements did not reach critical mass for control of the West Bank. After all the enormous efforts, only 100,000 people moved into the territories (excluding Jerusalem's immediate area). This number is dwarfed by the million and a half Arabs who are there.

Remember that the only way to reduce that Arab presence is a form of "transfer" or racist war, which is morally repugnant to the bulk of the Jewish people. For a Jew to propose, or to work to create, such an outcome in the generation after the Holocaust is particularly outrageous. This constitutes a proposal that certain aspects of Nazi policy be continued, except that Jews now act the role that the evil ones played. Such ethical hard-heartedness and historical obtuseness can be explained only by some loss of values. While some feel a deep skepticism of Arab intentions and resort to transfer as a backlash, many others have come to a judgment and perspective that glorifies land or power to the point of idolatry, e.g., a choice of death over life. This flies directly in the face of that part of the Torah that repeatedly invokes the memory of past Jewish suffering (such as slavery and outsider status in Egypt) to motivate greater compassion for the stranger (Exodus 22:20), for the weak and the downtrodden (Deuteronomy 24:17 ff.).

Most of the settlers and their supporters do not wish a full-scale war on Arabs even now. Still, the expansion of settlements began to create a situation where such an outcome would be inevitable. Alternatively, Israel would have to suppress the Palestinian Arabs in a process that would be undemocratic on the West Bank and could undermine democracy inside Israel. However, instead of becoming more realistic, the religious nationalist settlement movement became increasingly absolutist in its opposition to any territorial concessions or reasonable peace process. They were carried away by messianism, or by their dreams, or by their self-interest. This position obstructs the road to peace. My position is that, as much as I love the Bible and the land, peace and the survival of the Jewish people outweigh the holiness of territory.

Although it may sound naive, I believed initially that we could have our cake and eat it, too. If the Arabs want to live in peace with us, then the settlers can live on the West Bank in peace under Arab governance. If the Arabs are not ready for peace, then neither I, nor most Israelis, support giving them the territory. As I read it now, the government will give back most of the land for a real peace. I also believe that the Palestinians will have to prove their good intentions for peace by making territorial concessions and by living in peace with Israelis. They will have to suppress the terrorists who flourish in their midst.

Now, I still have a good deal of sympathy for the settlers, and even understand some of their behavior. When they feel embattled and when they are stoned or shot at, they become angry. Still, some of them have become out-and-out racists; and a small fringe did slide into murder and conspiracy in the 1980s.

Tragically, the polarization over the peace process and the territories led to a society-wide breakdown in civilized political discourse in Israel in 1995. This created a background of turmoil exploited by Yigal Amir, the assassin of Prime Minister Rabin. The overwhelming bulk of Israelis rejected and condemned this behavior, and accepted no excuses for it. In the wake of Rabin's murder, important criticisms of extremism were uttered by the settlers. Still, the situation in the territories proves again the dangers of one-sided or monolithic societies. There is still too little internal argument amongst the settlers, so that extremism gains plausibility, although it is not allowed to preach and display unchecked. People such as Kach members, who drifted to the settlements, have achieved a local respectability to which their despicable views are not entitled. Thus, a good idea is pushed too far and becomes a source of evil.

To conclude, then, I support the ideal that the settlers be allowed to stay in the territories under final peace arrangements. I respect many of them for being idealists. Some of them—including my nieces and nephews—are among the nicest people I have known, and they have retained their humanity vis-à-vis the Arabs. However, there are those who, driven by anger, have cheapened Arab life. Think of Rabbi Moshe Levinger—he is a disgrace to Jewry and a *chillul Hashem* in his barbarism. He has already been guilty of shooting and killing a person. His campaign for office and his commercials in 1992 were disgraceful. They offered gross appeals to scare the Arabs or shoot the Arabs. In his hands, a good idea—resettling sacred land—has been taken too far, and has become absolutist . . . even pathological.

My best guess is that we are going to have a real peace. We will have to give up some settlements. The Arab anger is so great that, even if their leadership really wanted to (as of yet, this is doubtful), they would not be able to protect the isolated Jews. It may well be that there are unfinished tragedies waiting to be written here. Yet I hope for a happy ending, reconciling the best of both sides' needs and capacities. I dream that the Jews would have full rights and full access, yet the Arabs would have their rights and their dignity, if they make peace with us. For this reason, I am critical of the "not an inch" position—not of the pioneering, and not of the willingness to live and let live.

Given the intensity of hatred and the unfortunate way in which the Oslo agreements have unfolded, it is probably true that additional settlements will have to be dismantled. This is a regrettable necessity that reflects not only the Palestinian failure to turn wholeheartedly to peace, but the Israeli government's failure to negotiate well and to hold the Palestinians fully responsible for their behavior. Peace—a shakier, less satisfactory peace—is still attainable. However, the margins have shrunk. The murderous terror bombings dramatized the failure of Arafat to confront Hamas and the failure of the Palestinians to decisively disown and restrain those who continue to wage war on Israel. If the PLO does not come through, the Israeli population may legitimately turn against the peace process in the belief that the festering terrorism and the virulent hatred reflects a deeper nonacceptance of the principle of peace. Under these circumstances, territorial concessions and, indeed, self-government is not justified. The most likely outcome is a freeze in the process, rather than a reconquest of the heavily settled Arab areas of the West Bank.

Q. Just one more question in relation to this. Rabbi, how do you deal with the question—the claim—that, after all, God promised the land of Israel to the Jewish people? This is so central to everything we believe through the generations, so central to Tanach. How do we then dare to say, "O.K., it's not working at the moment, so let us make a practical arrangement by which we abandon our foremost belief"? If Jews had felt that way one hundred years ago, they would not even have begun to rebuild the land of Israel.

And a second question: We have spoken about anti-Semitism, about its revival today. Bernard Lewis has written of the tremendous growth of anti-Semitism in the Islamic world. For instance, Saudi Arabia is the biggest distributor in the world of the anti-Semitic *Protocols of the Elders of Zion.* In Israel, we see every day incidents of attempted violence not only against Jews, but against the land itself. How do we hope to make peace with people who seem so filled with hatred and violence that they injure even the land they would have as their own? Is peace really possible at this stage, given that in all the vast Arab world there is no democracy? No tradition of compromise? No willingness to understand our pain as you and so many other Jews strive to understand the pain of the other side?

Greenberg. Your first question is, "If it is God's command, how dare we give back any territory?" Your second question is, "Do they really want to make peace with us?" I will answer the second question first.

We are facing difficult decisions. These are all judgment calls involving risks. I personally trusted Rabin as an individual capable of vision and sound judgments—the right kind of leader to have when one is taking risks. And I believed that Peres had been sobered by the peace process itself and by terrorism to move closer to Rabin's positions. Obviously, Peres did not persuade enough Jewish Israelis of his toughmindedness and sobriety in the negotiations, so he lost the election to Netanyahu. However, I believe that the voters elected Netanyahu not to stop the peace process, but to make peace through harder bargaining by a government that would hold the PLO to a stricter standard in keeping its side of the agreements. Whatever the conflicts and inner divisions in the Netanyahu government, and despite Arafat's waffling on renouncing the policies of violence and supressing the terrorists, I believe that the peace process will yield some agreement with the Palestinians.

There are people of good judgment, including generals, who believe that we can work out a peace that preserves Israel's security. Maybe we cannot have the ideal set of choices, but we can achieve a reasonable pact in the context of where we are operating. If we tried to keep every last inch of land and suppress the Arabs, I personally think that our security would be most endangered. Ultimately, American support would collapse. American Jewish support would weaken. So I do not think that we have great margins of choice. People whose judgment I trust say that peace is possible, that it is worth the risk. I think of my own grandsons born in Israel who may have to fight someday. Ideally, they should not have to fight. Enough sons and grandsons have died too young. Therefore, I would take a finite risk, a rational and defensible risk; otherwise they will certainly have to fight someday. I recognize that such a peace may not work; the sacrifice of territories may not help. It is sometimes necessary in life to make tragic choices in the best possible way.

When people assaulted Rabin and the peace process and cried "betrayal," I resented it. I felt closer to the people who criticized the peace process on security grounds than to the simple-minded who said, "We are here through an original sin (coming to a land where Arabs lived)," or those who said, "We are wrong because the Arabs are suffering. Do not ask questions as to how the situation came about; just give the Palestinians what they demand." These views are outrageous. The Midrash says: "Those who are kind to the cruel end up being cruel to the kind."

I do not want to romanticize this peace process. It is a hardheaded choice made from far-from-ideal options. The decision to pursue the peace process and make substantial territorial concessions is defensible and necessary. Let us hope that it will work. It will take years before we know for sure. But since we are ethically and politically precluded from the alternatives of transfer or killing, we should leave no stone unturned to explore the possibility of peace. Of course, if the Palestinians do not make clear in word and deed that they intend to live and let live, then the process will not go all the way to autonomy or statehood.

This leads to the other question. Both Rabbi Soloveitchik, *z'tl*, and Rabbi Ovadia Yosef have said simply that, as between the land of Israel and the blood of the people of Israel, the blood is more precious. As holy as the land is, the blood is even more sacred. It follows that if there is a realistic peace prospect, then giving back territory is a *mitzvah.* I believe that the Torah contains God's commandments, including God's revelation of policy and direction. I also believe that in our *brit* with God, humans are given responsibility to interpret. How do we apply this principle now? I believe that in the course of history humans have been called to take on more responsibility for the covenant.

In our time, we have the call to take full responsibility for policymaking in fulfillment of the covenantal task. To say today, in God's name, that "I [God] commanded you to conquer the land and you cannot give it back" is to refer to a no-longer existent theological situation. When God said to Isaiah, "Tell the Israelites that if they obey Me, I will drive off the Assyrians," when Jeremiah said in reference to the Babylonians that the Israelites' failure to obey the covenant drew God's wrath in the form of Nebuchadnezzar's army, that was true in the age of prophecy. That was a different age of Jewish history. Then, God spoke directly through prophecy. God split the Red Sea. God saved the Israelites in defiance of natural order and political power. Then one could speak in God's name, "Then if you will keep the land, then I [God] will protect you; if you do not stand fast, I will not protect you." In such a situation, leaders have a moral right to say, "Let us not give back the territories; God forbids it and God will protect us."

Today, in fact, we are in a different theological situation. (1) God does not speak unmediated through prophecy anymore, but rather through human interpretation. (2) God does not provide visible miracles. If you listen to God, you are not automatically protected. God did not save us from the Shoah. We have to face that fact together—under circumstances that God has chosen. God is not in any moral position to give orders not to give back land anymore. Does anyone really believe that if we do not give back the land God will protect us against Iran? Do you believe what the yeshiva *bochurim* claim—that through learning Gemara they protect the state, even though they do not serve in the army? I believe that such language is the true *apikorsus* of our day. I believe wholeheartedly that God wants to protect us. And I reject the secularist claims that God is nonexistent or that God does not care. I believe wholeheartedly that God wants us to take responsibility, to apply the Torah here. God is telling us that the holiness we create is "as holy as the holiness I [God] gave when I [God] sanctified Hebron." The new Jerusalem can become as holy—sanctified with Jewish blood, sweat, and tears—as Shechem of old. To save the inhabitants of Tel Aviv, one may exchange territory in Hebron. Since God does not save us by miracles, we are back to the issue of judgment, especially the generals and the army. If they think that they can protect this nation within new borders, I trust in their right judgment.

(Note: Rav Yosef and Rav Soloveitchik are not saying what I said about God not protecting us. They simply affirm that human life is worth more than land, and that policymaking is given to the human authorities under the halachic system. That is sufficient authority to take the necessary steps. I am trying to push the theological analysis one step further. In my judgment, Gush Emunim have become theologically like the *haredim.* Both operate out of a now-mistaken, once-applicable model of God's relation to us. In this view, if you simply obey God, just do the right command, you will come out all right. Whereas I claim that God now says, "If you apply My command, I am with you and I will protect you in a certain way only—not by miracles that go against the natural order." (The key to covenantal protection comes from making the right political and military decisions, accountable to God.)

Of course, I feel the pain and lament the cost of my position. To use a visa to get to Gush Etzion is emotionally painful. (It is also extremely unlikely, as Gush will be annexed to Jerusalem. But

Hebron is just as painful.) Still, that sorrow is softened by the consciousness of being responsible to God's commandment. The Jewish people lived outside the land for two thousand years. I cannot conceive how to live without Israel. I have been asked could the Jewish people survive another Shoah, God forbid; i.e., if Israel were to be destroyed, I do not think that we could. I do not believe that the Shoah is going to happen again—but no one can guarantee that it will not happen. We have to work harder to ensure the right outcome. Therefore, to absolutize the land is wrong.

Of course, if one worships peace at all costs, that policy will end up being wrong also. But if there must be a choice between the people and the land, there is no question in my mind that the people come first. They last longer. I remember Rav Soloveitchik quoting the Talmud, speaking of Moshe Rabbeynu as the greatest *sofer* (scribe) of all time because he wrote not on stone, but on the hearts of people. But does not the stone last forever? No. The people outlast the stone. The people of Israel are more precious than even the land. The land is very dear; it is given to us by God. But God is saying that, in our personal lifetime, we must reconcile the holiness of the land with the dignity of other people, Jewish and non-Jewish. I think that we can do this creatively and well.

In the interim, we have to keep our powder dry and not have any illusions. We have to work with God either way. If I am alert to God, I will not have this romantic notion that I can get away with political decisions that go against the facts. In the name of God, we dare not offer policies that cannot plausibly be upheld and carried in the face of realities—including international pressure and consensus. In making peace, we should act based on the best judgment as to what policy can best provide peace and security for Israel. Of course, I feel fully accountable before God for this position. This means that if I made a mistake in giving back the territories, I will suffer and feel very much accountable for that decision. But I will take responsibility for taking action. Rabbi Israel Salanter once said that *lo b'shamayim hee* (the Torah is not in Heaven—Deuteronomy 29:12, from the classic talmudic application in *Baba Metzia* 55A) means that we have full responsibility for the Torah. That means that our subjective judgments and even our mistakes, when ratified by the whole Jewish people, become part of Torah. God affirms them as God's will. If the decision is a mistake, then God affirms it—mistake and all—as the fulfillment of Torah.

If the peace process is a mistake in the sense that it ultimately leads to war and the loss of lives beyond what would have happened had Israel held onto the land, I would feel extremely guilty and responsible. But right now, as the Talmud says, the judgment must be made, based on the facts before the judge's eyes at this moment. Even if the decision backfires, such a judge will sit in heaven, before God, closer to God than the people who are so smart that they never made a mistake, before the people who are so righteous that they never got their hands dirty, before those who sat and made abstract moral judgments that condemned Israel when it was struggling every day. In a religious sense, I am not afraid. These kinds of mistakes for peace are more creative and more valuable than the alternative of standing pat. Ultimately, one can do only what accords with one's best judgment. Following through, making decisions, taking responsibility—this is what a profound level of commitment to the covenant demands from us at this time.

9

On Leaders and Leadership

Shalom Freedman (Q). Rabbi, I wanted to ask you about leadership. Of course, the Jewish people has had many great leaders. I think of Moses and Aaron: Moses, with his great strength and the great demands he makes upon the people in service of God. And Aaron, who loves peace, and is more loved by the people, perhaps, because he is too lenient with them. Do you have a concept, Rabbi, of how a Jewish leader should act today?

Rabbi Irving Greenberg. Leadership is an internal quality. Leadership is not a totally separate quality, nor are leaders separate from ordinary people. In that sense, all humans can be leaders. Certain people become leaders when they take certain personal qualities (which all people possess) and raise them to a higher level; then they move ahead and serve as a model (or avant-garde, if you will) for the rest of the people.

Let me draw an analogy: the definition of the *gibor* (hero) in Pirke Avot. "Who is strong? The one who self-controls." The definition plays off a paradox. The strength described is not the obvious physical force and power. Rather, the Mishnah takes a particular quality that all humans have—self-restraint—and says that the person who practices it at a more intense level—who attains self-control—is a hero. Similarly, the intensity factor enables the individual to serve as a focal point or leader for others.

Which are the qualities whose intensification makes a person into a leader? First, I would list vision—the ability to see the big picture. The leader focuses on the main purpose, whereas others concentrate on the details or specific tasks, and often lose sight of the overall goals. The quality of vision includes looking ahead to see the final outcome or the long-range consequences and letting them influence action. By contrast, the average person—perhaps out of a desire for instant gratification—is concerned with the immediate behavior.

An associated leadership quality is responsibility. A leader shows willingness to deal with a critical situation when others are reluctant to deal with it because they think it will be difficult or costly to act. Most people want to do the right thing, but the immediacy of the difficulties or other pressing needs diverts them. When an individual stands up and takes the long-term view, or pushes for the right policy despite the cost, the others recognize that their best side is represented in this person. Then they accept and support him or her as their leader. Of course, sometimes people lose out in this decision or are threatened by the process, so they do not accept the leader. This rejection is one of the risks of leadership. (This last observation implies another quality of leadership: willingness to take risks out of a sense of responsibility and obligation.)

The rejection factor also underscores a second dimension of leadership: the relationship of the leader and the community. The leader may be blessed with an extraordinary capacity for vision or risk-taking. But if the community simply is not interested and unwilling to move in that direction, then the leader will have no following, and so will not be a leader. Many a would-be leader has taken up the task and found that the community is so conflicted or so unconnected that the effort fails.

The reverse also happens. Sometimes the community is so eager to go that it pushes forward a reluctant or limited person and makes that individual the leader—really, the vehicle of the community's will—willy-nilly.

In the case of the Jews, leadership grows out of the function of the Jewish people. The people Israel is the avant-garde of humanity. In turn, Jewish leaders are people who serve as models, teachers, and co-workers at a higher intensity level for their fellow

Jews. The quality of vision is particularly needed, for the leader must remind people of the covenantal task that, after all, is directed over generations and centuries. Since there has always been a gap between current reality and the messianic end goal, it is critical that decisions reflect some thrust toward narrowing the distance. Therefore, the dream must in some way guide the daily decisions. There is a constant need for someone to mediate the gap; the leader must remind people that the effort is needed and assert that the results will make the effort worthwhile. Ultimately, the leader is defined as being someone who, either by example, by taking responsibility, or by helping the community deal with a crisis, opportunity, or challenge, has made a difference in the outcome.

The specific covenantal tasks of Jews are different today because the situation of the Jewish people is different today. In our time, the challenge is how to use power rather than how to survive powerlessness. But the covenantal mission is the same as it always has been—the Jews are supposed to teach, model, and work on the road to *tikkun olam.* Today's leader is one who makes it possible to meet the challenges imposed by this mission.

Q. Who is meeting those challenges today?

Greenberg. It is not one person alone. Since the mission is *tikkun olam,* the entire people must participate. And more than one group is helping Jewry meet the challenges to its existence. Incidentally, this is a self-correcting process. The Jews have faced dynamic, often rapidly changing situations. If there had been no leaders, and if they did not meet the challenge, then the Jews would have disappeared. Similarly, when the task is fulfilled, this brings changes in every aspect of life. Every solution brings a change in circumstances. This may well lead to the emergence of new leadership.

In biblical times, the great covenantal challenge was how to create a just society, how to create a people and a state able to live and survive by covenantal values. In that era, the great tension was: Will the Jews—in order to survive—lose their way? Will they abandon all moral restraint in fighting their enemies? If that happened, they would have betrayed their mission. On the other hand, if the Israelites had taken the Torah's covenant values to an extreme and turned ethical directives into an inability to cope with aggression, then they would have been destroyed. They would have failed their mission that way.

In biblical times, there was this constant tension. The kings felt that they had to defend the kingdom of Israel–Judah, or, sometimes, had simply to establish their authority. They often found the covenantal moral restrictions bothersome and irritating; therefore, they tried to cut corners. Side-by-side with the political leadership emerged a prophetic leadership. The prophets challenged the kings to live up to the standards of the covenant. They insisted that ethical behavior and covenant responsibility would protect the Jewish people (in part, because it would evoke Divine protection for Israel). They insisted that selling out—in the form of social exploitation or playing power politics in foreign affairs—would get in the way of survival. There was a constant dialectical tension between these two kinds of leadership.

Another quality was important to leadership in biblical times: access to God on an ongoing basis. This was needed for the sake of forgiveness from sins—individual and national—as well as for the sake of blessing and Divine protection and guidance. Sometimes this mediating function was filled by priests; sometimes by prophets. Historically, there was a tendency for priests and the kings to coalesce, but this did not necessarily happen. There was a potential tension between them as well. Over the course of Jewish history, only rarely has one type of leadership been able to solve all the problems. Different types of leaders played different roles at different times. This was particularly true because as time went on and circumstances changed, various types of leadership evolved.

An analysis of Jewish history suggests that there is a long-term movement through different methods of electing leaders. Initially, the leadership—such as priests—was genetically called; later, kings emerged the same way. Then came the prophets chosen sacramentally, that is, chosen by the Divine; they led whether or not the Jews picked them—although admittedly there was a strong personal interaction between them and the community. In a later period, the baton of responsibility passed to rabbinic leadership. This is one of the great transitions of Jewish history. Rabbinic leadership is self-generated; it is earned by learning and defined by its mission, and it has no genetic component. This new leadership came to the fore in historical crisis and took over from the genetically and sacramentally empowered. Without the new leadership, the Jewish people could not have made it as it went through a fundamental change from living in its own state to being a minority in a condition of powerlessness. Jews had to survive with a sense of covenantal mission intact even while living in drastically changed circumstances. The inherited leadership disintegrated because it could not fulfill its traditional function. A priest cannot play a central role when the Temple has burned down and that channel to God is not open. A king cannot lead a society in which there is no longer government function, army, and state. The inherited leadership fell by the wayside because it could not serve with its old functions, but it failed to give (or even guide) the response to the ongoing new challenges of Jewish experience.

Now to your question in regard to the Jewish leadership today. The Jewish people has a diverse set of challenges. One of the central tasks of the Jewish people today is to guide and secure the state of Israel, that is, to ensure Jewish existence with dignity, with the ability to protect itself—and to run a country with Jewish majority control. This calls for political and military, as well as social and cultural, leaders. In the Diaspora, Jews live as a voluntary grouping. Jewry must meet its tasks, create institutions, tax itself, support Israel—all through the agency of a voluntary community. This requires leaders with different skills, including the ability to create institutions to nurture and sustain the community. There is a critical need for religious leadership with educational and cultural skills that can compete for loyalty and attention in an open society. A rabbi who must win a following voluntarily needs different skills than a rabbi operating in a pedagogical situation that is politically established. One of the beauties and one of the fascinating aspects of Jewish life today is that there is such a wide distribution of leadership. There are many leaders whom one could pick out and admire.

Q. But I think there is a feeling, at least in Israel, that there is an absence of leadership. Many people speak of Ben Gurion as not only a great political leader, but a great spiritual leader. He had a vision of what Israel should be, a light to the nations. He had a sense of a great historical mission. This was felt in all that he said or did, whether you agreed with him or not. Now you have political leaders who, however competent or incompetent, seem more like technicians. What's missing is that added element. In this century, Churchill is the prominent example of one who had this quality, which makes a leader of stature.

Greenberg. That is a fine point. Again, leadership is a dynamic interaction between the people and the circumstances. The greatest leaders are the ones who, in their teaching and their work, marry the vision and destiny of the people with the practical solutions for the contemporary challenges. Ben Gurion was this type. He was ahead of his time. He was a great but shrewd risk-taker. Creating the state in the face of great danger was one of his main contributions. In that decision, we see an outstanding fusion of leadership elements—the ability to unite visionary and practical, avant-garde yet prudent, leadership at once. Such leadership is rare not only because such people are seldom found, but because the masses of people only occasionally are ready to accept leadership on such a grand scale. It is only in moments of crisis that the gap between what is and what is needed grows so great that people feel enough urgency to support and thereby enable that kind of leadership.

Consider what happened to Winston Churchill. He was dismissed in disgrace in the 1920s and early 1930s because he was perceived as too grandiose in his thinking and too demanding in his will to stand up to Hitler. Yet he was called back to power when the country realized that it was in a fight for survival. Churchill proved to be an extraordinary leader in wartime. Yet he was defeated by the electorate in the first election after the war because the people wanted somebody who would create a "normal" society, focused on achieving a better standard of living. They thought that for everyday life, the ordinary Clement Attlee would be a better leader than the visionary, charismatic Churchill. In sum, if people do not feel a need for inspired leadership at the crisis level, a person of the Ben Gurion or Churchill type is not given room to lead. Under "normal" circumstances, people often feel that a visionary is not "safe," or is not sufficiently "domesticated." Maybe the leader is a "fanatic" because he or she is committed to too strong a set of ideas or shows too much focus on the long-term principles.

Take Menachem Begin as a case study. For the first thirty years of the state, Begin was almost an object of derision. People considered him a failure; he lost every election, and by large margins. In order to go on, he had to have enormous self-confidence and extraordinary staying power. (There was a luck factor, too; there was no one in his party of sufficient stature to challenge him when he failed.) Then his moment came. First, a massive Labor failure (exposed by the Yom Kippur War) led to his election. Then Sadat made his historic peace move. At that point, Begin showed that he had more than the ability to stay the course. He had been considered doctrinaire, unrealistic; yet when the peace option opened up, he showed that he could make a pragmatic new set of policy decisions. He not only grasped the moment; he carved out policies that one hardly would have expected in light of his past record. A person who had upheld his vision of not giving back an inch of land for years decided to give back the whole Sinai. It was remarkable. He rose above himself.

Then why is there a feeling now that Israel is being run by technicians, not statesmen? My first answer would be that Israel needs more technicians. The economy is not yet functioning to its capacity. Too many details of life—daily amenities, the interaction with bureaucracy—are of poor quality. The Israelis have been so busy with the big questions of war and peace that they never have had time or energy to deal adequately with the questions of daily life. This is the most neglected side of Israel. Now Israel is capable of becoming a consumer society. That would constitute a big improvement in the quality of life.

Having said that, I believe that there is still room and need for greatness. Making peace now is going to take courage and vision. I was pleasantly surprised that Rabin, who had not been seen as the visionary type, opened up the peace process. He recognized the dangers of making peace—and of not making peace. While trying to deal with the dangers realistically, he was willing to make important concessions. Of course, he walked a narrow path. In his impatience, Rabin was tempted to demonize the settlers. This contributed to the polarization of Israeli society and the breakdown of political pluralism. Yet, after all, it was striking to discover that he'd had the talent of statesmanship all along, but never had the right moment or the right outlet for it until the Middle Eastern political situation shifted. This makes his assassination all the more reprehensible and his death tragic.

Note again the strange mixture. The people do not always want leadership. When the people do want greatness, it is not always given to them. Once in a while there is a luminous moment when the people are open to letting the person lead, and the right person comes along. In historical retrospective, those are the people who stand out as the great leaders.

Let me give another example. Great leadership is not always crowned with success. In order to be a great leader, you have to be willing to fail. A leader has responsibility for people; therefore the goal is to succeed and solve the problems facing the community in the spirit of the covenantal tradition. But, in many cases, you cannot lead without taking the risk of failure or actually failing. Moses, the greatest Jewish leader of all times, is a powerful example. In his vision, he would create a free people and get them into their own land. To know and worship God properly was the essential foundation and the goal for this process. Yet, while Moses liberated the Israelites from Egypt, he never succeeded in making them a free nation. The people that he freed died in the desert as slaves. He, too, never entered the land of Israel, despite his desperate yearning to get there. By many important criteria, Moses was a failure.

(Personally, I would dream of accomplishing one-thousandth of Moses' achievement. Then I would consider my life a great, great success. Still, by Moses' standards and hope, there was a great element of failure in his life.)

Consider the prophets. They had an extraordinary vision of the ethical–religious standards that the Jewish people should meet. They were so much ahead of the people for most of the time that the nation did not listen to them. (In fact, you might argue that, in that sense, the prophets were not great leaders. In their day, most of them failed overwhelmingly.) This is the prophetic paradox. These great leaders failed miserably in their own lifetimes. The notable exception is Isaiah, and that is probably because he brought a message of a miraculous deliverance that was soon actualized. What if his message had been a warning of "doom," as Jeremiah's had been? He, too, probably would have died un-listened to and unrequited in his love for God, the covenant, and the people. (Of course, one of the advantages of covenantal continuity is that failures in one lifetime can be redeemed by later leaders in later times.) In many ways, it was the rabbis who made the prophets into successful leaders—retroactively.

It is worth analyzing why the rabbis succeeded and why the prophets failed until the rabbis succeeded in their efforts and brought the prophets with them into the heart of the Jewish people. The prophets' great strength was their great weakness. Inspired by God, suffused with the electricity of the Infinite, they made absolute demands—fearlessly, totally, immediately. Listen to Isaiah (1:16–17): *Chidlu hareah. . . . Dirshu mishpat. . . . Ashru chamotz* (Stop doing evil. . . . Insist on justice. . . . Restore [make happy] the exploited). These are great demands, breathtaking in their elemental force. But they are not going to be fulfilled. No one ceases doing evil all at once; no ruler insists on justice in all matters. The gap was so great that people shrugged off the prophets' words. The prophets were doomed to failure because of their greatness in making absolute demands. Later, the rabbis came along. In their pedagogic wisdom, they recognized that they could not expect the people to live perfect lives. So they urged them to take one step more on the right path. If you cannot free all the slaves, then at least improve their food, health, and living conditions. (Do this again and again.) If you cannot create a fuller, equal society, you can at least upgrade the *tzedakah* resources. You can also create a web of friendship, kindness, and mutual regard between the wealthy and the poor, the powerful and the needy. As the rabbis upgraded the Jewish people's consciousness, as they inspired them to improve their standards of behavior, little by little they raised the Jewish people to the level where they *wanted* to listen to Isaiah. After all these years, the rabbis made him and all the other prophets (retroactively) great leaders—leaders that the Jewish people now listened to and followed!

One can argue that, especially in modern culture, the prophets are overrated because everyone loves a grand vision. The rabbis proved to be more valuable leaders because only when they solved the "little" problems did the grand leaders turn out to be grand leaders. If the rabbis had not accomplished their multiple little steps, constituting their incredible educational transformation of the Jewish people, then these great, prophetic leaders would have ended up with little influence on Jewish history. Imagine: Isaiah or Jeremiah would have been an *enfant terrible*, a far-out visionary who never accomplished anything.

This paradoxical case study applies to a special kind of leadership, i.e., spiritual leadership. A spiritual leader may last a hundred or even a thousand years before succeeding; a political leader cannot. Still, take the case of Theodor Herzl. Here is a man who died as a "total failure." Herzl offered incredible political visions. He established the political Zionist movement. In his lifetime, he essentially achieved next to no actual Jewish sovereignty over the land of Israel; when he died, there appeared to be no hope of ever achieving a Jewish majority in Israel. But if he had not started the movement, if he had not been willing to use his life "in vain" and die at forty-four, broken-hearted and almost penniless, then there would have been nothing for Ben Gurion to build on when he actually realized Herzl's dream.

The irony is that one can judge leaders and their policies only as of this moment. According to the famous talmudic dictum, the judge can decide only on the basis of the evidence that his eyes can see before him. The judge cannot rule against the burden of proof on the grounds that maybe in a hundred years from now, or five years from now, there will be new evidence. This is also the spirit of the classic midrashic passage about Ishmael. When his mother put him down under a bush in the desert in despair, she expected that he would die of thirst. God then opened her eyes to see the well of water that saved the boy's life. The Midrash portrays the angels arguing with God not to reveal the well; better to let the child die in the desert because some day Ishmael is going to be the father of all those Islamic Jew-killers in the Arab nations. As the rabbis interpret it, the verse,

"God heard the voice of the child crying *where he was*" (Genesis 21:17) means that God judged Ishmael as being innocent at that moment. The fact that future descendants would be guilty of murder and terror vis-à-vis Abraham's Jewish descendants was dismissed; God saved Ishmael.

Leaders, too, must be judged where we and they are now. One can make only a best estimate of whether they are ahead of their time. Sometimes, history surprises you with its judgments later. It is necessary for a leader to have an internal sense of history. The leader knows that one cannot do just what is immediately pleasing or follow a policy that pays off at once. Thus, the leader draws a thin line, reconciling the standard operating procedure and the doable, the ideal and the real. Striking the balance demands a constant exercise of judgment. And although I said that technicians are needed now, we are going to need someone with greater vision than technicians to lead through the breakthrough to peace. When that person steps forward, I believe the people will follow.

Q. Is there anyone in the American Jewish community besides Elie Wiesel who you feel is a true spiritual leader? Who speaks to a wide audience, to the Jewish community as a whole? Who is addressing the crisis of assimilation in the American Jewish community?

Greenberg. There are many people that I can testify have served as leaders for me. Rabbi Joseph B. Soloveitchik not only taught me and inspired me, he made a tremendous contribution to modern Orthodoxy as a model of how to interact with modern culture in a respectful and autonomous way. In his approach, one critiques as well as accepts modernity, so one is not simply accommodating to it. He focused our attention on the fact that the educational task is the central test of leadership if American Jewry is to survive and flourish. He also served as a model of moderation in Israeli politics. However, the public did not know him well.

Abraham Joshua Heschel did become much better known in and through the media. His spiritual model was widely recognized in American public life. However, Heschel exemplified the difficulties of leadership within the Jewish community; on the internal Jewish communal issues, he did not get the hearing that he deserved. Basically, Heschel was an outcast at the Jewish Theological Seminary where he taught. There was a lot of resentment and personal jealousy, too. There was a feeling at the Seminary that he was too socially active and therefore less of a scholar. They did not give true weight to his remarkable religious paradigm. Recognition of his stature has grown since his death. (As far as I was concerned, he was a great leader when he was alive.)

A third major spiritual figure and a leader in American Jewry from whom I have learned a great deal was Mordechai Kaplan. Whereas I accepted and absorbed over 90 percent of the ideas and policies that Rabbi Soloveitchik favored, and while I found most of what Abraham Heschel advocated congenial to my thinking, I had a much more ambivalent reaction to Kaplan. I was put off by his excessive naturalism and "secularized" interpretation of Judaism in the light of modernity. On the other hand, his ideas about community and the important role the people play in shaping religion affected my thinking deeply. Obviously, his conceptions of restructuring the synagogue and other institutions shaped the American Jewish community. The conclusion is obvious: There can be no one approach that solves the problem of modernity. The crisis of Jewry and modernity is not finished; it is growing intensely. Assimilation is rampant. Some of the spiritual leaders that I have learned from offer models of how to tackle these issues.

There are two rabbis, who made a distinctive and important contribution over the past thirty years, whose work has a continuing influence on American Jewry. One was Reb Shlomo Carlebach, *zichrono livracha*, the father of the Jewish religious music renaissance. Shlomo fused music and words to create a *neshama* (soul) music for our time. Decades ago, Judaism—even in its traditional forms—was in the grip of modernity and had been made too cold, too domesticated, too rational. Shlomo's countermodel of a fiery, burning spirit and his role of a wandering minstrel and outreach worker was an immense contribution. This musical vehicle for spirituality is a brilliant borrowing from contemporary culture; it is at once universal and distinctively Jewish.

The other rabbi who has carved a unique path for himself and has influenced many others is Reb Zalman Schachter-Shalomi. We first met in the 1960s, and I was struck by his remarkable liturgical creativity and insight. He is a genius of davening (he calls it "davenology"), and is a master of ritual and prayer's role in spiritual life. His career took a turn whereby he primarily reached out to the left, to the "new age" Jews, to the marginal and oppressed Jews. My work with CLAL turned toward the Federations and was skewed toward the established activists and the mainstream rabbinate. To my regret, therefore, we were not able to do much together. Still, my awe at his mastery of many world religious liturgies and his capacity to uncover the spiritual and the mystical in the heart of twentieth century social experimentation remains undimmed. Both Reb Zalman and Shlomo have disciples who carry on their work; both should have had their best insights filtered into the mainstream (which lost out, because this was not done). Both made errors or experiments that allowed others to belittle or even to dismiss them, but the detractors missed the big picture. Both men showed courage and perseverance in staying the course. Both will be remembered for providing their important creativity and models of access to the Divine in a time of need.

Currently, certain rabbis stand out because of their quality or their contribution to dealing with modern culture. Harold Schulweis is an outstanding rabbi and thinker. I have learned from him even when I disagree with certain philosophical or theological positions he has taken. Perhaps his greatest contribution was his development of the model and role of the *chavurah*, particularly within the structure of an established synagogue. Art Green, one of the pioneers of the *chavurah* movement, who established Chavurat Shalom, also serves as a model of postmodern spirituality. He has made a very important statement about mysticism and applying mysticism in (what seems to be) a scientific–rational age. He took over the Reconstructionist Rabbinical College (a classic Kaplanian institution) and was able to deepen its spirituality despite the growth of secularization within the student body and the movement. He was able to move RRC toward greater respect for the texts and the tradition despite the superrationalist tradition in the Reconstructionist movement. He is a person who has a continuing influence in American Jewish life.

The presidents of the major rabbinical institutions automatically play a leadership role in their movements and in the American Jewish community. Personally, I have been critical of the excessive denominationalism in American Jewish life, and I regret that none of the three presidents took a lead in checking or correcting the growing factionalism. Since Fred Gottschalk and Norman Lamm are at or close to the end of their careers, it is somewhat easier to make some estimate of their impact. Gottschalk succeeded most in keeping Reform on its pro-Israel, Zionist path, including upgrading Reform rabbinic education with a year's required study in Israel. This has deepened Reform's spiritual connection to Israel and has moved important elements in the Reform rabbinate toward greater respect for tradition. Gottschalk was less successful in trying to maintain or improve Reform's religious standards for lay living. Indeed, in a number of cases where standards were lowered, he was an unhappy bystander. He had good intentions, but he was going against the tide of history. Let us hope that his successor, Sheldon Zimmerman, who is committed to raising Reform's learning and Jewish living standards—will succeed better.

It is encouraging that the successor of Rabbi Alexander Schindler as President of the Union of American Hebrew Congregations, Rabbi Eric Yoffie, has proclaimed that upgrading learning and religious vitality within the movement is his top priority.

Norman Lamm greatly strengthened Yeshiva University, saving it from bankruptcy (a crisis that he inherited) and giving it the greatest financial strength in its history. However, he also presided over a ruinous decline of modern Orthodoxy, demographically and theologically. For modern Orthodoxy, these have been catastrophic years. Spiritual leadership in Orthodoxy—within Yeshiva and within the community—passed to the *haredi*–yeshiva philosophy. Lamm's heart and mind were in the right place. His writings in this last decade have surpassed the quality of his earlier work, but, alas, he could not enable modern Orthodoxy to stand its own ground in the face of the radicalization of American culture and the yeshiva world. As a result, his influence was set back at Yeshiva University even as modern Orthodoxy was set back within American Jewry. This is a classic case. In normal times, his leadership would have been more than adequate. But in a situation of rapid change and erosion, he was overridden.

Ismar Schorsch is still struggling to find his way. In recent decades, the middle or center of Jewry has suffered erosion to the right and to the left—and the Conservative is in the middle. Sometimes, he communicates the feeling that he is an academic trying to lead a spiritual and religious institution, and that is hard to do. In sum, all three men are generally constructive people who have lent their influence to positive trends in American Jewish life. But they have not been able to turn their denominations around. During their watch, the influence of the synagogue has continued to decline in American Jewish life. That is a loss for all of us.

Who else has affected the spiritual resources of the American Jewish community? Eugene Borowitz has been very influential. His publication, *Sh'ma*, has been an important popular influence. Borowitz played an important role in getting Reform Judaism to change its relationship to the tradition for the better, in particular relating Reform to the idea of covenant. There was a whole group of rabbis and scholars that came out of the movement, people who spent time together at Economowac, Wisconsin, who played an important role in turning Reform Judaism toward tradition. On the other side, a generation of *roshei yeshiva* has taken control of Orthodox Jewish life. Many built their *yeshivot* with incredible *mesirat nefesh*—dedication, sacrifice, passion. Their side impact was to incline Orthodoxy toward separation and toward *haredi* values. *Haredi* life has flourished. Artscroll is a publishing phenomenon. The indirect influence of the right has grown out of their commitment to generate an atmosphere of greater respect for learning and text orientation in all aspects of Jewish life.

During the past three decades, Lubavitch has emerged as a highly visible force in the American Jewish community; much of the credit must go to Rabbi Menachem Mendel Schneerson, *z'tl.* The Rebbe took the responsibility to create a religious civil service for Jewry and to send them to all corners of the globe. Many of their outreach initiatives (i.e., *mitzvah* tanks, media advertising, campaigns for candlelighting and putting on *tefillin*) were imaginatively conceived and embodied brilliant public education. However, the intellectual gap between Lubavitch and contemporary life is so great that I think the movement has had limited impact on American Jewry overall. The messianic turn has hurt them and has further weakened their influence. Although he was a visionary and an organizational genius, and I consider him one of the great leaders of American Jewry since the 1980s, the Rebbe must take responsibility for the intellectual and cultural limitations of the movement, i.e., its inability to integrate modern culture—and for the messianic fiasco at the end.

Interestingly, some of modern Orthodoxy's finest figures—Hartman, Lichtenstein, and Riskin—went to Israel, where they made a significant contribution. Avi Weiss' activist model has made him the best-known Orthodox rabbi and influence in America. Saul Berman is a gem in modern Orthodoxy.

Few leaders have been willing to transcend the lines or think in bold new terms. Sometimes, one feels that the leaders are energetically shuffling the chairs on the deck of the Titanic. I feel that way about my own work sometimes also. Of course, I rationalize to myself that I have been pointing to the iceberg coming for twenty-five years now—but that is little consolation when the crash looms before us.

Elsewhere I have argued that, given God's intensified hiddenness and the outward secularization of American life, only a more "secular" vehicle like literature or film can transmit the Jewish spiritual message widely. So, it is not surprising that some of the most important leadership spiritually has come from writers who are not rabbis. Elie Wiesel and Cynthia Ozick come to mind. Wiesel played a central role in bringing home the significance of the Holocaust as a turning point in Jewish life. There is a lot of jealousy and sniping, but I think that his contribution is of historic proportions; no one can take that away from him. Cynthia Ozick represents indigenous Jewish values coming of age culturally. She is a model of a self-reaffirming Jewish thinker–writer able to speak and be heard in the general media. Hers is an extremely important and valuable role.

Norman Podhoretz, especially through *Commentary* magazine, also had a powerful impact on American Jewish values. At a very important point, Podhoretz began a critique of the excesses of liberalism. While I consider myself a liberal, I internalized and accepted many of his insights and was reshaped by his thinking. Podhoretz showed real courage in going his way. Since Jews are overwhelmingly liberal, his shift was perceived as a betrayal. Despite the often ugly personal attacks on him, his influence was felt broadly in American life, as well as in the Jewish communal realm. Even though the percentage of American Jews who switched political positions was disappointingly low, from his perspective, I believe that his influence transcended the numbers. His defense of America and of Israel in the face of a fashionable left radicalism was particularly valuable. It may have prevented a catastrophic mudslide of support for Israel that could have had disastrous effects on American Jewish loyalty.

The variety of American culture and the wide range of Jewish *sitz im lebens* ensure that no one person or position can supply all the answers. When *Tikkun* magazine was begun, I was on a weekend with Michael Lerner. He told me that he was starting this new magazine to articulate the more radical–liberal version of culture and politics—but with a strong spiritual thrust and a positive relation to the tradition. I could assure him with confidence that, although my position would probably be closer to *Commentary*'s on many issues, he could make an important contribution by stimulating a needed discussion in American life (Jewish and non-Jewish) as well as by reaching an important element of American Jewry whose connection to the Jewish community was weak. While I was ambivalent about a number of *Tikkun*'s stands, especially on Israel, I believe that it reached an important segment of American Jews with a positive spiritual message—which they would not hear were it coming from someone with less than impeccable left or antiestablishment positions. The need for a diversity of voices is an inescapable implication of the pluralism of America and of modern society. Of course, pluralism and free discussion help clarify viewpoints and develop better policy. But pluralism is necessitated by the fact that no one can speak for everyone any longer. People will feel left out by the majority view and policy unless they hear someone articulate their viewpoint; without someone speaking out for their minority position, people will be less likely to accept the regnant policy.

We must learn to think of percentages whenever we speak of values or offer spiritual approaches. Defining the spectrum of acceptable speech too narrowly is counterproductive. Any viewpoint, no matter how valid, can persuade only a percentage of the total community. Even if the position is right on the issue, a certain percentage of people will not be able to "hear" the viewpoint. Every spokesperson must constantly weigh the extent to which his or her words will exclude or include. Sometimes it is worth not pushing your whole argument, in order to allow more people to accept the essence of the viewpoint. One might say that Podhoretz's own strength of viewpoint made him difficult to accept in circles that Michael Lerner was reaching. Only when Lerner established his *bona fides* as a political radical would certain people become open to being connected to Jewish spirituality and religion through his views. So, although I did not always agree with specific Podhoretz stands, I was highly impressed with his role. I can say the same about Michael Lerner and his positions: While some of his attacks on Israel infuriated me, overall his attempt to connect the left (or parts of the left) to the tradition are constructive and influential. This proves that one can be a leader and make a constructive contribution even if one's views evoke strong counterreactions. All of us should welcome and nurture multiple leadership models because we need the participation of the widest variety of people. It is worth paying a certain price in cognitive dissonance and even in the circulation of viewpoints that may have a negative effect on our own positions, if the overall gain in attachment to the Jewish community is greater.

Q. But don't you also have an absence of leadership—if you have 50 percent intermarriage, if you have so many Jews who are indifferent to the tradition? Then you have a lot of leaders who simply are not reaching the people who most need to be reached.

Greenberg. As a corrective statement, your comment is correct. Considering the disastrous situation, the spiritual leadership of American Jewry has to plead guilty to some failure. I apply that comment to myself. I saw this surge of assimilation coming; I certainly tried hard to develop alternative institutions and policies in many areas. But when the CJF study came out and reported such a high rate of disaffiliation, my basic reaction was that if I were a politician I would have been finished. When a leading political figure is doing a good job and means well, but political catastrophe hits nevertheless, then a record of trying to avert disaster does not hack it. The decent thing to do is to take the consequences and resign. Unfortunately, in the spiritual area, there is not the same kind of accountability, and people do not resign. In fact, many people get away with a continuation of the policies that contributed materially to the disaster.

Let me qualify the above judgment. The rabbinate is a tremendously difficult profession. The rabbi has to give all the time. Living in the heart of the rabbinate's mission involves constant personal sacrifice. Individual rabbis who have made contributions large and small deserve our credit; many have the right to judge their individual lives to be a success. However, as a collective group, the rabbis should be highly self-critical. Overall, there has been a failure for which the collective rabbinate must take responsibility.

The rabbis have not succeeded in relating most Jews to Judaism, or to the contemporary scene. If one were to sit down and write a *j'accuse,* then we, as rabbis, should plead guilty. When I was a professor, life was much easier. The professor's and the expert's role is almost like the prophet's. The consensus is that the task is to critique and to show what must be done right. But it is always easier to imagine better alternatives than to realize them. When I became involved with the community, the experience taught me a very important, chastening lesson. I came to see how difficult it is to make ideas work in the real world. My CLAL experience taught me how hard it is to actually meet a payroll, to handle the nuts and bolts of policy. I became a little more tolerant and understanding of people who were not meeting the great challenges. Of course, that is no excuse for the failure.

Let me tell the highly exemplary story of a person for whom I have the greatest admiration, yet who might be put down by others as a "failure." Blu and I met Jacob Birnbaum in the early 1960s. He is of English birth, a descendant of Natan Birnbaum, the famous *baal teshuvah* who became a pioneer in Zionism and later in the anti-Zionist Agudas Israel movement. Jacob Birnbaum visited Russia in the early 1960s and came back with a remarkable story: there was a Russian Jewish community, and it was coming to life after fifty years of Stalinism. Blu and I had never heard of this before, and we were deeply affected—especially in light of the colossal failure of world Jewry to respond to the Holocaust in time. Birnbaum started an organization called the Student Struggle for Soviet Jewry. He was not a fundraiser; he has never been a master of personal public relations or a smooth organizational-politician type. But consider the purity of his commitment! He gave up the easy jobs with good remuneration and became, if you will, *meshuga l'dvar echad*—driven, focused totally on one cause. It became his mission to awaken American Jewry to the Soviet Jewish situation. He struggled all the years. Student Struggle never became a powerful organization—if you define power by numbers or by financial clout. But I look back now and say: It was so close. By a hair's breadth, American Jewry did not close its eyes and miss the issues because of business as usual. In my judgment, Birnbaum made a difference.

Blu and I were deeply moved by Jacob Birnbaum. By 1967, I had become the Rabbi of the Riverdale Jewish Center. I gave up teaching at Yeshiva for that year. I took a salary cut to become part-time rabbi at my synagogue in order to work on the Student Struggle project. Unfortunately, I was not a good enough fundraiser, so I did not help him all that much. Looking back now, it is clear that I did not know the overall Jewish community. I did not know what to do or how to go about moving it. Oh, the tremendous rage I felt! The threat of the Holocaust repeating itself haunted my dreams. Here was the chance for Soviet Jewry, threatened with suppression or assimilation, to be saved. Oh, the people I talked with; the *machers* of American Jewry whom I approached in vain. They listened, but did not hear. "I have to do my payroll." "I have my organizational concerns." "Who are these students? Whippersnappers." "Who is this Birnbaum guy?" I remember an intense feeling gnawing at my stomach. A bare twenty years after the Holocaust, it was the same phenomenon of "by-standing" that dominated the situation.

Still, awareness of Soviet Jewry's condition gradually spread. The Leningrad trial put it on the front page. Then came the JDL, which drew broad media coverage. Then Jewish communal response became organized. The Establishment set up the National Conference for Soviet Jewry. Birnbaum had the reputation of being difficult to work with, so he was not invited to join it. Since Birnbaum was not a great organizer or fundraiser, SSSJ struggled. Finally, on the broader issue of rescuing Soviet Jewry, there was a success beyond anyone's wildest dreams. The Soviet Union collapsed; it let the Russian Jews out. Ironically enough, SSSJ was fiscally devastated by this development. As an organization, it had always been on a financial shoestring. When people perceived that Soviet Jewry was being saved, financial support dropped off, and SSSJ was finished. Birnbaum toiled on in obscurity and neglect. Yet when I look back, I consider his a life of greatness; his leadership is historic—nay, biblical—in its greatness. Here was a person who truly put his life on the line—and he made the difference. He was the key to that first opening, that first awareness of the issues. Without that initial effort, there would have been no breakthrough. That was an incredible contribution.

I often muse on this process, including the purity of his sacrifice and his selflessness. I also admire Jacob's wife, Frieda Bluestone Birnbaum, enormously—because she has supported and stayed with him all these years. Birnbaum has had ups and downs in health, and he and Frieda worked indefatigably together. The Divine words to Abraham, "Walk before me and be whole hearted" (Genesis 17:1), keep echoing in my ears. Birnbaum and his wife are models of historical leadership and saintliness. (I realize that "saint" is considered a corny word and not even Jewish!) Their heroic saintliness made the difference between a disaster and a triumph of historic proportions. When a dam breaks, it breaks along little fault lines that stem from an initial small cavity or puncture in the structure. The person (or force) that bored the initial cavity deserves a lot of credit for the break, even if it took all the pressure of tremendous water flows later to break the dam. So, Birnbaum made a tremendous contribution to Jewish life, even though he was not on the list of the top ten (or even the top hundred) well-known leaders. This only proves that fame and leadership do not always go hand-in-hand.

One need not go through the entire list of people who spoke

up for increasing Jewishness in the 1960s and 1970s. Perhaps it is too early to say who will prove to have been successful or not. My experience with CLAL taught me that, even with good intentions, it is very hard to accomplish goals. Compared to Jacob Birnbaum, maybe I was more lucky, or perhaps a better salesman. As a result, I was able to get a little further into establishing my specific project. But I have a greater appreciation for the enormous difficulty of changing history—and a deep conviction that there can no longer be one organization, one direction, one leader, to meet historic challenges. One must have multiple efforts; applying pressure through many channels is necessary to make anything of historic scope happen.

Q. How do you see yourself as a leader? Which community, specifically, are you addressing yourself to?

Greenberg. I grew up in, was nurtured by, and remain very attached to the Orthodox community. I served as a rabbi and teacher within that community. However, thanks to the influence of my parents, and of certain teachers along the way, I always felt part of the total Jewish people, not just my own immediate community. You will also recall the impact of the Holocaust on my emotions. In the light of the Shoah, it seemed self-evident to me that all Jews carry the message and the risk of Judaism. All Jews who care about being Jewish are heroic risk-takers and are responsible for Jewish destiny, or so it seems to me. I came to the conclusion early on that I did not want to speak to the Orthodox only, but rather to the whole Jewish people.

One of the more painful discoveries in my life was that the decision to speak to the whole Jewish community forced a trade-off. Respectful discourse with others was held against me in the narrower community. Some of the policy decisions I made because they were best for the total community were exploited to attack my legitimacy within the Orthodox community. My work in CLAL reduced my influence on the Orthodox. My views and teachings would have been taken more seriously within Orthodoxy had it not been for my association with liberal Jews through CLAL. I have wrestled much with this issue because I am deeply attached to Orthodoxy. Also, I believe that many of my natural students and followers are found in Orthodoxy; being cut off from some of them is devastating. Nevertheless, after twisting and turning and considering what positions might be most prudent or most influential or most integral, I concluded to persist with my principled policies. After all, I wanted to speak to the whole of the Jewish people, not just to the religious part and not just to the Orthodox part.

Of course, these insights about pluralism apply to my work, as well. In trying to deal with culture, values, religion, and lifestyle, one person cannot do everything. To this day, there is a conflict between my writing and my desire to reach spiritual heights, and my urge to help the community try to solve problems, particularly the problem of the crisis of modernity. Judaism's two-centuries-long struggle to master the conditions of modern culture is coming to a climax. The tremendous openness of the society opens two paths: successful integration while retaining one's distinctiveness and/or total assimilation.

I have tried to develop ideas and thought able to meet the competition of the general culture, as well as to develop organizations and program models of learning. When my obituary is written, I suspect that innovating new organizations to deal with the historic challenges facing Jewry will be the most striking feature of my career. The list will include: Yavneh, dealing with the impact of college; SAR Academy, a model day school for the educational challenge of the open society; Student Struggle for Soviet Jewry, anticipating the fight to liberate Soviet Jewry; The Association for Jewish Studies, pointing to the emerging positive role of a college Jewish presence; CLAL, facing the coming crisis of assimilation and the dangers of polarization; The Institute for Jewish Life, a failed attempt to speed up the American Jewish community's response to assimilation; the U.S. Holocaust Memorial Council and Museum, to stimulate Jewry and the total American society to face up to the watershed nature of the Holocaust.

Yet, although I have been involved with initiating important new organizations, there is a long list of organizations that I believe are needed but have not been able to establish. There are projects and books yet undone. Unfortunately, there is direct conflict between these areas. Writing and thought require uninterrupted time and a chance to concentrate; organizations call for extensive time commitments and constant interaction with people. Serious thought demands depth and following through the implications of ideas wherever they may lead; yet some of these ideas upset people whose help is needed to accomplish organizational goals. Also, there are subtle ways in which politics and organizational considerations distort thinking or move thought toward political rather than integral conclusions.

On the one hand, my thinking has been deeply enriched by my organizational experiences. But, in recent years, my ideas have caused difficulties for my organizational goals. Most of all, I fear that I do not have time to do justice to all the ideas I have for books. Which should get priority? The matter is unresolved. I have come to accept the fact that leadership involves costs, sacrifices, and trade-offs. No one can meet all goals. Furthermore, leadership is not inherited or simply granted. To choose any one path really means that one must put in time, earn trust, give up options. On the other hand, leadership is democratically earned in an open situation. Perhaps if I had gone the institutional route and taken over or controlled one particular institution, I might have attained more power. But, in the final analysis, I determined to offer a wide-ranging model rather than focus on just one institution, not even CLAL. I have taken attacks in some areas in order to be better heard in others. It is still too early to say how successful I have been. That remains to be seen.

Q. What do you feel are your weaknesses and strengths as a leader?

Greenberg. I find it hard to answer this question. My *musar* training makes me feel uncomfortable talking about my accomplishments. Nevertheless, let me try to answer. One of my strengths is a very flexible and dynamic approach to life. I enjoy the clash of ideas and savor the range and variety of life's possibilities. My pluralism is instinctive. Although I take strong positions and principled stands, I love good arguments, and am open to being persuaded of other views. I genuinely listen to others and am often taught, persuaded, corrected, or upgraded—which I appreciate. I welcome substantive criticism, and I make extraordinary efforts not to let disagreements be personalized. As a result, I have been able to work with a wide range of people and movements.

I have a sense of where I think Judaism is and where it should be going. Many people respond to the vision beyond the margins of survival. I have always believed that the affluence in modern life brings with it great spiritual and political promise. If people know where the next meal is coming from, they are willing to think a little bit longer-term. People (naturally, not all) respond to my sense of direction and vision.

I never ask people to do what I would not do myself. People are more willing to follow if they feel that the person asking is there with them. I am willing to pay the price for my beliefs; I would not ask others to sacrifice unless I was ready to do the same.

People feel the love that I feel for them. Throughout my life, I have drawn strength from the people with whom I work. When I lecture, the audience radiates its strength to me. I can always tell when I am not getting through, because I am exhausted and "used up" at the finish; when the audience and I are in sync, I come out recharged and feeling stronger. My thinking and my institutional leadership have been driven by the messages and friendship that the audience and co-workers have communicated to me, nonverbally as well as verbally. And when I have gone through periods when I felt that I could not go on (there have been such times), the people have renewed my strength each time and propelled me onward. This is as it should be. A leader should not simply follow, but should be sustained by the people.

One of the great dangers of leadership is that the leader wants it. If you do not seek leadership, rarely do people pursue you to take it. Therefore, whoever wants leadership is, by nature, a driving and a risk-taking type. The result is that those who become leaders frequently and easily move into excess. Often, leaders lose their sense of the people. In leading, I have tried to reconcile conflicting urges. The leader needs to be strongly driven by ideology, vision, and purpose. Yet, an ethical leader should not override human considerations, the needs of the people, or the principle of mutual respect.

The model is right there in the Torah in the concept of covenant. The covenant and the Torah's way of life are embedded in the family. The family focus teaches us that one is not allowed to sacrifice family for the sake of the vision. God sets up cross-purposes. Love of family sometimes gets in the way of ideology. Sometimes I totally disagree with my brother, but I still love him. Dictators preach the way of ideology; they say: "Kill this person [your brother]; he is in the way of the Revolution." The covenantal way teaches: "Let him live because he is your brother, even though he may contradict the very goals of the movement." That is the strength of the Torah's concept: One does not sacrifice the human for the sake of a vision; nor does one sacrifice the vision for the sake of the human. The house of God—the *mishkan*—is in the midst of people. God loves the Jewish people and accepts them in their sinfulness and their impurity. But God does not yield the vision of *tikkun olam*, of a perfect world, either.

One learns to live with this tension. I have tried to live this dialectic; I have tried to live without pandering, to challenge people to reach to higher levels, and to do so without rancor. I have not succeeded all the time. Too often, I allow anger to overcome patience, or resentment to weaken my quality of judging others *l'chaf zchut*—giving the benefit of the doubt.

Some of my weaknesses are obvious. I have not always been able to translate my dreams into practical, doable steps. Often, I have been very frustrated by that gap. I try to do too many things. I am not a good fundraiser. Many of the things I tried to do would have been more effective if they had been done on a larger scale with more people, but I was not able to put together that kind of financial package or the broad community sponsorship that leads to large-scale support. Sometimes, in my will to make something happen, I fail to be realistic enough. Although I really listen to people, people who work for me have not always felt free to bring me bad news or to voice their problems. Perhaps my intensity is intimidating even when I try to be supportive and sympathetic. This last point is a repetition of the fact that sometimes a strength is a weakness. Because of my commitment to be out front, in some cases I have gone too fast and spoken too quickly or too openly. Sometimes this has scared people off; sometimes it has aroused opposition, unnecessarily or prematurely. For these weaknesses, I have paid a price.

In reviewing my life, I feel that the price was worth it.

However, if I could have done everything in a perfectly balanced way and brought more people with me, particularly from the Orthodox community, I would have liked to do it that way. I also feel, owing to my ambivalence about leadership and my openness to alternative viewpoints (not to mention my conflict between the private person and the public one), that sometimes I am not strong enough. Instead of staying with an issue—or forcing my views through—I draw back. Perhaps I compromised and allowed people to differ with me (or not support my work adequately), yet still enjoyed full friendship benefits. Looking back, I rationalized that in my mind as "Mr. Nice Guy," but, in fact, it was also an indicator of and a mask for weakness.

Q. Rabbi, I don't know whether this is a criticism of you as a leader, but I have heard that you are far more critical of your own community, the religious community, than you are of the secular community.

Greenberg. Those closest to you should be held to the highest standard. As the prophet Amos said: "Only you have I known of all the peoples of the earth; therefore will I hold you responsible for all of your sins" (Amos 3:2). My thinking has been shaped by that model. Precisely because I am deeply attached to and have higher expectations for Orthodoxy, I am motivated to holding it to the highest standards. On the other hand, I do not agree that I was as differentially critical of Orthodoxy as my critics claim. Because of my commitment to *clal Yisrael*, I have tried to be fair, sometimes even even-handed, in criticism of all the groups. Orthodoxy is sometimes sheltered from criticism because of its association with tradition and nostalgia; this is a feeling I do not share, because I take it seriously and because I live it. Some Orthodox, unused to criticism or stung by my specific criticisms, hope to evade the critique; the solution is to dismiss my views as excessive or one-sided. I believe that my criticism has been balanced; my message is appreciative of as well as critical of Orthodoxy's excesses.

Nevertheless, on occasion, my critique of Orthodoxy has taken on a stinging quality. Why? I suspect that the excess represents the insecurity or conflict of being in tension with my own community. My wife, Blu, has been especially perspicacious in pointing out to me the anger in the critique, when it goes too far. She has often suggested to me that anger is a sign that I am not at peace with my own criticism. Maybe I feel that I am wrong, or maybe I feel guilty vis-à-vis my childhood authorities when I am in conflict with the community. In such moments, I overreact. In retrospect, I regret those moments, and I have tried to work through the angers and anxieties to prevent a repetition. And I must say that I am guilty of occasional critical excesses toward others, not just the Orthodox. Obviously, no one can be perfectly balanced in every judgment and attachment. When I overstep, I count on the understanding and love of my community or on the goodwill of the listeners to discount the excess or to forgive. Remember my example about family and the covenant? Relationship covers errors and forgives sins.

Throughout my life, I have been guided by a rule of thumb that might be described as a law of group behavior. A leader can be, at most, 10 to 15 percent ahead of his people. If the leader goes beyond that margin, people cannot take it. The cognitive dissonance is too great, so they begin to turn off the words or reject the speaker as a leader. On the other hand, if you want to be a leader, you have to push people forward. If you simply tell people what they want to hear, then you are not a leader. (Rabbi Israel Salanter says that any rabbi whose congregation never [becomes so upset by the rabbi's words that they] wants to fire him is no rabbi.) Feeling a sense of obligation to move people and to lead them to a better day, I try to push people—to extend them to reach their fullest potential strength. Yet, a leader must lead people; he cannot allow the gap to grow so great as to cut himself off from people—that would be a failure of leadership. (Rabbi Israel Salanter continues: But any rabbi whose congregation does fire him [for his speaking] is no *mensch.*) Walking this narrow path without falling off into "prophetic" isolation or into morally compromised opportunism is the art of leadership. I have always tried to live in that tension, neither breaking it by moral absolutism nor evading it by ethical abdication.

When CLAL first started, I sensed that there would be real tension. Pluralism was not, and is still not, ideologically respectable in Orthodoxy. So I tried to calculate the limits (intuitively, not literally). Keep in mind that I want to be a rabbi, not a prophet. In my analysis, the rabbis succeeded in their program to cultivate Jewry, getting them to live up to the covenant by educating them in stages, whereas the prophets failed in their lifetime because they demanded immediate compliance. I see myself in the rabbinic role, but I try to push the limits of that role. I try to move the rabbinate closer, as it were, to the prophetic stance.

I tried to estimate what CLAL could do and say for unity and pluralism up to the limit point. However, I then decided that stopping at the 15 percent limit would be too calculating, too comfortable, too cowardly. One is not fully responsible if one says: "I do not wish to damage myself and my standing—even for an historically necessary task." This would mean that I was guilty of giving primacy to covering myself, rather than to achieving the urgent communal task. So I determined to pursue needed policies that involved taking steps beyond that point (of 15 percent). In this way, when I looked in the mirror, I would not need to say: "You played it safe because you never stepped across the 15-percent line." Going beyond the line meant that there would be some breaks, some damage to my standing, some loss of credibility in the Orthodox community. I gambled that enough accomplishment within Orthodoxy or *l'shem shamayim* would pull me through—with wounds.

Let me confess that I did not anticipate the degree to which the modern Orthodox community would retreat because of the rise of the right-wing. To me, it seemed self-evident that the implications of the Holocaust and the rebirth of Israel implied more ethical concern, more openness to *clal Yisrael*, more sacred secularity, more religious respect and unity. So I did not imagine the surge of the right or the collapse of modern Orthodoxy. The next thing I knew, CLAL's position and mine, which I had calculated as 18 percent ahead, were suddenly 25 percent ahead. The difficulty was that for me to go back 10 or 15 percent (just to get back to the 15-percent limit!) was not easy—particularly because many issues were a matter of principle.

Take the matter of pluralism. This is the single issue for which I—and CLAL—have been beaten mercilessly within the Orthodox community. Given the reigning authoritarianism and retreat from modernity, the idea that there can be legitimacy in the non-Orthodox (as differentiated from some behavioral tolerance for them as individuals) was too big a stretch for most Orthodox. Obviously, they could be reached and taught on this matter, with difficulty, but CLAL did not have the resources for such an effort. (See how fundraising becomes a factor in leadership!). Now what was I to do? Could I retreat 15 percent on pluralism? It is very hard to be a little bit for pluralism; it is like being a little bit pregnant. In light of the Shoah, I felt that a retreat on this issue would be a betrayal. I had to risk failure.

What else could I have done? Professor Menachem Friedman of Bar Ilan University has a theory as to why the Lubavitcher *Hasidim* pushed the "Who is a Jew?" issue so hard, although it hurt them with their secular or non-Orthodox Jewish supporters. The Lubavitch are deeply involved in outreach, and mix freely with other Jews—which is very threatening to the Satmar and other Hasidim, and, indeed, to the *haredi* world within which Lubavitch locates itself. Therefore, they must generate an issue that sets a boundary, a cause for whose sake they can beat up on the non-Orthodox, thereby reassuring the *haredim* that the Lubavitchers are safely within the *haredi* boundaries. Many times, I have asked myself, "Is there an issue for whose sake I can beat up on Reform or liberal Jews to reassure the Orthodox?" There were issues that could have been used that way, but I just could not bring myself to do it. For the moment, then, the greatest bloc of antagonists or fundamental rejectionists of my views is found within the Orthodox. (Incidentally, the percentage is not that high. The majority of lay people still agrees with CLAL's general call to show respect for other movements, even if they do not agree with pluralism. However, the modern Orthodox establishment collapsed and backed away from me; that has been damaging.)

Sectors of the Orthodox community, especially those on the right, have not merely disagreed with, but have delegitimated CLAL. Then, leadership elements of the modern Orthodox establishment went along with the delegitimation, leaving my position considerably weakened. After much reflection, I have concluded that this situation is a reflection on the community, rather than a substantive criticism of me. At first, when I realized that I was being delegitimated within Orthodoxy, I felt guilty and tended to blame myself. Perhaps I had gone too far in my thinking or had been excessively critical of the Orthodox. However, I have considered the matter quite a lot since then. My conclusion is that the problem is not in me. There is a certain "sickness" within Orthodoxy that has hurt me as well.

Once I was at a meeting at Mercaz Yaacov Herzog. We were planning a conference and discussing whom to invite in the process of trying to creating an ideological circle to explore issues of modern Orthodoxy. We were discussing people whom I happen to admire. A key person—mind you, active in this liberal wing of Orthodoxy—said about two people in question: "I could go with this one, but not with this one." In other words, even within this focused group, someone whose thought went beyond that consensus was disallowed. I said to myself: It is not just I that am being marginalized. People like David Hartman and Shlomo Riskin, each in his own way, are being marginalized. In certain Orthodox circles, Riskin is excluded; in others, he is certainly under attack. Rabbi Adin Steinsaltz is attacked frequently in the *haredi* world, although he has leaned over backward not to offend them.

When a community marginalizes people of the quality and record of Shlomo Riskin and David Hartman or attacks Adin Steinsaltz, then the community has a real problem. Maybe the task of the leader is to stay with the people no matter what, and not to rock the boat so much. But if the margin is drawn so tightly that any passage beyond that one line turns the community against its own best people, then it is weak—and it is weakening its own best leaders! My conclusion is that my marginalization is a reliable indicator of the pathology that is undermining modern Orthodoxy. My marginal state will be corrected as the community reasserts itself.

Finally, while I take the blame for saying things at particular moments that have been excessively critical, I believe that, overall, I have not been too critical. Indeed, there are many areas where I have not been outspoken enough. The classic example is the women's question. I do not speak out as much as I should because I fear that I will pull the string to its ultimate snapping point. I am also not as critical publicly as I would like to be on the rise of the right-wing political views in the Israeli community. The process has gone much too far. The National Religious Party has painted itself into the extreme fringe of Israeli politics with its position of not giving back one inch of territory. The image of modern Orthodoxy is that it puts land ahead of lives, that it is anti-Arab to the point of nurturing racist tendencies, that it is a bitter and vulgar opponent of the peace process. To make matters worse, in the Gush Emunim and Merkaz Harav circles, there has been a tendency to "trade" more *haredi* lifestyle elements in return for legitimating extreme political positions—so there is a retreat from moderation in all sectors of religious Zionism. I would like to say more publicly on these matters, but have held back somewhat to protect the community's willingness to listen to me in other urgent areas.

10

On Holocaust Commemoration

Shalom Freedman (Q). One criticism that I have not heard about you personally, but I have heard about American Jewish leadership (which does relate to you) concerns the Holocaust Memorial Museum in Washington. The criticism is that resources are being given for the dead, not for the living.

Rabbi Irving Greenberg. To the charge that I have played a disproportionate role in drawing extraordinary attention to the importance of the Holocaust, I will gladly plead guilty. Elie Wiesel, Stuart Eizenstat—who was President Jimmy Carter's chief Domestic Affairs advisor—and I are probably the three individuals most responsible for the Direction of the President's Commission on the Holocaust and its program. The President's Commission recommended that the U.S. Holocaust Memorial Council and Museum be set up. I believe that the museum is a new institution in Jewish history. Just as the synagogue emerged as a major institution after the Temple, so the Holocaust Memorial Museum—not just this one in Washington, but all of them as a type—is a new institution to express Jewish values and beliefs and to advance understanding of the Holocaust as a turning point in Jewish and world history. At CLAL, we set up a project called *Zachor*: Holocaust Resource Center in 1975. *Zachor* not only taught the importance and the implications of the Shoah; it proposed the creation of a Holocaust Memorial Museum in the spirit of Yad Vashem. Eizenstat, who was touched by his experiences at CLAL, proposed the idea of a holocaust memorial to President Carter; the three of us worked to sell this particular model to the Commission and to the government. Because of my commitment to CLAL, I could not stay on as director, but I remained completely committed to the concept. (Michael Berenbaum, the Deputy Director of *Zachor*, served as Deputy Director of the Commission and stayed with the project; perhaps more than any other professional, he deserves credit for staging the museum.) My support remains steadfast. Although actual construction costs totaled $150 million instead of the original projection of $50 million for the building, it is worth every penny.

For almost two decades now—almost since Holocaust awareness broke out of a narrow circle and reached into Jewish and American public consciousness—there has been a drum fire of attacks on the institutional and educational costs of Holocaust commemoration. Sometimes, the very need for such efforts is denigrated. The standard party line is that Judaism is not a religion of tragedy or death; it is also claimed that focusing on the Holocaust creates anti-gentile feelings or paranoia (which is blamed for causing Israel's supposed intransigence). The standard put-down is that the money is being spent on the dead, not the living.

There are elements of jealousy in the response. When spending on Holocaust education increased, there was the cruel jibe, "There's no business like Shoah business." In witticisms like this, a grain of truth is magnified into a sandstorm—blocking correct vision. The bottom line is that the Holocaust is an event of historic magnitude that tests and transforms our understanding of Judaism—and of all human culture (not the least, of the culture of modernity). Responding to major historical events is the way that Judaism has always grown. The impact of the destruction of the Second Temple, of the Spanish expulsion, and of the Chmielnitski pogroms are classic precedents for such development.

The Holocaust is not a substitute for Jewish religion; rather, it sheds great light on how Judaism must develop and be understood in the future. Without coming to grips with the Shoah, all people (not just Jews) cannot have a true moral, religious, and cultural compass. When people better understand the implications of the Holocaust, they will appreciate and treasure democracy as never before. This new consciousness is the key to shattering the idolatry of modernity; it is the key to Christian repentance and moral renewal. When people understand better, the memory becomes a shield for the Jewish people and a profound confirmation of the necessity and moral-spiritual significance of the state of Israel. That is precisely why anti-Semites and anti-Zionists have been drawn to denial of the Holocaust and to any attempt to reduce its significance. Therefore, the Holocaust is a central challenge for Jewish and general education. It is a prime component of any responsible education. Any money spent on Holocaust education is being spent for the living, not for the dead.

There is an additional dimension to the Holocaust Memorial Museum. When certain major events and the values they imply have become central in Jewish religion, they have been transformed into sacred acts (*mitzvot*), sacred time (holy days), and sacred space (physical institutions). The Exodus was expressed and transmitted through sacred acts (eating matzah, freeing the slave, loving the stranger), sacred time (Passover, Sukkot, Shabbat), and sacred space (the holy Temple, the *sukkah*). Early on, I became convinced that the Holocaust is of such monumental proportions that it, too, will be translated into sacred acts (creating a defense force, saving Jews at Entebbe, guaranteeing the right to return, giving to UJA), sacred time (Yom Hashoah, community yahrzeits), and sacred space (Holocaust memorial museums). The rabbis saw, after the destruction of the Temple, that a new institution was needed to express connection to the more hidden God through prayer (a more "hidden" form of service than sacrifices), through study and a more "secular," less sacramental setting. Then they brought the synagogue front and center as a new central institution.

The Holocaust Memorial Museum will not be as central as the synagogue; still, the spiritual genius of the Jewish people grasped that we need a sacred space to study and explore the profound implications of the Shoah in a setting that enables a serious empathetic encounter with it in a total environment. For this reason, the Holocaust Memorial Museum was developed in

Jewish settings (first Yad Vashem and Lohamei Hagetaot in Israel, then the Memorial for the Unknown Jewish Martyrs in France). Starting in the 1970s, *Zachor* pushed to create such institutions in America. (Yad Vashem's leadership was skeptical and worried that such places in the United States would undercut its own standing—a fear that proved utterly baseless.)

In the case of the United States Holocaust Memorial Museum, the additional benefit is that the United States government offered to lend its sponsorship and to house the museum on the sacred ground of America: the National Mall. This meant that, properly done, the museum could reach many more people, with greater credibility, than any Jewish institution located on Jewish ground. There was a risk involved—the danger of a forced but false universalization—but the danger was prevented. The exhibition strikes a superb balance; it is deeply Jewish, yet all the universal implications are drawn. Thanks to its location and sponsorship, the museum will reach hundreds of thousands of Jews and probably millions of gentiles who, under any other circumstances, would not have been open to receiving a Jewish message (with universal implications) at this level of power. It will stimulate a much higher degree of interest in Jewish life and in the world and culture that was destroyed, as well as in the life that continued after. In that sense, the museum will have paid for itself as a vehicle of education for Jewish life and loyalty. That makes the $150 million (most of it undoubtedly Jewish money) a bargain.

Let me add the irony that, in my opinion, most of that $150 million could not have been raised directly for Jewish education; much of that money would not have been given at all, but for the excitement of this cause. Therefore, in my judgment, very little of this sum will have come at the expense of alternative Jewish causes that might have received these gifts. Finally, as a result of the forceful impact of the museum exhibition, millions will be given to Jewish education by people who otherwise would not have cared enough about Jewish life in any form—or not even cared enough to study about the Holocaust.

One of the amazing truths about Jewish life is that the encounter with the Holocaust—which logically could scare people away from being Jewish—actually continues to be a major stimulant to renewed Jewish life. To this day, I am stunned, moved, and electrified by this experience. I have met hundreds—even thousands—of Jews who, because they came in contact with information about the Holocaust, decided that they had to come to grips with their Jewishness. They became serious, deeply involved Jews in the process. For this reason, I disagree strongly with Harold Schulweis' complaint that too much attention has been paid to the evil and destructiveness exhibited in the Holocaust and not enough to the kindness and human compassion shown, notably by the Righteous Gentiles who saved Jews. Schulweis' clinching point is that most Jews know the names of the Germans who led the mass killing, but very few know the name of the gentiles who saved Anne Frank, for example. The statement is true, but it is an exaggeration. First of all, the redeemers were, in fact, a handful (otherwise, 6 million could not have been killed). Equal focus on saviors and murderers gives an historically false and morally misleading message. Equally important: It is not true that exposure to the death and killing is education only of cruelty and death. The encounter with the force of death in the Shoah evokes a response of life in many today, even as it did in the Jewish people in the 1940s.

The most important piece that I ever wrote on the Holocaust—the first piece that I published after twenty years during which I could not bring myself emotionally to publish—opens with the following line: "Judaism and Christianity are religions of redemption." The main message of Judaism is the triumph of life, the Divine promise of redemption to be realized through the God–human partnership—for the perfection of the world. But one who preaches this message without coming to grips with the Holocaust is naive and a fool. Such a person is a dangerous Pollyanna, inspiring people who have no idea of how powerful the forces of death are in this world. No one grasps or begins to understand the spiritual grandeur of the Jewish people unless he or she understands that this people lived through the Holocaust and still believes in God. Jews still have the messianic dream and still risk their lives as guarantor of this commitment. Those museums are a tremendous statement of Jewish life, of a vigor and hope that has defied the worst assault of all time—and has overcome.

The vast majority of givers (and teachers about the Holocaust) are showing deep wisdom and spiritual heroism. They understand that the Shoah is an historically transforming event, and that it is worth spending millions to get this message across. The U.S. Holocaust Memorial Museum turned into a major fundraising draw because of the prestige of Washington and the association with the president, Congress, and so on. Of course, the glamour factor can be exaggerated and can lead to abuses—including excessive focus on death or the cannibalizing of needed Jewish causes. But this has *not* happened so far. Yad Vashem and the other quality memorial museums are truly educational for life, not just for death. Indeed, these are religious institutions where people have religious experiences with powerful moral consequences and motivation toward ethical responsibility for all humans, not just Jews.

Elie Wiesel was much bothered by the "commercialization" of the Shoah. Then I argued with him that if the Holocaust had not become visible and well-known, there would not have been any vulgarization. If commercialization is the cost of becoming well-known, it is worth the price. When Elie Wiesel could not get a job in the late 1950s, when no one wanted to publish his works—who wanted to read about the Holocaust?—that was much worse. Ignorance and indifference were rampant; apathy truly breaks the heart and the spirit. Of course, every upsurge of interest brought with it elements of exploitation and abuse. This is true of many aspects of life. But the Shoah is a classic case where the negative, uncontrolled abuses have been far outweighed by the constructive channels developed for commemoration, education, and liturgy.

Look back at the United States Holocaust Memorial Museum and at the other memorial centers with which CLAL or I was directly involved (in planning, counseling, guidance, and the like)—such as the Museum of the Jewish Heritage in New York City (which will cost $30 to 40 million) and the museums or exhibitions in Miami, Dallas, Los Angeles, Montreal, Detroit. Add together all the costs (including programs that failed, as in St. Louis and Pittsburgh), and I would say that the net results were outstanding contributions to Jewish living—and a bargain. When I look back on my life, I am happy with the thought that one of my main contributions to Jewish life will have proved to be a role in the creation of a new historic Jewish institution. Knowing that the risks of future failure still exist, I still wager my life that these museums are not going to turn into places of worship of the dead.

The vast majority of people, and Jews in particular, have a natural feeling for life. They respond to death by increasing life. Worldwide, in wartime and just after wartime, the birthrate jumps. People's gut instinct is to renew life. One should respect that force and bet on it, rather than make clever jibes and put down this effort.

Of course, there were cases of exploitation. There are museums that go for shock effects, but these are the exceptions. For the most part, the fundraising has been legitimate and positive. UJA has fundraising missions that go to Yad Vashem, where they solicit people. UJA has been repeatedly attacked for using this approach. But let me be the devil's (actually, angel's) advocate. There was an enormous assault on the value of Jewish life in the Shoah. Refusal to save Jews only added to the cheapening of Jewish life. There was even an S.S. department whose function was to maximize the profit and reduce the cost of killing Jews. When a group of people has visited and has witnessed these facts, what is the appropriate response? What profounder theological statement can you make than saying that, despite the counterevidence of Nazi devaluation and allied indifference to Jewish life, you still believe in the preciousness of Jewish life? "To prove that Jewish life is precious, I hereby pledge to give a lot of money right here and now." This money will be spent to save, to upgrade the dignity, to restore the value of Jewish life! That is what a UJA pledge is all about.

Q. For me, the effect of the Holocaust is, above all, the sense that you must do whatever you can to help make the Jewish people live. Is that what you are expressing?

Greenberg. That is what I am expressing. And I do not even claim to be original. People often ask me, "What have you tried to do in your writing and philosophizing?" My answer is that I have not spun out new theories. I simply describe the Jewish people's behavior, taking it seriously, generalizing from its concrete actions, describing in broad theological terms what it is actually doing. If one does that well, one can write important thoughts. I once had this exchange with Richard Rubenstein. Rubenstein made the extremely powerful statement in his book *After Auschwitz* that, in light of the Shoah, "God is dead," i.e., the only messiah is death. My response was that, logically, he was probably right. But religion and theology are based on life, not logic. These claims and results are ultimately empirical, tested by reality. Basically, the Jewish people did not react as Rubenstein argued. The Jewish people grasped a deeper truth. Traditional notions of God are wounded by the Shoah, but the awareness of God and of covenant was renewed. Jews responded with intensified faith expressed in increased creation and recreation of life and new religious expression. That is exactly where I take my stand in my religious writings.

For the record, the story told in the museum in Washington does not end with the war; it ends with the renewal of life. The exhibition does not start with the killing; it starts with Jewish life before the war. The New York museum is focused on Jewish life and culture. I feel very strongly about this holistic view that must guide our encounter with the Holocaust. I will never forget the first year that I spent reading and studying about the Holocaust in 1961. The combination of being in the land of Israel and living and seeing the life of the Jewish people every day made the whole experience incredibly moving. Even though all day long I was seated in the library reading about destruction, even though my brain was saturated with images of death, my days were simultaneously totally immersed in the blossoming life of Israel. One cannot separate the two events. Israel is a response to the Holocaust.

Of course, Zionism does not start with the Holocaust. Jews had dreamed of, and prayed to God for, their return to Zion for centuries. Settlement in Israel started sixty to seventy years before the Shoah. But the crystallization of the Jewish international consensus to support Zionism and Israel; the world's shock of recognition that there must be a Jewish state now; and the overwhelming action and support of world Jewry represent profound responses to the Holocaust.

Sometimes, I look back and ask, what if the Yishuv—especially Ben Gurion and the leadership—had not decided that it must establish the state right then, in 1948? What if they had played it safe and said, "Let us build up the Yishuv more—maybe the Arab hostility will decline ten years from now"? What if they thought, "Why risk the whole Yishuv's life now? Let us try a decade from now." Could they have won a state in 1961? Not likely. From that point of view, Israel is deeply linked to the Holocaust, but linked in the most positive way. Israel is the Jewish people's affirmation of life in the face of the Holocaust—which was a monumental assault of death on its life.

The miracle of Jewish life and religion today is that the very event that should be a source of hatred and death and killing—i.e., the Holocaust—has been turned into a sustaining force for life. The models of evil, and cruelty, and hatred evoked a counterreaction of love; the memory of death is a driving force for increasing life. This is true not just among Jews; there are heroic thinkers who responded to the Shoah with the determination to never again allow Christianity to nurture hatred for Jews. They carried out a moral critique of Christianity from within. These people have led the Church to reject its anti-Jewish teaching. They were shattered, challenged, and driven by the Holocaust to do this. This is like alchemy—turning hatred into love. The dictator Idi Amin's reaction to the Holocaust was that the Nazis should have killed more. He and other evil people took the model of mass death and tried to make it into a stimulus for more murders. But the power of human love defeated him and people like him. By a huge margin, humans took the death experience of the Shoah and turned it into a powerful motivator for life. The Jewish people and other decent people have taken the memory of evil, and by this miracle of human love, have turned it into a powerful weapon of the good. This is a fulfillment of the classic Jewish message of the Song of Songs: Love is fiercer than death (8:6).

Q. It has been over thirty years since that first year you spent in Israel, which, as I understand, was largely devoted to research on the Holocaust. In that time, there has been (in part, thanks to your efforts) a great increase in awareness of the Holocaust. At the same time, we see something that would have seemed impossible then—so-called "historians" who deny the very reality of the Holocaust. This is connected with the rise of all kinds of anti-Semitic movements. Looking back, how would you assess the change in "awareness" of the Holocaust in these years?

Greenberg. There has been a remarkable growth of awareness of the Holocaust in the past three decades. A fever of recording and witnessing has taken hold. An incredible amount of testimony has been collected; Steven Spielberg's Shoah foundation has played a noteworthy role. The number of scholarly publications, documentation, and films has skyrocketed. To illustrate the contrast, let me recount a story that I believe I heard from Mark Dworetsky, *alav hashalom*, a survivor who later taught about the Shoah at Bar Ilan University. (Dworetsky had been a prisoner in labor camps in Eastern Europe.) When Dworetsky proposed to study the camps for his Ph.D thesis, his professor at the Sorbonne told him, "You will never find enough material for a Ph.D thesis." Dworetsky came back with a huge bibliography. The amount of material listed was so vast that the professor thought that Mark was putting him on. The faculty, furious, were going to charge him with forgery and misrepresentation. His advisor was so convinced that Dworetsky was fabricating that he said sarcastically: "Considering the amount of material that you are claiming is available, it would appear that every prisoner must have spent all his time in the camps writing his memoirs, instead of being enslaved by the Nazis." Yet the volumes and the records continue to expand exponentially. This outpouring of testimony has been a triumph of the human spirit. The Nazis wanted to degrade the Jews not only physically, but spiritually. They wanted to destroy them and then wipe out all trace of the crime. In fact, both during the Holocaust and after, in a fundamental assertion of life and dignity, the Jews wrote and witnessed. Now, the Shoah is the best-documented crime of all time. The truth is now so widely published that it cannot be suppressed or the record destroyed.

Only now is the rest of the world beginning to understand what a fundamental transformation of life and understanding humanity has to go through in light of the event. The tip of the iceberg is exemplified in Christianity. Most people do not realize the extent to which there has been a revolution in Christian understanding and thought. Major theologians and teachers within Catholicism and within the Protestant churches have rejected Christian supercessionism, recognizing that it was a primary source of anti-Semitism and Jew-hatred that was exploited by the Nazis for their demonic purposes. There is a widespread determination to stop Christianity from being an ongoing source of hatred. This has led to a rethinking of the value of the Jewish religion and a real change in relation to Judaism. Unfortunately, the changes have not yet reached all Christians and are not yet fully incorporated into the basic structures of the Church. Still, among a very important and influential element within the church, there has been a real *teshuvah.* There is no question that the driving force of this transformation is consciousness of the Shoah and the guilt that they should rightfully feel about Christianity's long history of the persecution of Jews.

In 1993, I was at a planning meeting with Father Ari Crollius, who is responsible for Jewish Studies at the Gregorian University in Rome. He is also in charge of the joint program for research at the Federation of Catholic Universities of Europe. Crollius reported that Jewish Studies was still growing, and that there was great interest in pursuing these courses. Since these students are non-Jews, who are priests or future priests, I asked what accounted for the great growth in interest. His explanation was simple. Mostly, they have become aware of the Shoah, which has generated a tremendous response. When decent people are exposed to the record of the Shoah, they are driven to repentance, renewal, ethical purification, and theological growth. Regrettably, not enough Christians and Jews have understood that encountering this event means that they have to undergo a revolution themselves in order to be worthy, so to speak, of living properly after this event. That is why we must continue and expand education about the Holocaust.

If public awareness of the Shoah has grown extraordinarily in the past three decades, how, then, do we account for the negative phenomena that you mention? There have been two main regressions in dealing with the Holocaust in these thirty years. One is the rise of revisionism. This is connected to sheer chronological distance from the Holocaust. The passage of time allows for a certain amount of emotional distancing. Unspoken, the memory of the Shoah remained a shield for the Jewish people during the 1950s and even the 1960s. The Holocaust was not articulated, not even well-known then. Yet, in political circles, anti-Semitism had become so delegitimized by its association with this horror that no mainstream politician could vent anti-Semitic ideas and survive politically in America. In Europe, the taboo was not quite as strong. There was still a lot of residual anti-Semitism from prewar times, so anti-Semitism did not automatically and totally disqualify politicians. Still, anti-Semitism was associated with burning children and gassing old people; therefore, nobody respectable could afford to dabble in anti-Semitism. In that sense, Holocaust sights and memories were a protection for the Jewish people. To the extent that people become aware of the Holocaust now, it still is a form of protection. Still, there was a breakdown in the 1960s, and more significantly in the 1970s and 1980s. As distance grew, as the generation that saw the sights of the Shoah—at least in newsreels—began to die out, it became possible for people who hated Jews to begin to revise history by denying the undeniable.

This led to an associated breakdown—the absolute taboo on political mainstream anti-Semitism was breached. To this day, I am grievously disappointed with Jesse Jackson; his unthinking anti-Semitic comments removed the barrier—though he is now trying to make amends. In the decade before he ran for national office, the seeds of anti-Semitism grew among black nationalists. These nationalists were marginal in American life; they were politically unsophisticated and initially powerless. But they were faddishly radical, initially. People were reluctant to confront them when they used classic images of anti-Semitism in the course of their political struggle. They got off scot free, politically, because they were rank outsiders and card-carrying victims of white racist America. Nobody in respectable American political life had been able to survive politically with anti-Semitic views for thirty years. But because black nationalists were seen as oppressed victims, they were not "disbarred" from mainstream political life. In turn, Jesse Jackson became a national figure and let slip some anti-Jewish comments that had not been challenged in the internal culture of black nationalism. Up to that point, it made no difference whether the politician meant it or not: An anti-Semitic slip finished you politically. When Jackson got away with his anti-Semitic comment, I felt angry because this was a weakening of the taboo. (Nevertheless, there was some political cost. Jackson himself has been trying hard to make amends and clear himself of the stigma. He has made some progress, but he continues to lose ground politically. However, the infection is still rampant among the more radical groups, such as the Nation of Islam.)

In Europe, too, there were setbacks in the political area. As traumatic memory faded, neo-Nazism came forth. Ironically, the fall of Communism brought forward a population whose moral sense was dulled by decades of totalitarian Communist suppression. As these people encountered the frustrations of freedom and the loss of certainty, they became subject to neo-Nazi appeals. Anti-Semites reared their heads again. All took advantage of the changing image of Israel. As worldwide publicity pilloried Israel, the anti-Semites deliberately borrowed and turned the Holocaust terminology onto the Jews. The step after that was the rise of revisionists' denial that the Holocaust had been inflicted on the Jews.

The revisionists represent the triumph of hatred. How could one even dream of denying the best-documented crime of all time? The answer is that if you have enough hatred in you, then when someone is spitting in your face, you will say that it is raining. The facts smack you in the face, and you kiss them off. That is the basic truth behind revisionism.

Many survivors are shocked and driven to despair. Since they experienced the agony in their own flesh, they find it demeaning that anyone would dare to deny their pain and loss to their faces. I urge survivors and people of good faith not to despair. Of course, revisionism is upsetting, but the encounter with revisionism arouses me to further effort. And, in actual fact, it is no contest. We are winning the battle for the mind of the public and the historical record. The frantic efforts of the neo-Nazis and revisionists show that they are on the losing side of the battle. They are trying so hard because they know that consciousness of the crime and the documentation has spread enormously. For two thousand years, when Jews sought to counter Christian canards, we were ineffectual. The fact that Christianity was spreading lies against us did not help us. We were talking to a majority that was indifferent or negative. We never could catch up with the spread of hostile stereotypes and vicious, demeaning falsehoods about our character and the nature of our religion. Anti-Semitism spread into literature, folk art, and language, and into circles far beyond Christianity. The modern general culture incorporated secularized versions of Christian anti-Jewish stereotypes. Christianity poisoned the mind and the cultural ground of Europe, and provided the cesspool of hatred within which the Nazi virus grew. By contrast, the great accomplishment of these past thirty years is that Holocaust consciousness has spread widely. The world recognizes that these deniers are trying to obliterate the facts for the sake of hatred and death, whereas the truth about the Holocaust has been spread for the sake of life. Of course, there is a setback in the very fact that revisionists have been able to raise their heads. But, if you ask objective people to make a judgment, it is obvious that the forces of truth are winning this battle. There are thousands of books of testimonies; videotapes and full-length films dealing with the Holocaust have spread much farther and have persuaded many more people. Now Holocaust memorial museums are rising worldwide. Every time I hear of a Holocaust denial, it is infuriating, but the revisionism has driven survivors and our other allies to make extraordinary efforts to spread the word. I see the haters' frustration, for they are, in fact, spitting into the wind.

It is important to see that even though neo-Nazism is a very disturbing phenomenon (as is Pamyat in Russia, and as are the hateful fundamentalists in Iran and in many Islamic countries), the bottom line is that they are the marginals in their societies or in the family of nations. If we play our cards right and work hard, they will remain marginal; they will be defeated and overruled by the historical record.

Over these three decades, there has been a different sort of deterioration that, paradoxically, is connected to the achievement of these years. As Holocaust awareness spread widely, there was a certain popularization that led to some cheapening and commercialization. Elie Wiesel, in particular, has been very disturbed by this phenomenon. From time to time, he has expressed regret at his role in raising consciousness of the Holocaust, because he is so grieved at the vulgarization of the topic. I am not being cynical when I say that the commercialization and the cheapening is a "good sign." No one could have exploited the Holocaust commercially but for the stunning success in arousing awareness of the Holocaust among the public. Look back at the 1950s. When I first met Elie Wiesel in the early 1960s, he was literally starving. No one wanted to hear about the Holocaust; no one wanted to publish books about the topic. Wiesel's first book was published in America in 1959. I came across it accidentally. Hill and Wang, the publisher, was a small firm; the book—*Night*—soon went out of print. This classic was almost lost to sight—an outrageous, almost ridiculous situation. To this day, I have this enormous admiration for Wiesel. How he had the strength to give his witness and persist through the 1940s and 1950s into the late 1960s! That was a heroism almost beyond belief. The absolute indifference was horrifying to me. From my point of view, if the price of getting the attention of the public is popularization—even if the price is a measure of cheapening—then, sadly, so be it, but let us do the right thing and get the word out.

Over the years, we have discussed this many times, especially as we participated in the President's Commission on the Holocaust, which set up the United States Holocaust Memorial Council and the museum. Wiesel was on guard, fearing every step of the way that the museum would "betray" its sacred mission by dilution or vulgarization, or by false universalization of the topic. He is a purist, which is understandable given his personal experiences in the Shoah and his remarkable, prophetic stature as a witness. I felt from day one that there would be some costs to getting the museum accepted by the whole American people and to get it located on the Mall in Washington, but what an incredible opportunity this was. Of course, we had to be on guard; only the highest level of moral imagination, ethical integrity, and creativity could achieve the necessary level of presentation in the museum. I was convinced that that standard could be met, but that no museum (or representation) could ever achieve perfection. To give one example, the museum would have to deal with some other forms of Nazi genocide (thus risking some "dilution" of the understanding of the absolute nature of the total assault on the Jews in the Holocaust).

Wiesel was such a purist that, at times, I feared that the museum would not be built. Finally, when there was a shift in direction, he so feared that the dilution would now come that he resigned as a member of the council. Sometimes, in the course of our arguments—which were respectful—he would come close to despair and slide into anger. A few times, he privately accused me of compromising the purity of the project. My reply was invariably that I would stand judgment at the bar of history before God. Undoubtedly, I would be found guilty of falling short of this unattainable goal, but I would feel blessed that my failures made this incredible project possible.

This principle has been a lamp unto my feet in a number of important projects in my life. The very concept of covenant implies a "dilution" of the Divine standard of purity with a human admixture. God affirms this process because humans must be reached in a human way, that is, an imperfect way. Throughout my life, I could not afford the level of being a purist in any matter. Our goals are absolutely pure and wonderful, I argued to Wiesel, but to get the job done you have to be willing to get your hands dirty. This means living with qualifications and compromises. (This is conditional on not betraying by selling out.) My affirmation assumes that one's commitment is covenantal; the pledge is permanent; the deviations are never allowed to divert or redirect the fundamental direction. Standards are essentially kept; the chance for further upgrading is built in. Then the (flawed) outcome is noble.

I feel personally responsible for some of the commercialization and cheapening of the Holocaust topic in that I helped popularize the Shoah in the mind of America. I also recognize that sometimes scholarly treatment and education are taken or supported to excess. But of all the sins I have committed in my lifetime, this is the one with which I would be proud to come before God on my judgment day. I would plead that I am guilty of this "crime." This activity was needed; it is still needed. I would throw myself on the mercy and good judgment of the court.

On balance, spreading consciousness of the Holocaust and the importance of learning from it—nay, of transforming life and society in light of it—is one of the great achievements of these three decades. It is not merely that the educational impact and public policy awareness have reshaped aspects of the world. The world is so aware of the Shoah that the Palestinians and black radicals feel constrained to use—and misuse—this imagery. In a way, their language is a compliment to our achievement, although I regret very much that they exploit the image.

There is another major moral accomplishment in this educational achievement. Think of the model of death, the message of hatred, in the Holocaust. The catastrophe should have become a permanent source of hatred. Any time that someone commits a crime of that magnitude, any time people break the elemental taboos of respect for life, the paradigm of those behaviors weakens resistance to future evil. That is why Jews are insistent on the terrible fallout from *chillul Hashem*, the desecration of God's name, by bad example, and on the enormous resonance of *kiddush Hashem*, martyrdom, in making God's name holy. Every act witnesses to humanity. When people see that killing is easy and goes unpunished, then respect for all human life vanishes. According to *halachah*, we restrict the forms of kosher slaughter because if you kill *animals* cruelly or mechanically, then *respect for human life declines.* Life is inseparable; respect for life is indivisible. Then the logical conclusion is that the Holocaust should have weakened respect for Jews and encouraged hatred and more killing. It should have led Jews to become killers in return. The corruption of evil should have spread; talking about the Holocaust should have scattered the virus of hatred even more widely. But this is the opposite of what happened. Overwhelmingly, Jews—and other decent people—elected to turn the memory and the model into a force for goodness and life.

This was the subject of my fundamental quarrel with the late Meir Kahane. Meir was a friend and a classmate in high school. I was very sympathetic when he started the JDL. "Never Again" was right. We needed to defend Jews. It was important not to stand by when Jews were trapped in declining neighborhoods and were being terrorized. But he did not keep the passion and anger under control. As time went on, in his hands, the slogan "Never Again" meant that one could do anything one felt like in defense of Jews—including abusing innocent people, appealing to anti-black racism, and the like. But if you want to be faithful to the agonizing dialectic of the Holocaust, the event does not give one-sided answers. We not only have to remind people of what the world has done to us. . . . We not only have to fight for Israel and make sure the world gives Israel the benefit of the doubt. . . . We have to apply the same lessons to our own behavior. We have to try hard not to act beyond the necessary means of self-defense in regard to the Arabs. We have to be good to them.

The JDL once planted a bomb in Sol Hurok's office because he arranged a musical tour for some Russian artists. When the bomb went off, an innocent secretary was killed. Kahane denied doing the act. But we spoke once, and he indicated to me in a very cynical way that JDL had nothing to do with it—meaning just the opposite. One of the students who attached himself to Kahane may have been involved in planting the bomb. (Years later, the FBI was investigating a student of mine at City College. The student spoke to me and hinted strongly that Kahane had been involved.) When Kahane winked and smiled at me, I could not contain myself. I lashed out at him: "When you kill innocent secretaries, that is not stopping the Shoah, that is a continuation of the Shoah! In the Shoah, they also killed innocent secretaries." There is a thin line between memory and moral activism on one side, and memory and hatred and blind revenge on the other— But that thin line is like the hair's breadth which (the Talmud says) separates heaven from hell.

Now comes the amazing revelation of the past thirty years. Despite the moral powder keg implanted in the memory of the Holocaust, Jews in the mainstream—because they are driven by the memory of the Holocaust—actually increased their love and their kindness. They made a greater effort to build Jewish life everywhere. The bulk of the survivors did not sit around filled with self-pity; nor did they become bitter and hateful as they had every right to. The vast majority of survivors rebuilt their lives and succeeded in raising good families. They tried harder in some way to be more responsible in life. Similarly, most of the Christians I have worked with, when they were challenged by the Shoah, were led to become more humane, more morally responsible and more critical of past Christian failures. In all these cases, the memory of the Holocaust has been turned into a force for life and love.

Sometimes I get angry. How often has Fackenheim been attacked for substituting Holocaust for Judaism? People often take potshots at Holocaust education. "Why don't you spend the money on Jewish education?" They exhibit a failure to grasp the greatness of vision and the soul of the Jewish people. People continue to make fun of taking people to Yad Vashem and afterwards asking them for pledges. Instead of taking cheap shots at Holocaust education and memorials, one should proclaim the opposite. The Jewish people has kept up its moral judgements; it has observed limits and exercised good taste and restraint in most of the commemorative activity. It has turned the memory of hatred and death into a force of life and love.

Am I satisfied? No. Do I believe that, as history unfolds, Judaism will be further restructured and reinterpreted in light of this event? Yes. Do I believe that Yom Hashoah, as well as Yom Haatzmaut, will become a major holiday? Absolutely. Do I believe that we are just beginning to transmit the memories? Yes. Do we yet have rituals at every wedding and in every home as we have to remember the *churban*? No. But, in thirty years, the gains far outweigh the losses. The memory of the Shoah has become an irreversible force for life. This is something that does honor to the Jewish people and to all people who have joined in the sacred task. Someday, this work will be recognized as the equivalent of the creation of the canon after the destruction of the first temple and the development of the Talmud (over a period of centuries) after the second destruction. This is further witness that neither the Jewish people nor Judaism is dead. It is proof of the incredible power of life and of the post-Shoah song, *Am Yisrael Chai*! (The Jewish People is Alive)!

11

Israel and the Jewish and Human Future

Shalom Freedman (Q). As one who has done much to bring awareness of the Holocaust to Jews and non-Jews alike, and as a student and teacher of the history of the Jewish people, you are well aware that this greatest of evils suffered by our people was nonetheless preceded by many other great tragedies and destructions. The fall of the two Temples; the great destruction after the defeat of the Bar Kochba revolt; the Crusades; the Inquisition; the pogroms in the Ukraine in the seventeenth and twentieth centuries . . . not to mention hundreds of other persecutions and expulsions that occurred both in Christian and Muslim lands. Do you feel—perhaps this is a question no human being can really answer—that the pattern of mass communal Jewish destruction has been broken by the founding of the state of Israel? Or do you believe that it can recur? This is asked in the context of the Jewish people having returned to its ancient homeland, having founded a state of its own—a state that is a prospering and developing state, yet that has, in its short history, fought five major wars; a state that is still, through no will of its own, at war with most of its neighbors, and is presently threatened by the rise of Islamic fundamentalism, one of whose major aims is the destruction of the Jewish state.

Rabbi Irving Greenberg. Living as we do after the Holocaust, every Jew must accept the fact that life does not come with guarantees. If this ultimate evil could be inflicted, then any evil can happen. The first time is always the hardest.

One of the most important lessons we can learn from the Holocaust is to demythologize the idolatry of modernity. The avant-garde of modernity claimed the ability to abolish evil—especially in the form of war (or the conditions or forces that generate evil [war]). Some modern movements argued that human nature was at last liberated (or becoming perfected), so that, thanks to __________ [you fill in the movement] there will be evil (war) no more. In yet another variation, some movements claimed that evil/war is religiously or culturally based, and that now that the Enlightenment had triumphed (or was about to), we would overcome evil (war). A lot of these illusions were shot down in the Holocaust.

One of the most important lessons that followed from the shaking off these illusions was the recognition of the need for the Jews to take power. Because Jews were powerless (i.e., they did not have their own state), they were victimized more easily. This led directly to the establishment of the state of Israel and to the consensus—initially of the Jewish people, and eventually of all the people who are not haters of Jews—that Israel was needed. There is no other guarantee of the Jewish right to defend ourselves, let alone our ability to fight.

Just as Jews sobered up from the inebriation of modernity and utopianism, so, too, they had to renounce theological escapism. It is a sad and bitter truth that Jews turned the classic Divine promises into an illusory fortress. The covenantal assurance that God cares was interpreted as an iron-clad guarantee: If the people of Israel were faithful to God, God would protect them as no human efforts could. On the long road of exile, the biblical idea that God fights alongside Israel's army was transformed into the idea that only God fights, and that Israel has no right to (or need for) an army. Carried away by their own spiritual heroism (and, in retrospect, by the self-restraint and limited capacities of their enemies), Jews underestimated the importance of military forces. This overemphasis of the significance of the spiritual kept Jews going for 1,900 years when they were powerless. Finally, they internalized the lack of political power and even glorified it, to their misfortune. Too many became convinced that the Divine promise of Israel's eternity released them from realistic military considerations. This left them vulnerable to evil and to the sheer overwhelming power generated in the twentieth century that evildoers could use against Jews. For this set of illusions, for this tragic miscalculation, the authorities of the tradition have to take the blame. The rabbinic leadership, which fought Zionism, has to take responsibility because it argued that God would protect Jews with miracles. The ultra-Orthodox concluded that Jews do not need their own army, that it was impious or worse to try to form a Zionist state. The credibility of that theological position went up in smoke over Birkenau. Despite the surge of power and influence of the *haredi* world over the past four decades, I believe that the *haredis'* theological credibility will never recover.

The recognition of the inescapable duty of taking power spread beyond the Jews to the whole world. This is another expression of the classic role of Jews serving as pacesetting models and as "a light unto the nations." This new recognition of the essential need to liberate and empower explains the worldwide phenomenon of post-World War II independence movements and third-world revolutions. The same insight stimulated indigenous civil rights campaigns and the women's liberation movement. All are driven by the common assumption that humans can use their free will to choose to do evil and that unlimited force is available to such potential aggressors. Therefore, potential victims must be strong enough to repel any assault. The downtrodden must organize to help themselves. In light of the behavior of the democracies and the Vatican and the world Jewish community, which did not intervene adequately to stop the Nazi assault, it follows that potential victims should assume power and not be dependent for their existence upon the goodwill of others, no matter how good.

We dare not flinch from the full implications of the lessons of the Holocaust. A truth that cost us six million lives to learn is too dear to evade. Hitler came very close to destroying the whole Jewish people. God did not stop him. We must consider this to be a message from God that humans are expected to take power and stop such evil. The "guarantee"—especially the belief that the salvation work will be done for us—is a mistaken notion. The Jewish belief in the "happy ending" to history is neither guaranteed nor automatically bestowed. I do not say this in a spirit of despair or depression. For me, this is an electrifying revelation about Judaism and its future. After the Holocaust, the Jews, knowing that there is no guarantee, nevertheless took responsibility for the covenant. Their most extraordinary statement was to establish a state where they could build their life, society, and power. Thus, they affirmed their full awareness of the continuing threat to Jewish existence and their desire to nevertheless persist with the Jewish covenantal mission. The Jews of this generation have proven their willingness to defend themselves against all assault with their own power and lives.

The sad truth is that new and old enemies have persisted in their hatred. Far from learning from the Holocaust how wrong their hatred was and the dangerous lengths of evil that contempt leads to, enemies—especially among the Arabs and the Communist world—attempted to destroy the Jewish state for the past fifty years. To validate and accomplish their goal, they engaged in the systematic degradation of Jews and the delegitimation of their state. They tried to place Israel outside the pale of human dignity and security.

Before the Nazis could kill the Jews, they had to move them outside the universe of moral responsibility. They had to make them subhuman, to portray them as so evil that it would be legitimate to destroy them. The Arab countries, aided for many years by the Communist totalitarian dictatorships, systematically delegitimized Israel in order to keep open the option of genocide. Happily, the evil Communist empire collapsed; therefore, the threat to Israel is significantly reduced. Nevertheless, the negative images have been so widely spread that Jewish blood (and Israeli citizens and interests) are still less protected by international norms. Amazingly enough, between Israel's remarkable efforts to protect itself and Jews around the world, and the extraordinary achievements of Diaspora Jews (especially American Jews) in winning the support of the United States and other forces of decency in the world, the vulnerability of Jews is offset by greater efforts to save them. People are starting to recognize that being Jewish is now a survival advantage. The extra efforts to help a Jew will likely outweigh the burden of the extra hostility and the greater likelihood that the rest of the world will stand by when a Jew is attacked.

Still, even now, Israel does not get the kind of protection and understanding from the rest of the world that it deserves—so Jews remain vulnerable. All Jews share certain nightmares, such as fundamentalist Islamic states obtaining access to atomic bombs and long-range missiles in order to inflict heavy destruction and loss of life on Israel. While the reduction of the bipolarity of the world has significantly reduced support for genocide against Israel, it has made it harder for Israel to take drastic actions to protect itself. (Compare the international reaction to the Israeli bombing of the Iraqi nuclear installation at Osirak.) All Jews know in their hearts that the risk is there, and that the miraculous guarantee that it will not happen is *not* there. Unbowed, the Jewish people—soberly yet hopefully—continues to build its power to prevent another destruction. This is a true fulfillment of its covenantal commitments. This is what God wants us to do. God is with us every step of the way as we create Israel, the single greatest bulwark—not a guarantee—against the possibility of another Holocaust.

During the past five decades, Israel has fought five full-scale wars and battles too numerous to count to ensure its survival and the safety of Jews around the world. As Jewish strength grows, the probability of another destruction declines. Fortunately, with every major Israeli war, the margin of survival has widened. (This claim is a bit exaggerated, since victory in the Yom Kippur War was a much closer call than in the Six-Day War. Nevertheless, the general pattern is correctly described as an historic reversal—a move from powerlessness to power—in the course of which Jewish security has improved enormously.)

Israel barely made it through the War of Independence in 1948. The human lives lost (in percentage terms) were much greater than in the other wars; Israel lost 1 percent of its population, an incredible percentage for most populations in most wars. But for the grace of God, at a couple of key turning points, the Israelis were almost overwhelmed by the Arabs. Israel was nearly cut in half. No later setback—not even the first week of the Yom Kippur War—came that close to the heart. Looking back, this generation can say that its hope and courage has been rewarded. By taking enormous risks, it has moved the danger of a new destruction much farther away.

Today, we live with faith in Jewish religion and in Jewish history. Our faith was expressed in 1948 in the decision to proclaim independence. Ben Gurion defied the odds, overriding the analysis of the generals that if the state was declared, it would be destroyed. The Jewish people were behind him because they were determined to reestablish Jewish life and uphold the covenant. People everywhere put their lives on the line. The Six-Day War results were obviously a spectacular expansion in the margins of Jewish security. It is true that, in 1974, the army was almost out of ammunition and Israel's survival was in danger, but in the comeback, the Israelis came close to total victory. If the fighting had not been stopped by international intervention, there could have been as overwhelming a victory as in 1967. Now, with the collapse of Communist support for the Arab states, and with Egypt out of the picture, Israel's margins of safety are greater than they have been before. The age of guarantees is over, but your inquiry is in the process of being answered positively by Jewish action in history. All this suggests that the question of whether Israel guarantees the end of Jewish disasters deserves a twofold answer.

Let us rephrase your question in theological terms. The process of building Israel and Jewish power as a bulwark against renewed catastrophe grows out of religious sources. It is sustained by deep religious faith and driven by covenantal qualities: steadfastness, giving of oneself, taking the risks and the opportunities, and winning out. One concrete religious image captures the accomplishment of this age: Jews resumed the creation of joyous holidays. For 1,900 years preceding this half-century, the religious calendar became sadder and sadder, filled with more and more tragic dates.

The Torah contains only happy holidays; even Yom Kippur was a joyous day. (The Talmud says that Yom Kippur was one of the two happiest days of the Jewish year.) Because of the destruction of the First Temple, fast days—mourning days—were added to the calendar. During talmudic and medieval times, the official mourning commemorations spread to three weeks in the summer, and then to the seven weeks between Pesach and

Shavuot. The continuous suffering and the unrelenting assaults on the Jewish people tinged the whole religious way of life with grief. As the exile grew longer and Jewish agony increased, the whole religion took on a darker, more depressed tone. Jews kept adding periods of mourning or semi-mourning, and customs of asceticism and denial.

One classic example: Originally, the tone of the holidays was so joyful that it was prohibited to say Yizkor for the dead on Shabbat and the holidays. Then the Rhineland communities were decimated by Crusaders on the Sabbath before Shavuot. The following year, the grief was so great that the popular will insisted on saying Yizkor on the anniversary, even though this meant contradicting the joyful spirit of the Sabbath. From there, the saying of Yizkor spread to Shavuot and eventually to all the biblical holidays. Thus, sadness saturated the layers of the culture and the Jewish psyche, gradually drowning the sense of joy that heretofore had bubbled up and made expressions of grief totally inappropriate. Only a long-term immersion in continuing grief and oppression could have accomplished such a fundamental transformation.

That tidal wave of grief in Jewish history, which swept unchecked for almost two millennia, reached its high point in the Holocaust. This devastating blow was the climax of the exilic age of suffering. The Shoah was so shattering that, unlike the previous catastrophes that occurred during the exile, it could not be incorporated into the existing fast day of Tisha B'Av. Therefore, the Jewish people added another day of mourning and tragedy to its sacred calendar. In the process, Jewry converted a day in the month of Nissan—hitherto a month reserved exclusively for joy because it was the month during which the Exodus occurred—into this new day of grief. Understandably, traditional religious groups resisted this "takeover," but the urgency and power of the pain of the Holocaust could not be denied. Yom Hashoah could not be subsumed under the rubric of Tisha B'Av because the catastrophe and the suffering that the new day commemorates were too massive to be overshadowed and absorbed by the memory of the destruction of the First and Second Temples. The majority of the Jewish people intuitively made the right religious response, i.e., adding a distinctive mourning day to the calendar to express the profound sorrow caused by the Shoah. But this proved to be a climax that exhausted the historical wave of grief. In this sense, Yom Hashoah is the high-water mark of the tide of tragedy in Jewish history.

The reestablishment of the state of Israel signaled the beginning of a new age of joy and triumph in Jewish life. To celebrate the birth of the state and the reestablishment of the value of Jewish life and the reassertion of Jewish dignity, a day of rejoicing, Yom Haatzmaut, was added to the calendar. It is striking and symbolically appropriate that the day of celebration transforms a day hitherto designated for semi-mourning (e.g., during the seven-week *sefirah*—the *omer* period) into a day of joy. Thus the movement of Jewish history—expressed in the calendar—shifts to the side of life, joy, and rejoicing. Again, some traditional groups resisted this reversal, but for the majority of the Jewish people, the weight and significance of this new Exodus could not be denied. I believe with a wholehearted faith that the reversal of this tide is the happy lot and sacred task of this generation. The goal is the fulfillment of the prophet Isaiah's promise: "The days of your mourning are completed" (Isaiah 60:21).

To celebrate Yom Haatzmaut is to make a statement of faith. This victory is not a temporary interruption of the age of exile and suffering. The birth of Israel represents a fundamental change of the Jewish condition, which will never be reversed—if we can help it. We pledge our lives. The age of sorrow is over. The time has come to add happy days.

Now see what God and Israel have wrought. Within nineteen years, with the liberation of the Old City of Jerusalem and the unification of the city in the Six-Day War, another great triumph for life was accomplished. In the enthusiasm and happiness of that event, the rabbinate proclaimed "Yom Yerushalayim" to be a day of celebration. Again, a day of semi-mourning during the *sefirah* period was moved from the side of sorrow to the side of joy. Here, I invoke a stock-market principle. To establish a trend, one cannot judge from a one-time event. To establish whether there is a bull market or a bear market, there must be a series of higher highs (bull market) or lower lows (bear market). Adding the second day of rejoicing provides a very important benchmark. Yom Yerushalayim proves that Yom Haatzmaut is not a historical "fluke"; on the contrary, Israel Independence Day is the first of a series, and Yom Yerushalayim is the second. When Israel has a full peace treaty with all its neighbors, another day will be added to this cycle. In time, I believe that the days between Yom Haatzmaut and Yom Yerushalayim will be filled in—as one whole period of rejoicing and celebration. During those days, mourning and grief will be overshadowed. These three weeks of joy will become the counterpart—the "antimatter" of joy that annihilates the "matter" of grief—to the three weeks of sorrow between the seventeenth of Tammuz and Tisha B'Av.

Consider the following small but powerful symbol. Yom Haatzmaut occurs in the period of the *omer* during which, traditionally, Jews are not allowed to be married. Yet the Israeli rabbinate has affirmed that this should be a day of joy; therefore, it is permitted to hold weddings on this day. Yom Yerushalayim is in the same category. Thus, we liberate day after day from the shadow of grief and catastrophe. As we celebrate these days, as we add joy to new periods of the Jewish calendar, we witness with our lives that in this age, Jewish history will pile joy upon joy.

Is there a guarantee of this projection? No. Are the continuing risks clear? Is it more dangerous to live in Israel than to live as an individual Jew elsewhere in the world—especially in America, where Jews are safer? Of course. But with faith and faithfulness, the Jewish people acts out of a deep, quiet conviction that the change of course is irreversible. My prediction is made with full confidence: the days of sorrow are behind us; the days of rejoicing are only beginning. Of course, there is no automatic necessity for this scenario of joy to come to pass. The matter is in our hands. The partnership of God and Israel, the partnership between Diaspora and Israel, are both needed to make sure that this prediction comes true. But I believe that every Jew who celebrates is making a statement—not only of thanksgiving for the miracles, but of faith that all of this is part of a process of transformation that is as yet unfinished. I am confident that the words of Zechariah will also be fulfilled. The four special days of mourning for the Temple will be turned into holidays because we will live to see the full restoration of the Jewish people. (See Zechariah 8:19.)

Q. Rabbi, do you connect this process of restoration in Israel to the rebuilding of the Temple?

Greenberg. Yes and no. In the Jewish tradition, there is a very strong association between the return to Israel and the restoration of the Temple. Both are classic signs of the validity of the covenant and the eventual triumph of life. I pray for the restoration of the Temple every day, especially since the final triumph—the messianic age—is so connected with the restoration of the Temple.

However, by one of those paradoxical surprises of history, it turns out that on the Temple Mount, the place where the Third Temple should exist, there are two magnificent Moslem mosques. To me, this concatenation is a symbol of a more general tragedy. The Jewish restoration and the revival of Jewish Israel turned out to be in some conflict with the Arab presence in the land of Israel and with the awakening Arab hopes for themselves. As a result, there have been terrible conflicts and great defeats for the Arabs with suffering for Jews and Moslems alike. I believe that the Arabs brought conflict and suffering upon themselves, for the most part, because they refused to make room for the rebirth of Jewry. Still, I understand their suffering. To me, and for most Jews, it is a tragedy that Arabs had to die as a consequence of our new life. If only they would stop the fighting so that we would have less of this suffering. But whatever their share of the blame, I mourn their losses. The Jewish people never wanted that its spiritual dignity and national fulfillment should come at the expense of Arab existence.

When Arabs attack Israel and Jewry and, in the course of defending ourselves, some Arabs are killed or some Arab settlements are uprooted, I regret this outcome—but I feel fully justified in taking the necessary steps for self-defense. However, I see no morally defensible, plausible scenario whereby the Arab mosques could be removed from the Temple Mount. The lunatic attempt to hasten the redemption by blowing up the El Aqsa mosque was all wrong. Therefore, there is no natural way that I can project that will clear Mount Moriah and enable Jewry to rebuild the Temple. If the price of getting Arabs off the Mount is some ferocious war or gross conflict between Jews and Arabs, I do not want that outcome. Spiritually, Jews do not need the Temple that badly. Winning a Temple at some grotesque human cost to Jews and Arabs would make the acquisition so inherently flawed that it would not be constructive. So I pray and I wait. While we wait, there are many constructive things to do.

Q. But then what is the point of praying for the Temple? And what is the full meaning of religious restoration for us?

Greenberg. The Temple was meant to serve as a microcosm for the world of perfection that Judaism seeks to achieve. The Temple was an ideal place where only life (and no human death) was allowed. Here, perfect human specimens, priests without flaws or physical handicap, served. The Beit HaMikdash was the model of the future messianic world. This model is based on a very powerful Jewish idea. To perfect the whole world in a realistic and doable fashion, you should start with one place and then widen the circle of redemption. First, the Temple is liberated for life; then we expand its parameters to include Jerusalem, the city. Then we make Israel—the whole land—a perfect place of peace and prosperity, of social justice and human kindness. Eventually, Israel will be turned into a Garden of Eden for the whole Middle East. Ultimately, the whole world will become God's "holy mountain." That is the prophetic projection.

The Temple incarnates this dream. It spurs us to try to realize the ideal. Therefore, I pray with a full heart for that stimulus to be restored. But we do not need an actual physical Temple, at such a horrendous price, to serve as a galvanizing model. In the mind's eye, through prayer and ritual, the future Temple can continue to express our dreams symbolically even before it is actually restored.

Second, in praying for the restoration of the Temple, I am praying to be close to God, to feel that ancient sense of immediate presence. A direct line to God (as the Jews experienced in the Temple) would be a blessing. With good faith, I pray for that restoration, whether or not it is the will of God (or the need of humans) that it be brought back in a structure laid out with the exact building plan of Solomon's Temple. As far as I am concerned, I pray for the substance of the relationship. The design of the exact costumes of the priests, the choice of the tabernacle model—be it Solomon's, or Herod's, or Ezekiel's projection—I leave to God. In fact, since I do not see any human way to achieve rebuilding without a tragic cost to everybody, I conclude that I am going to leave the whole matter to God.

Rav Shlomo Goren made the same ruling. Rav Goren stated that the Temple will be handed straight down from heaven miraculously. According to the sources, it will come down whole and be placed on the Temple Mount. Together with Rabbi Goren, I would like that to happen. After coming to this conclusion, it flashed through my mind that God has a sense of humor. Maybe when the heavenly restoration occurs, the sanctuary will descend and sit on top of the Dome of the Rock without crushing it. Maybe it will be held up by jets of air, like those tennis courts with a bubble cover overhead. As I said, I leave all of that to God.

Let me also confess that while I would very much like to have a Temple, I share some of Rambam's ambivalence about the actual *korbanot*—because I am a priest (*kohen*). Please understand that I considered becoming a doctor—until I realized that I could not stand the sight of blood. Secretly, I have always had this nightmare: They restore the Temple; they take me into the Temple as the service priest of the day; they take out the first ox; the Levite choir sings; they cut the ox's throat; I faint. That is the end of my grand moment! (Sometimes, people are lucky when their dreams are not fully realized.)

Nevertheless, I pray with all sincerity for restoration because I yearn for the closeness to God. I yearn for the purity that the Temple invoked. Consider Psalm 24, the entrance prayer chanted by pilgrims going up to the Temple. "Who can ascend God's holy mountain? Who can stand in God's sacred place? [Only] a person of clean hands and pure heart, a person who never used God's name for a fraud and who never swears falsely." Think of the power of a place where visitors felt that, before they could enter, they had not only to immerse their bodies but to stop lying and stop taking advantage of people. I would love to have in our midst a place that inspires that degree of awe and ethical integrity.

When people fixate on literal recreation of the Holy Temple now, they are led to the *reductio ad absurdum* of Ateret Kohanim and other such groups seeking to reestablish the Temple. To clear space and advance these projects, there have been assaults on Arabs, bribes and pressures on Arabs to leave, resort to various means to raise tensions between Israel and the Arabs. These tactics are the best proof that the proponents are on the wrong track. The Temple is meant to be restored when it can be done with clean hands. If it turns out that it is not possible because of the Arab presence, then it would be a great tragedy to restore the Temple through a cruel expulsion or a genocidal war. Rather, I will continue to pray that the ultimate reconciliation of these conflicts will come from God.

Q. But what can God have in mind? What can be the message of the Temple Mount being preempted by Moslems? The mosques are located there because, in those centuries, Moslems felt no "liberal" pangs of conscience. They simply destroyed whatever Jewish or Christian holy places existed and replaced them with mosques.

Greenberg. Maybe God wants to teach us respect for other people's religions. Maybe the message is that all of Abraham's children should have access to the Temple Mount. Maybe the lesson for religious Jews is that the concepts behind the Temple have been lost and that we need more years—even centuries—to absorb these values before we are worthy of building the sanctuary. Maybe the fact that the actual Temple eludes our grasp serves to remind us, even against our will, that the restoration of Israel is far from perfect.

I believe that Israel's rebirth constitutes a Divine sign of presence and redemption. This idea could be easily extended and turned into a false absolutization of the religious significance and ethical standards of Israel. The inability to achieve the symbolic liturgical completion or perfection may serve as a constant reminder that the redemption has begun to take hold, but is far from complete. There is much to be done to give full dignity and equality to all Jews in Israel, and to Jews and Arabs alike.

Q. Rabbi, you have indicated in previous interviews what some of Israel's accomplishments have been in the roughly five decades of statehood. What are the accomplishments you look for in the years to come?

Greenberg. The most important model that the world is looking for now is an exemplar of successfully living with affluence, power, and freedom. Modern culture has given us tremendous affluence, but also enormous problems. Materialism, loss of purpose, and excessive consumption erode the human environment even as they lead to the pollution of nature. The world needs models of how to live with affluence so that everyone does not turn selfish. Judaism teaches how to appreciate and enjoy wealth and yet to properly share it. The *halachah* helps us take action to produce, yet also teaches how to feel that the wealth is a gift to be shared. The *halachah* instructs us that the world is not just for humans; it is to be preserved for all God's creatures.

Sukkot is the great holiday of rejoicing—celebrating the year's harvest and wealth in general. At the same time, Sukkot teaches us how to share; it teaches us about our vulnerability and fragility. The holiday's halachic practices teach that wealth is not the most important thing. For example, people leave their fancy year round homes and dwell in the *sukkah.* Israel needs to further develop some of these models.

I look forward to Israel overcoming the problem of poverty, and not just for Jews. Twenty-five percent of Israel's population lives below the poverty line; among Israeli Arabs, poverty reaches 40 percent. Israel must become a world-class model of how to make a lot of money and bring people out of poverty. This would be particularly helpful for countries with limited natural resources and with significant portions of the population born in premodern cultures. Israel's entrepreneurial model should include ethical restraints and environmental protection. To accomplish this goal, Israel will have to remove the restrictions of socialism and nonresponsive bureaucracy. The productivity, the use of technology, and the enterprise for which Jews are known must be unleashed. Worldwide, the Jewish people is known for its business skills. Let Israel raise its affluence level and simultaneously show people how to use the wealth properly. I would like to believe that, with a higher standard of living, Jews would know how to share with those who need help. If Israel could overcome its current poverty, it could use its resources further to help other people in that part of the world. The Arabs are afflicted with poverty, and Africa, which is nearby, suffers the most deprivation of all. There is a fertile field in Africa for Israeli help.

All that was said about affluence applies to power, as well. On the one hand, Israel could show the world a model of how to use power, technologically as well as politically. Let Israel apply its power to stop war, to protect itself, to be safe. Then it can serve as a regional model of how to wield force to preserve the peace, using control, restraint, and fine tuning. The same principle applies to Jewish power—economic, political, technological, and medical. The whole world is struggling with ecological problems. Israel has serious problems of air pollution, and lags behind in recycling. Medicine is another field to be upgraded. There are a large number of Israeli doctors, yet they are not paid well; they often leave to find better conditions abroad. Yet Jews have always been outstanding doctors. Israel could become the medical center of the Middle East; clinics could become self-supporting. They could become so outstanding that people would fly in from all over the world. If Saudi Arabians fly to the Cleveland Clinic, why should they not fly to Petah Tikvah?

Irving Schneider, a great personal friend, underwrote a children's medical center next to Beilinson Hospital. The center moves me deeply every time that I visit it. They take children who are frightened, sick, and facing painful treatment. The institutional setting has been made responsive to children's needs. The layout, scale, colors, and staff set an atmosphere of love for the child that removes some of the fright of being sick in a hospital. In giving his incredible gift, Schneider set a condition that this center would be open to children from throughout the Middle East. He made that request (which the Israelis accepted) long before the prospects of peace opened up. What a magnificent act of faith in the future! Miraculously, the vision is now coming true. The hospital establishes Israel as the state-of-the-art for children's medicine. Let this become the standard Israeli role. Israel ought to have the world's best hospitals, and people will fly in from all over the world to be cured—and to learn how to cure.

Finally, there is the challenge of freedom. Will freedom lead to the total flowering of individualism? I hope that it will. Will freedom lead to anarchy, narcissism, and total egoism? I pray that it will not. Let Israel become a living example of the proper use of freedom. There are models to draw upon in the *halachah* and history to guide the experiment. The Jewish tradition affirms the dignity of every individual, asserting that every life is worth the equivalent of a whole world. At the same time, Torah incorporates a powerful dialectic of family and community. The Jewish tradition nurtures people in their freedom. Let Israel show how, instead of using that freedom to give up their past heritage, people freely use their loyalty to renew that tradition. The whole world needs this model. I look forward to the next forty years when, it is to be hoped, the arrival of peace will free Israel to concentrate on these concerns.

One final point. In these last decades, the state of Israel has received enormous financial support from world Jewry. This has been good for Diaspora Jewry. Now, with the crisis of intermarriage and assimilation in world Jewry, Israel can become a major resource for the Jewish communities. We must provide opportunities for people to come to Israel to study, to nurture their religious souls. Learning in Israel is incomparable. Take our children's experience: After graduation from high school, each child spent a year or more studying in Israel. They felt that they accomplished much more learning in those years than they did spending equivalent time in American study centers. Let us enable every Diaspora Jewish child to study in Israel. New schools, new *yeshivot*, new frameworks must be set up for them because there are not enough Israeli institutions to handle the youth of America. The whole network of study options—from yeshiva to university, from short-term to long-term—should be expanded and made available. Thus, Israel would become a major source for Jewish renewal and survival throughout the world.

Israel can also send out *shlichim* to serve local communities worldwide. It can send money to help fund Jewish education throughout the world. This may sound utopian, but it will be possible when Israel becomes truly productive. Israel already has some of the largest concentrations of Jewish wealth in the world. Take the Israeli banks (which went broke, and had to be bailed out by the government!). One or two of these banks (now restored) are greater in resources than the fabled Rothschild fortune. I look forward to Israel's economic might allowing it to help Jews and non-Jews alike. Those are some of the potential accomplishments of the next half-century.

You will note that I have not projected that Israel will give birth to a religious renewal of Judaism in this next generation. Such a rebirth would narrow the gap between religious and secular, would inspire and strengthen Diaspora Jewry, and would project Torah Judaism on the world scene as a world-class faith to be reckoned with. I pray for this development every day. There is a deepening of Jewish learning and a "thickening" of Torah culture under way. Sooner or later, when such vitality interacts with a dynamic general culture, it should generate a renaissance. But I cannot detect it yet. I fear that religious withdrawal, polarization, and hardening is going to increase before things get any better. Still, we must never stop praying for the fulfillment of the prophetic promise that "out of Zion shall go forth Torah and the word of God from Jerusalem." Israel is a great religious center now, but the renewal that will motivate nations and peoples to go up to it for guidance has not yet occurred.

Q. Israel is now the only major Jewish community in the world that is growing significantly. The Diaspora population is aging and, some demographers believe, declining. The indication is that, some time early in the next century, Israel will become the largest Jewish community in the world. Is there, to your mind, the danger that these Diaspora communities, principally the United States, are about to lose their critical mass and power, thereby weakening Jewry as a whole, depriving Israel of principal support?

Greenberg. Israel is central to Jewish faith. It is also becoming demographically and statistically the center of the Jewish people. In 1933, 1 percent of the Jewish population of the world lived in Israel. At the time the state was declared, the *yishuv* constituted 5 percent of world Jewry. Today, Israel's population makes up over one-third of the world Jewish population. The trend continues upward. There are two primary causes of the trend. The Israeli birthrate is higher; the average Israeli family is larger than the average American Jewish family. This growth is compounded by *aliyah* from communities at risk, such as in the countries of the former Soviet Union. This population transfer is "good for the Jews." However, the other causal factor in the growing percentage of world Jewry that lives in Israel is the cultural disintegration of Diaspora communities. That is a source of great concern.

The issue of a "critical mass" is particularly important. There is tremendous magnetism in the host society. In an open society, the smaller the group, the harder the struggle to maintain itself. A higher concentration of Jews is a positive factor for identity; the impact of higher Jewish percentages already affects American life. For example, the rates of intermarriage are much lower in the central Jewish population clusters such as New York City. As the Jews moved South and West into smaller communities, intermarriage rates rose sharply. Intermarriage rates are highest in the Southwest, where Jews are most spread out and there are fewer Jewish neighborhoods.

The question reasserts itself. What can we do about this demographic decline in the Diaspora? Some Jews make *aliyah* in the belief that this is the way to ensure the future Jewish character of their family. However, many Jews are not going to leave the Diaspora unless there is a security crisis that forces them out. It is hard for people psychologically to transform their lives, to adjust to a new language and culture. For some, it is hard to move to a new place even if they are at ease and welcome there. Therefore, the percentage of Diaspora Jews that will come to Israel voluntarily likely will remain small. The conclusion is: We dare not write off Diaspora Jewry. We must look to upgrade Jewish communities worldwide. Israel should include strengthening Diaspora Jewry in its own mission. This would make clear that Israel is not just another Middle Eastern state, but that its people see themselves as responsible for the outcome of Jewish history. The only consolation prize I can offer the Israelis is that if they do strengthen Diaspora Jewry, *aliyah* will increase!

Q. Through the years, the political and economic support of American Jewry has been an important element in Israel's struggle for survival and development. There are those who speak now of a falling-off in interest in Israel within the American Jewish community, and especially in the younger generation. Do you believe that this is true? Is there anything more that Israel can do now to strengthen the ties between the two communities?

Greenberg. Steven M. Cohen, who has done studies over the years, insists that there is a significant drop-off in attachment when you compare the generational cohorts. The people who lived during the Holocaust and the rebirth of Israel have a tremendously high intensity of involvement. My recollection is that 65 percent said that if Israel were destroyed, it would be a tremendous shock. That percentage drops in every subsequent generation. When Cohen asked people to rate Israel as very important, average, or not very important, the lower rating numbers go up in the younger generation. It is hard to argue with statistics, but my personal observations tell me otherwise.

I am convinced that the statistics are describing a surface phenomenon; they do not plumb the depths of Jewish feeling. In 1956, when President Eisenhower put heavy pressure on Ben Gurion to withdraw Israeli forces from Sinai, the American-Jewish leadership panicked. Basically, they insisted that Israel get out as soon as possible. In the year before the Six-Day War, Stanley Lowell of the American Jewish Congress participated in a dialogue with Israelis, which I also attended. Lowell was very insulted that the Israelis gave him the usual lecture about making *aliyah.* He complained, saying that he was an American citizen, and was proud to be one. In his climactic oration, he stated that if there were a war between Israel and America, he would support America. Within one year's time, the Six-Day War evoked a tremendous outpouring of American Jewish feeling. To put it bluntly, Lowell's words were an utter misrepresentation of what Jews would do and how they really felt.

I am convinced that the same factor is operating today. Therefore, Cohen's statistics are misleading. In any crisis, I would wager that there would be a repetition of this overwhelming outpouring of love and support for Israel. Moreover, I affirm that the underlying attachment was always there. The Six-Day War triggered the expression of feelings that were already there; it did not generate those feelings. The same holds true today.

Of course, I do not deny that there have been some shifts. The media have been broadcasting negative views of Israel for a long time, especially since 1967 (and more so since 1982). Among people who want to be "politically correct," Israel has not been "in" for some time now. However, that group is not that important. In a real crisis, I wager that American Jews would be shocked at the positive intensity of their own response.

One proof that Cohen is seriously underestimating the depth of American Jewish commitment to Israel is found in American Jewish response to political confrontation. In 1979 and 1982, Presidents Carter and Reagan hinted at dual-loyalty issues when Jews fought the sale of AWACS to Saudi Arabia. Unlike their behavior in 1956, American Jews acted to publicly defy both presidents. The tremendous growth in Jewish involvement in American politics over the last decade was primarily driven by the desire to ensure American political support for Israel. These trends are not controlled in a centralized fashion. The informal network of Jews connected with each other politically does not operate by giving orders. In the 1960s, and particularly in the 1970s, there was a feeling that Israel was going to have a hard time. Then Jews started to flood into political life. These Jews were proud of being Jewish; they were not embarrassed to tell politicians that Israel was their main issue and to ask for support. I remain convinced that, at the deepest levels of the Jewish soul, that same profound attachment to Israel continues.

It may be that the assimilating Jews are exhibiting the weakness in attachment that is showing up in Cohen's studies. Even for them, I believe that Israel remains one of the most powerful attractions. Perhaps we will never know whether Cohen's statistics are right or my intuition is right. I pray that there will never again be the kind of crisis—with a threat of the destruction of Israel—to prove which one of us is correct.

On the other hand, there is a way to take out an "insurance policy" on Israel's centrality. Israel should become the center of Jewish life by building Jewish identity. The minute an individual's Jewish loyalty intensifies, Israel becomes a natural emotional attachment for those feelings; study in Israel and connection with Israel become more important. There is no doubt in my mind that, as the percentage of American Jews who study and visit in Israel increases considerably, the attachment to Israel will deepen. Thus, more time and study in Israel should be part of an overall, comprehensive Jewish education and identity program to save world Jewry. Israel—directly as a focus for loyalty, and indirectly as a nurturing ground and connecting link—must play a major role in American Jewry's future. That is the best guarantee that the strength of attachment to Israel will always be there.

Q. Israel's connection with American Jewry and its political problems is one kind of concern for the future. Another concern relates to Israeli life internally, the cultural life of Israel, and the secular–religious character of Israel. There are religious people who contend that Israelis are not "Jewish enough." What is your thought on that?

Greenberg. People do not appreciate the extraordinary richness of Jewish life in Israel. The Jewishness appears everywhere in every way! The street names are suffused with Jewish history and values; the language of the street is a deeply Jewish Hebrew. Consider one fact: Living in Israel in 1992, I did not know that it was Christmas season until it was practically over. By contrast, I was fully aware when Yom Kippur and the other Jewish holidays were occurring. (That is to say, one need not be religious to know when holidays are. The media, the stories, the entire environment broadcast the message; it is impossible to miss it.) Israel's Jewishness is revealed in the proliferation of kosher food; often it takes a special effort to get nonkosher items. Wherever one turns, one is struck by the availability of Jewish books. Historical associations thrust themselves at you wherever you go in Israel. The staggering historical texture of the land nurtures a rich Jewish life.

Ironically enough, the depth of the Jewish atmosphere and the extent of government and communal support also encourage a measure of extremism and fanaticism. People are so wrapped in Jewishness that they can afford to be increasingly more extravagant in their expressions and expectations. In Israel, the *haredim* become more *haredi*. Paradoxically, they do not appreciate the state of Israel, but the environment that Israel provides makes their lifestyle possible. The government supports their institutions as well as all others.

The education system is another example of Israel's richness.

Day schools now educate over 30 percent of American Jewish youth. The percentage used to be much lower. (The day-school percentage share of Jewish youth attending Jewish school doubled in part because many less affiliated Jews stopped sending their children to Jewish school altogether.) In Israel, the number of children who attend all-day schools that include substantial Jewish education reaches 90 percent. Even though Israel has only one-third of the worldwide Jewish population and maybe 40 percent of the children, Israelis constitute 70 percent of those who are receiving intensive Jewish education (that is, the number of Jewish children around the world who are studying all day in total Jewish environments that include Jewish studies).

The incredible density of Jewish life in Israel and the nurturing environment provided by government action and cultural norms is not adequately appreciated by Jews around the world. For example, Lubavitchers focus on 770 Eastern Parkway as if Crown Heights can be as holy as Jerusalem. But Eastern Parkway lacks the same extraordinary density. One will never have the experience on Eastern Parkway that one has walking the streets of Jerusalem, where one actually absorbs Jewish history or the message of the prophets. In Israel, you experience the tangible presence of Jewish religion and Jewish history as you can nowhere else in the world.

Now, what about secular Israelis? On the one hand, the Israeli medium is so rich that observance levels are much higher. Secular Israelis keep the holidays in a secular fashion, but they observe them at a much higher rate than do Jews worldwide. The percentage of Israelis who keep kosher is in the 60th percentile. This is quantum leaps higher than anywhere else in the world. The rate is a compound of food availability, media attention, and social expectations; the sense of history; friendship circles; paths of least resistance; and so on. Nevertheless, there is a certain vulnerability among secular Israelis. Much of their observance and general Jewish behavior is done without deep commitment or conscious choice. Many of their Jewish feelings are conditioned by the self-evident nature of Jewish living. This foundation is vulnerable when they go abroad and live among a gentile majority. If they go on *yerida,* they cannot bring this element with them. The secular Israeli often does not have a consciously articulated Jewish identity and preference for Jewish values. Therefore, when peace comes to Israel, and relations with Moslems, Christians, and the world expand, there is a definite possibility that the new friendships could lead to assimilation and further loss of purpose.

Q. Rabbi, when I hear you speak about Israel, I have the feeling that any Jew who cares about being Jewish, but lives outside of Israel, must go to Israel in order to live a full Jewish life.

Greenberg. Obviously, I am not practicing what I am preaching. Blu and I are still living in America, although we plan to make *aliyah.* We have not made *aliyah* yet partly because there was a job to do for Jewish cultural and religious life in America. In general, I am very much against making *aliyah* out of disillusionment with America. I do worry about the future of American Jewry, but I am equally convinced that *shlilat ha-golah* (denial of the validity or viability of the Diaspora) is mistaken. *Shlilat ha-golah* is a negative definition of Zionism and of Israel; it is not helpful to Israel or to Diaspora Jewry. More Jews should go to Israel drawn by its attractions, rather than repelled by Diaspora's dangers. Jerusalem—what a magnet! (I am showing my traditional "claws." Tel Aviv and Haifa do not have the same impact on me. I am probably overestimating traditionalism. There is a lot of richness in the cultural life; important literature, music, and art are coming out of Tel Aviv. Even though I have a deep love for Jerusalem, I do not mean to say that nothing is going on elsewhere.)

Q. In thinking of the future, Rabbi, I would like to ask you about the notion of evolutionary historical and spiritual development. I detect a certain parallel here between your thinking and that of not only Jewish thinkers like Rav Kook and Mordechai Kaplan, but someone like the theologian scientist Teilhard de Chardin. Have they influenced you? Do you have the sense of the human future as some kind of progress in spirituality toward greater closeness to God?

Greenberg. The fact that I was trained as a historian has had a powerful influence on my thought. My religious conceptions have been affected by modern historical thinking. One of the main contributions of modern culture has been to incorporate the historical dimension in all understanding. This historical sense has often turned into historicism. The axiom of constant change has become a big threat to the timeless, unchanging image of Judaism. Despite this shake-up of Jewish tradition, historical evolutionism has been a constructive force because it has brought our thinking into concrete reality, down from the timeless eternal into the world of human beings. As Rabbi Soloveitchik stresses repeatedly, Judaism is not oriented to find religious meaning by escaping from this world. Rather, God "comes down" into this world. God self-limits in order to be present with us. Holiness is brought from heaven to earth. So, the historical concrete is at the heart of Judaism's understanding. There is not just one universal earth, homogenized, that will some day be all-holy. There are concrete holy lands; there are clusters of human religion and cultures, each with specific memories and specific family attachments.

Still, some of the influences on my thinking have come from modern conceptions of progress and improvement. Even though I rebelled against them, and even though I was deeply distraught by the Holocaust and felt that it shattered many of these categories, still the concept of progress left a trace in my thought, even as I fight it. But there were other positive influences. The prophetic visions are strongly future-oriented. Rav Kook has certainly had an influence. Looking back, we can say that his native optimism sometimes reads as naive optimism. His palpable sense of cultural progress sometimes strikes me as excessive. Nevertheless, I was moved by Rav Kook's teachings and inspired by his model, especially his hope.

My American background has certainly influenced me. America is an optimistic country. David Hartman always teases me that I am typically American because I think that for every problem there is a solution. Like Rabbi Soloveitchik, he is more pessimistic and tragic in his thinking. Apparently, I cannot so easily shake off the innate American conviction that the good will win out and that things are getting better.

In truth, I did not read many of Teilhard de Chardin's writings. However, I explored medicine and biological thinking partly because of my fascination with that area of science (which Rabbi Soloveitchik initially inspired in me) as representing the frontier of human power and dignity and the growing human ability to improve life. As I studied those areas more and more, I intuitively identified with de Chardin's views. De Chardin was a spiritual person who had a deeply religious reaction to the world (an inherited tradition of Catholicism that should not be dismissed). When I did encounter his work, I was touched by it. The tradition of Orthodox Judaism has influenced me equally. Reflect upon the Bible, especially its Genesis and other creation texts, and you will find the same framework. There is a Creator God who cares. The world is developing under God's gaze. The goal is an end of days in which life will be perfected. De Chardin and I are responding to the same complex of God, Creation, covenant, and redemption. Whether it is a conscious identification or just a parallelism, I am happy to be identified with his positions because I think that they are truly inspired as they paint the sweep of cosmic history. (Mind you, one must demur at this point. We are living in the age after the Holocaust. We must be on guard against slipping into any idea of automatic cosmic progress. In this century, we have seen higher highs for human culture, but also lower lows.)

Still, in all our policy considerations, we cannot ignore the remarkable breakdown of totalitarian regimes, the spread of democracy, the spread of the ideas of human equality and dignity. Perhaps I am responding optimistically because I am temperamentally optimistic. But, if so, let me offer the mirror image of Delmore Schwartz' famous line that "even paranoids sometimes have enemies." I would argue that "even optimists are sometimes realists." There have been moments and levels of progress in this century from which we can deduce that reality is supportive of our greatest hopes. To offset that tendency to be optimistic, I work to ensure that I never look away from ugly threats or the potential for evil that still resides in human hearts. The persistence of evil is why Israel has to be powerful, why its army must be kept strong. For this reason, I have striven always to think realistically in foreign policy judgments.

My strong streak of optimism makes me more willing to take certain risks and to look for optimistic scenarios for breakthroughs. All these elements have played a role in shaping my world outlook. My mother was a deeply optimistic woman who always communicated that attitude to life to her children. In fact, she usually denied that any problems really existed. She always insisted that the world was better or that life was going to be better. Whether the personal models of my life or the temperamental chemistry or the influence of thinkers who have shaped me, the bottom line is that I do believe that we are living in messianic times. After the Shoah, only a messianic breakthrough would constitute an adequate response to this tragedy.

Q. Rabbi, the idea of the end of days, the goal toward which all history is moving—Do you see that as a "fixed state"? A "stasis"? Is this the completion of history, of man's having worked with God to reach an ideal order? Or is this something that always has to be approached? How would you envision the "ideal end," such a state, such a world?

Greenberg. I have a very strong messianic yearning. Sometimes it is easier to slip into a frame of mind that believes that, when we get to the Kingdom of God, all the improvements will be made. In my more sober moods, I wonder whether a static messianic age would be very boring because there would be no problems or challenges.

There is another way of thinking about the messianic age, however. Consider Genesis. What does God do on the seventh day after completing Creation, after the world is perfected? The answer the Torah gives is: He rests—Shabbat. God does not sit around feeling bored. God *is* on that day. Being, savoring existence, reflecting, expressing love, appreciating life—that is a remarkable state of being. I can conceive of a thrilling messianic age in which people would *be*; they would live and savor friendship, love, being. Of course, it is hard to imagine that we will overcome all evil, war, and killing. But if that miraculous level of life is achieved, there will still be an infinite number of possibilities and stages of growth for people to enjoy.

What will people do when they are in the messianic age? They will love. They will learn. Remember Maimonides' image of *tzaddikim* sitting and studying the Divine Presence and reflecting the radiance of the Divine in their learning? There is a profound truth in Maimonides' vision. The human soul is inexhaustible; the capacity for love—and for learning—is infinite. Therefore, even if one could imagine history reaching the end of all conflict, this does not mean the end of all accomplishment.

Will this messianic age be, in fact, the end of history? My answer is that there is no need to resolve the question now. (There is also no way to resolve the question now!) I would be delighted to get there and face the crisis in actuality. Think of all the people who lived and died trying to get humanity close to that day. I am willing to waive my "rights" to know the answer in advance. Some great anti-utopians have warned us about the dangers of stasis. I share some of their concerns. But it would be a nice problem to have. Consider the billions of human beings on this globe who face hunger, sickness, oppression, arbitrary rulers, war, random violence, and death. How they would long for a life of welfare, health, plenty, and peace that would be utterly boring. Let us bring it to them and then face the crisis of entertaining humanity. It sounds like a crisis to look forward to; I would be delighted to face it.

12

The Teacher of Judaism in the Modern Age

Shalom Freedman (Q). Rabbi, you spoke in an earlier interview of how Rabbi Soloveitchik was a model for you as teacher, in part through his ability to make the most complex subject clear to his students. You also are primarily known to many as a teacher. You have taught in the university world and in the framework of adult Jewish education. All your life, you have been involved with traditional Jewish learning. Can you speak about the conception you have of the ideal teacher? And of which kinds of teaching you prefer?

Rabbi Irving Greenberg. First principle: The Torah is our model for teaching; God is our model for teacher. The Torah communicates some of the most important messages of all time; yet it teaches them in a rich, powerful, and simple way. Very frequently, it teaches through stories. Thus, the sophisticated philosopher is able to hear and learn from its teaching, but so can the (supposedly) simple person. Rabbi Soloveitchik had a strong influence on my teaching style by exemplifying the power of narrative to communicate profound ideas and the power of simplicity. He also showed that if you think through the most complex and difficult concepts until you reach clarity, then you can communicate them in elemental, direct ways. No matter how complex the idea, one can break it down into simpler building blocks that the student can grasp and utilize; it is almost like identifying the basic atomic particles out of which you make very complex molecules and structures. As the student grasps the ideas, he or she is able to apply them. Thus, the teacher empowers the students. That is a truly ethical teaching model. The teacher is not there to show his power, or to show the extent of her knowledge. Frequently, the display of the teacher's accomplishment is distracting or even intimidating. Often, when the teacher starts using scholarly language or displaying erudition, the students feel incompetent, and frequently give up.

One of my father's favorite stories was about rabbinic speeches. In Eastern Europe, rabbis were chosen for their halachic erudition rather than for their speaking ability. Communities vied for the glory of having the greatest scholar. This would increase their prestige vis-à-vis other communities. Typically, the rabbi would sit and learn; he would speak publicly perhaps once or twice a year. The criterion for the really great *talmid chacham* was that his talks were scholarly to the point of incomprehensibility. If the lay individual who hardly ever studied could understand the talk that the rabbi (who had studied full-time all year) had created, then what had the rabbi accomplished in his learning that year? If people understood the teaching, then they would be disillusioned; this meant that their rabbi was a journeyman scholar, not one of the greats. The community could hardly be proud of such a rabbi. The test of rabbinic greatness soon became how quickly the people failed to understand the rabbi's talk. If the audience understood the whole lecture, then the rabbi was a failure; if they were totally lost after a minute, then they would be proud that they had such a great rabbi! My father poked fun at this model because he believed that this was just the opposite of what a true teacher is supposed to be.

This emphasis on comprehensibility for the beginning student does not mean that important material or complex issues should be eliminated from teaching. God and the Torah offer us a different model. A story or a model text can be so rich that it can be grasped at many different levels. Thus, the unlearned and the simple student will understand thanks to the simplicity and the coherent logic; the hidden scholarship and the deeper issues will not confuse or distract them, but will enrich the person who knows more. The person who becomes better informed later can go back to explore the richness and dig out the deeper meanings.

There is an extra joy in discovering the wisdom and self-control that has gone into "hiding" the complexity in the simplicity of the structure and in getting the message across without "showing off" the teacher's great knowledge. A great deal of additional thought must go into breaking down the complex ideas into the constituent elementary "particles" that every kind of student can fully grasp. Thus, every session or piece of writing is deceptively simple, for it really adds up to a complex structure of multiple meanings and patterns.

Second principle: In my career and creations, I have tried to narrow the differences between university and adult informal education. This means that there should be no lowering of content and level standards on the grounds that informal education is not to be taken as seriously as formal settings. Ethically speaking, whatever the context, the student has the dignity of infinite value, equality, and uniqueness. Then the teacher owes it to the students to teach at that level and not to waste their precious time. In every setting, the teacher's goal is never to fail to use time to its maximum value.

An even more important application of this principle is that, whether in synagogue, university, or any other setting, one should try to say the truth. Unfortunately, it has become almost a convention that in the synagogue people do not ask questions. In the university, a student not only asks questions, but is free to challenge and even to say bluntly to the teacher's face that the professor does not know what he or she is talking about. That freedom (or free-for-all) is a strength, not a weakness. If you do not ask, if you do not question, then even if you hear a good sermon, it turns out to be not as good as it could have been. When the learner listens without challenging or even offering adversarial analysis, the student learns less. The tradition of *not* asking or challenging in the synagogue has created an environment in which rabbis need not tell the truth. Sometimes, this convention means that the people expect to be lied to and maybe will be shocked to hear the truth. The university encourages controversy; it may even encourage shock for shock's sake. But the free-wheeling atmosphere puts a check on lying or on conventions of not facing the truth. The touchstone of all good teaching must be integrity, honesty, and free exchange.

These teaching principles flow from the basic principle of human freedom and human dignity. If the teacher shows respect for that freedom, the student learns more, not less. The student's question strengthens, not weakens, the teacher's authority. When I was rabbi of the Riverdale Jewish Center, I went out of my way to invite questions. One of my goals was to try to bring fresh thinking into Orthodoxy. Many people were resistant, even angry, because they did not want to hear a rabbi express ideas they were not familiar with or that they felt were questionable. Then I made it clear that they had a right to argue and question. We would set up times in the afternoon so that they could return to ask questions on views with which they differed. It took a lot of venom out of the opposition. The questions that people asked opened them up to actually hearing and absorbing what I was saying. In general, then, bringing in multiple voices and encouraging questioning is part of good teaching.

Third principle: Here again, God is our model. The ultimate goal of teaching—as the ultimate purpose of the Divine word—is to create an image of God. The task is not to pack in this amount of knowledge or to get across that amount of doctrine. Of course, truth is a very important component in shaping the image of God. When you lie to someone, you tacitly assume their inferiority, which violates their equality and their dignity. Evidence and information are certainly important to teaching. But remember that most of the evidence and information is somehow forgotten. One of the great Bible teachers of our time, Nechama Leibowitz, said that after sixty years of teaching, the one principle she learned that she can absolutely vouch for is that the students remember nothing afterwards. (My variation of that principle is to assume that within six months they have forgotten 90 percent of the material.) The process of transmitting information is low-yield. The teacher should assume that the students will learn a lot on their own.

What is the point, then, of teaching? To develop the student's own image of God, the basic framework of the teaching must respect the equality and uniqueness of the student. The principle of equality means that students are entitled to access the same information that you have. Teaching learning and analysis skills and showing how to approach material is essential. To hide or suppress information in order to persuade the students is wrong. An atmosphere of equality allows for discussion and debate and for multiple voices. The student can contribute to the debate. Equality is practiced when the teacher listens to the students' comments and questions. When the teacher listens, the teacher learns. This is the truth behind the talmudic dictum (which I find to be an empirical fact), "I learned a lot from my teachers . . . but most of all from my students."

One of the most moving experiences in CLAL teaching grows out of this truth. I teach certain texts—for instance, Genesis—that I love deeply. As a student of Genesis for almost fifty years, I read it every year with different commentaries. And I have systematically sought out books on Genesis and read them. Yet, when I teach the text to people who have never looked at it before, I am perpetually astonished. On their own, applying their native intelligence to the text, they come up with 90 percent of the insights that all those scholars, rabbis, and experts have gleaned through the years. I am even more astonished to see how often they come up with something totally new that no scholar, to my knowledge, has written.

A story comes to mind: One day, in studying Abraham's call (Genesis 12:1–3) we rehashed the age-old discussion as to why, by what merit, Abraham was chosen. Did Abraham discover God? (A classic midrash.) Was there some intrinsic greatness in Abraham (and, by implication, in Abraham and Sarah's descendants) that God discerned? (After many commentators and talmudic passages.) Or was the choosing of Jewry some inscrutable movement on God's part, an act of grace, unmerited? (Compare Deuteronomy 7:6 ff and 9:4 ff.) One student spoke up and said: "I believe that God addressed many people then, but Abraham was the (only) one who responded."

The teacher should also factor in the student's own confidence. The rabbis say, *Lo habayshan lamed* (a shy person [afraid to ask] will not learn). If the person who teaches creates an atmosphere of intimidation, students will not learn; if they are afraid to ask, they will learn little.

Another expression of equality is to empower the students, which is to follow the Divine model in the covenant. The first step is not to overwhelm the students. If the students are flooded with information, they may lose their footing, choke or gag on water, develop a fear of the subject. Giving just enough content to allow the students to absorb and to grow in the process is the correct step. But the aim is that the students continue to grow so as to take over responsibility for learning and teaching. The teacher's goal may well be defined as showing the students how to grow in responsibility. This implies that the teacher plays a role as facilitator and gives people a method of analyzing rather than just information. You know the old story: If you give someone a fish, you give that person a meal; but if you teach someone how to fish, you give that person a way of life and a lifetime of eating.

At every step, the teacher should show how the text or the topic was analyzed. Show methods; show comparative approaches of different people. All this is more important than the specific details. The rabbis' assumption is that God gives us general rules. Every *mitzvah*, every word of God has multiple layers of meaning and is subject to further interpretation. Thus, the text includes what every future student will innovate. This conveys a real sense of continuity *and* development. The rabbis stressed interpretation, not just passive acceptance; interpretation implies the importance of personal creativity rather than simply privileging tradition or convention.

The basic framework of a class starts with the axiom of the student's equality and uniqueness. Uniqueness means that a teacher does not give a canned answer. Many times, it seems that the student's question is a known, even standard, question. Yet if you listen carefully, in many cases, the student puts a different shade of meaning behind the question. To respond to that nuance, you cannot just give a standard answer. Teachers who show respect for the student's uniqueness thereby develop the student's uniqueness. A new insight that emerges when a good question is responded to—be it the teacher's or the student's origination—becomes a reward that stimulates even further exercise of the student's capability. Furthermore, teachers develop the student's uniqueness not only by discovering it in the student, but by revealing their own distinctiveness. Let a teacher share the struggle that has gone into crystallizing a teaching. Let the answers to questions be not defensive, but frank. Let teachers reveal where they have found their own path or where they no longer follow the party line. To do this, the teacher must trust the students. (Trust flows from respect for their equality and from love for their infinite value.) The trust (and the revelations) nurture the students; in return, the students sustain and help the teacher grow. Thus, a good teacher is unfinished . . . as is a good student.

These principles are at the heart of the philosophy and ethics of teaching. Note that there is a strong element of ethics in teaching. If you do not observe these rules, you can easily turn teaching into a form of crippling. Schools often educate to stop the process of insight; many teachers operate to deprive students of the freshness of curiosity with which they enter the classroom.

Never forget: teaching is a very important religious calling. It constitutes an imitation of God, the ultimate teacher. The Talmud says that God spends one-third (some say one-quarter) of the day teaching and studying. The whole model of the covenant is a teaching model; the method is designed to bring out the best in people. The end goal is a free person, a person with dignity; that is possible only through education. If you want people to truly become free, you have to help them mature and take responsibility. Indoctrination makes people less free. Intimidation shrinks their image of God. Teaching is the ultimate religious calling, comparable to parenting in that the outcome is the most infinitely valuable creation of all—an image of God. (Note that the laws of *kibbud av v'aym* [parental honor] apply to the *rav muvhak*, the teacher who primarily shaped the student mentally and spiritually.)

It is said that Rabbi Israel Salanter was once approached by a *shochet* (ritual slaughterer). The man wanted to give up *shechitah* because he was constantly haunted by his tremendous responsibility. If he made one false move, he might cause people to violate the law and eat nonkosher meat. He found the burden of responsibility too heavy to bear. Salanter expressed sympathy, but asked what profession would he enter next. The man wanted to become a teacher. At that point, Salanter argued with him. Being a teacher is a far more serious responsibility. If you make one false move, you may destroy not a cow, but a human being. In *shechitah*, one mishandling can cause a certain wound or flaw which may disqualify the meat. But in teaching, one can cause serious mental damage to a child, which can ruin a mind. Rabbi Salanter advised him strongly to remain a *shochet* because that is a much less challenging, much less serious religious responsibility.

Q. How do you deal with the problem of teaching and, in fact, learning with people at different "levels"? Do you have a preference in this? Do you prefer to learn with a certain group at what might be called a "higher level"?

Greenberg. People studying at CLAL come from a wide range of backgrounds of observance and views, as well as from totally different previous learning levels. This is a distinctive pedagogic challenge, and I love it. Remember, the students are not passive. Their contribution and questions profoundly deepen the learning. In principle, the wider the variety of backgrounds, particularly religious backgrounds, the richer the results because we learn so much from each other. Therefore CLAL sets, as a pedagogic goal, the recruitment of students over a wider range than is normally thought to be desirable. Nor are the variations without complications. Not infrequently, the more observant bring a more extensive learning background. This deepens the risk of intimidating the liberal Jews (or of communicating a notion of intrinsic superiority to the observant Jews—also of setting a level too elementary for them).

How, then, can one teach at all these levels at one time? How can one speak meaningfully to conflicting backgrounds simultaneously? One of the ideas I have developed over the years is to use "continuum concepts." Most words and concepts do not have one fixed, narrow band of meaning. The ideal concept is like a radio wave. It may be centered in one spot, but it spreads and has overtones over a wide range. Particularly in the case of rich, well-chosen concepts, the range over which the concept remains meaningful (by analogy, the radio wave is still coherent and has not yet dissipated) may be quite extended. Such concepts have the power to speak to people who are located at many different points and who, in fact, because of their life situation, may be able to hear a different part of the continuum concept. (For some people, their existential situation may permit them to hear at only one point of the very same continuum). These concepts that have a wide, rich continuum of meaning I call "continuum concepts."

At CLAL, we have sought out such concepts and developed them at the core of our repertoire because they have the ability to speak to a wide variety of people with different levels and backgrounds at the same time. Over the years, I have learned to apply this extra test to all ideas that I work on. Sometimes I have found, after developing a good idea, that it does not have this multiple resonance. Then I will dig deeper to find the concept that can get the same needed lesson across, but which, being a continuum concept, can speak to our whole range of students simultaneously. Incidentally, I have found that even the people who would have been satisfied with the narrower band of meaning concept (which might have spoken to them directly, but to others in the same group not at all) are even more excited by the continuum concept, which brings with it other ideas in comparison. Apparently, people's ears pick up the many resonances of meaning and are more deeply touched by the concepts even if they do not "need" or even fully understand the farthest reaches of the idea. It is like hearing stereophonic music; it comes across richer, more resonant than monophonic music.

An example: The word "covenant" has an enormously complex and broad continuum of meaning. It can describe a situation where God "comes down" from heaven; God is revealing and exhibiting miracles, while the human is passive. At the other end of the spectrum, the human can be active and primarily responsible for the action and outcome, while the Divine Partner is deeply hidden and all but inactive (at least in terms of human perception). The concept can describe a wide range of Divine and human intervention and joint projects with a mix of roles that falls between these poles. Yet the whole range is truthfully covered by the same term "covenant." When I bring up the concept in class, the agnostic or atheist sitting there is not turned off by its religiosity. The agnostic or atheist may well interpret it as a purely human covenant—say, between the generations, or between humans and a vision. By contrast, the devout Jew sitting there "hears" it with the mental image of the Divine disposing while people passively receive. Each may be challenged and even moved by further exploration of the idea into changing their initial positions. But the great gain is that they were not repulsed or "swamped" by the idea initially. In its richness, it spoke to them where they were—although the students (all of them) were in very different places. It is like listening to a great concert; the more overtones you capture, the more richness and variety of people who hear it.

Such continuum concepts stretch across whole bands, just like AM or FM. Revelation was intended by the Divine Author to reach widely with the richness of the idea—since God wishes to speak to all. Since humans differ one from the other, they must be reached by separate messages (which separate them) or by continuum concepts (which unite them).

When I was the rabbi at the Riverdale Jewish Center, the congregation consisted of an observant, learned sector and of a non-observant, Jewishly uneducated element. I like to speak extemporaneously. It enables a certain interaction with the audience that a written text prevents. When I would sit down to work on a sermon, often more than one idea would come to me, and I would work out their implications. Often I found a good, even excellent theme, which nevertheless spoke on only one wavelength. This meant that it would touch one group only. But I felt that the rabbi's task was to speak to the whole congregation—both sides, all levels—so that it would live and grow as one (diversified) community. Therefore, I would choose the alternative theme that had the richness to speak simultaneously to each group in its own way. After a while, I could tell very early on if an idea had the strength and range of capacity to become a "continuum concept."

I have come to believe that the "continuum concept" is a key element in the power of revelation. All human concepts grow from the place or spiritual location of the human who has created them. Furthermore, the capacity of the idea to stretch across the spectrum of cultures, languages, and locations and be heard widely is necessarily limited. The Divine idea grows out of an infinite consciousness that stretches across all time, place, and cultures. Humans are limited by their own culture, location, language, and life situation, and therefore may have difficulty hearing the word of God. The revelation has the great advantage of starting everywhere and therefore being intrinsically more accessible. This does not mean that there are not ongoing difficulties in hearing revealed messages. As a body of interpretation builds up, this, paradoxically, brings the word of God closer to people in the culture in which it is written, but makes it that much harder for others to grasp when they are located in other cultures and places. The word of God exhibits its eternal power by including within its continuum such a large range of differing individuals (in various life situations), cultures, languages, and places.

Perhaps this is the meaning of the midrash, "The voice of God is power (lit., in strength)" (Psalms 29:4). This means it is present according to the strength of each and every individual. Psalm 29 celebrates the majesty of God through the majesty of the storm, the power of the storm, and the ocean. But the deeper meaning is that the voice of God is proven by its capacity to make itself available and heard by each individual uniquely, in accordance with the individual's capacity, openness, and life situation. Thus, the Divine word (as the human word) has one meaning to one person, whereas the same word has a different meaning to a different person with a different background. The difference lies not in ambiguity, it is not a tricky shell game, where one shows one thing to one person and something else to the other. Rather, the idea whose meaning stretches across different wavelengths will be able to be received by different receivers. Each person hears the range of the idea that he or she is capable of absorbing; if the person keeps growing, that individual may come to the same place and hear the same meaning as the other person. Conversely, if each locks into the narrowest aspect of the meaning they comprehend, the two ideas may appear to be in total conflict, despite the fact that the two positions are part and parcel of the same idea. Thus, the metaphor's range of meanings is not a reflection of lack of clarity or of inner confusion, but a reflection of the richness of the concept and the variety of people who hear it.

In my view, the depth and breadth of the continuum concept is an important criterion of the validity and value of an idea. In giving the Torah, God wants to speak to all the people—and over all times and places. Indeed, if the Torah did not have this multilayered meaning and texture, how could it speak to nomad shepherds living in the Bronze Age (i.e., the Patriarchs), and speak equally to a commercial merchant in the Middle Ages (say, like Rashi), and again to a computer-science expert in a postmodern technological age? Clearly, many of the Torah's fundamental concepts have been heard and understood quite differently by people in different eras of history and cultures as wide apart as different locations—geographically and in life. But the richness of its concepts has allowed Torah to speak in all these different settings, to different people, in different communities.

The word "continuum" has another implication. The concept is like a conveyor belt. The individual can get on in one place and can move along the conveyor belt to another place. To bring a person fully into the covenant of Torah, this person has to be moved. But the initial point of attraction is the connection. First, one has to capture this person's attention and assent. Remember the creature Pan, who first played the pipes so as to draw people's attention; once hooked, they then followed the melody to their destination. Similarly, the concept reaches out to where this person is, which often is quite far from the center of the idea. Once the "fringe" of the idea has seized people's imagination or has captured their assent, the people involved step on the conveyor belt. As they search, explore, and relate the idea to their own lives and understanding, they move along and may come ever closer to the center of the idea. Had one insisted in advance on offering only one central, narrow concept, these people would not have been reached; perhaps they would have been totally cut off. Because the idea had richness and one was able to articulate it with all its overtones, the concept was able to reach out and draw these people on to the continuum. Eventually, the movement may bring the person to a certain place; yet had I originally demanded that outcome, the person would have been turned off, and the whole experience would not have happened.

The use of continuum concepts is not only more effective in reaching people; it also enables people to make their choice in true freedom. In other words, people can move along, stop at a certain point, or go a little further. In this method, we do not twist the arms (or break the necks) of recalcitrants; we give them the chance to go as far as they can or care to go. Thus, we respect their dignity and freedom and bridge some of those gaps between people at one time.

At CLAL—by using these simplest, most fundamental statements of ideas that are so rich that people take them at one level and later combine them or synthesize the idea with their life condition at a more complex level—we are able to learn with different people at different levels simultaneously. The great bonus is the tremendously exciting variety and color of the interchange. When you have naiveté and complexity in two different students, they listen to each other. Aside from the excitement of the contrast, sometimes the "simpler" person sees things that the more sophisticated one misses . . . or vice versa. The more sophisticated person who sees past the surface is able to analyze the idea into a much richer pattern, and open the eyes of the naive person by saying, "Here is a deeper pattern." Those rewards turn the whole experience into an aesthetic as well as a religious experience.

Q. From what you say, Rabbi, I understand that teaching is, for you, too, a continuous process of learning. But I was wondering, on a more formal level, how you divide your own time between study, learning, and teaching. For instance, the time you give to Torah studies or to *maddah*, modern secular wisdom. Do you have any rules in relation to this?

Greenberg. The classic Maimonidean division is one-third of the time for *Torah She-bichtav*, one-third for *Torah she-b'al peh*, and one-third for the wisdom of the world. However, I fear that I am not that well organized. Maimonides is a much more ordered mind. Personally, I am more like a streak hitter. My time is not divided in regular rhythms. When I read or study, I am totally concentrated on different fields or topics at different times. Therefore, I would be reluctant to offer my personal model as a guide to dividing time for study.

For example, I love reading; that is one of my strengths, but also one of my weaknesses. When I am writing, I may look up a reference; the next thing I know, I am reading and reading—and not writing. I also receive tremendously rich nurturing from people. So I enjoy talking to people and learning from people rather than just engaging in formal study. Along the way, I have found that when I obligate myself to write, that discipline forces me to clarify the issues. Thus, writing refines ideas in a way that almost no other activity can. Personally, it is easier to articulate ideas in speech and in talking with people; I find it harder to discipline myself to put words on paper. Unfortunately, I still spend a great deal of my time in administration and travel. These activities leave limited time for the writing and conceptualizing. However, I still get quite a bit of reading done, especially when traveling; at night I stay awake to read. At home, this happens quite often also.

Editing is the most difficult activity of all. Once I write down the idea, I "remember" it this way as I reread the words. The words appear to have been always (and appropriately) organized in this sequence. The soul of editing is to conceive of the ideas organized in a simpler, clearer, more necessary, and compelling sequence. But once the words are written down, it is hard for me to conceive of an alternative layout or structure.

It is also very difficult for me to carve out time for writing; that involves a different kind of discipline. Getting ideas out into the world through writing is harder for me emotionally. When I speak, there is instant feedback from people. I see their eyes and their body response; afterward, there are questions. In writing, there is isolation. The interaction in speaking pulls me toward the people; the strong sense of presence, as it were, opens up my channels of communication. The words flow. When I write, I feel a sense of living in a vacuum. When I sit down to work, it is like facing the *mishkan,* the Temple of Silence (as Israel Knohl calls it), and hesitating to go in. At first, there is difficulty in putting words down. Something inside me shrinks from entering a world of silence. However, once I enter it, in time, words begin to flow. Interestingly, when I am deep into writing and the phone rings, it is startling; many times it takes me out of my rhythm of writing. Afterward, I have to struggle to reenter this world. All in all, writing is a different kind of learning. When I write out my ideas, people from the past speak to me more, as against interaction with my contemporary interlocutors. Currently, I spend most of my time reading, less time teaching, and the least time writing.

As to your question, how to divide the time between religious and secular learning, I object to the assumptions behind the question. In *Halakhic Man,* Rabbi Soloveitchik repeatedly points out that the *halachah* is monistic, not dualistic; it does not pit this world against the heavenly world or the body against the soul; rather, it strives to unify them. The secular is a constant source of religious insight. Many times, I find movies very stimulating because of the religious issues they raise and the human insights they communicate. Many times, the lessons of politics or of daily life are inseparable from those of religion. In fact, it is a basic principle with me that a good theology "works." If a religious concept does not work in the real world, then it is not good theology, even if it looks good on paper. After all, the Torah is not a book of theory! Nor is it a book of philosophy. The Torah was given to the Jews "with laws and rules . . . to do in order to live by them" (Leviticus 18:5). The real test of the Torah is: Can you live by it? "It is a tree of life to all who hold onto it, and those who uphold it are happy." (Proverbs 3:18). The Torah offers itself as a way of making a better life. The Torah is prepared to be tested empirically by the criterion of how people live it. Rabbi Israel Salanter said, "The Torah came to make a *mensch*"—i.e., not just to communicate esoteric knowledge or brilliant doctrine.

The division of time must reflect the actual life situation. Therefore, one cannot arbitrarily set up a standard day: say, half secular and half religious. The elementary fact is that quantity does affect quality. If one does not study Torah sufficiently, one cannot be good at living by it. By the same token, if a person does not study medicine sufficiently, that person will not be a good doctor. Whatever the field, you have to give it enough time to do it right. You cannot do all the things you want to do. You have to accept limits. One may, therefore, spend whole days, weeks, even years in formal secular study or formal religious study to the exclusion of the other because that concentration is needed to do the matter right. I feel comfortable saying this because I believe that my "secular" work—and that of many others—is truly religious in its nature.

In modern times, the issue of time division has sharpened because there has been an explosion in the quantity of knowledge available. This has led to the growth of specialization, which in turn demands more extended training, but results in higher-level achievement. This has strengthened the conviction of traditionalists that one cannot do justice to Torah study and be a serious scholar or scientist in another area of specialization. I deny this conclusion. It is true that those who spend all their time "learning" will know a lot more Torah than those who do not study so much. But it is also true that many students show limited achievement in the yeshiva world. Therefore, the excuse that because you have to learn Torah there is no time left for secular studies is quite mistaken. The yeshiva methods of learning are not well developed; there is a lot of time wastage. The study of Talmud creates language problems because the text is written in Aramaic. The yeshivas rarely, if ever, give the language training that would make entry swifter and less difficult and the text less likely to baffle and then repel the student. With proper preparation, with development of bibliographical aids and research skills, the average yeshiva student could accomplish much more in the same amount of time. If we can introduce a serious efficiency factor into learning, there can be time for both secular studies and religious studies.

There is also a question of methodologies. At present, the Western methodologies are more sophisticated than the identified Jewish techniques. Those people—such as Rabbi Joseph Soloveitchik—who were positively exposed to Western analytic models found that their insight into Torah was deepened. Such students get more out of the text for the same amount of effort. Maimonides divided the day into thirds, but gave the secular subjects, such as physics and mathematics, subtle but important religious standing. The choice of Torah against secular studies has been overstated in our time. It is possible to say, in some cases, that this subject is purely secular, or purely religious, or mainly secular or mainly religious; but this classification is not ideal. The better way is to develop more effective use of the time that the student has. I refer not so much to a mechanical distribution of time, but an effective utilization of the time in maximizing learning. We could create great Torah scholars who would have sufficient time to study secular culture and to be immersed in modern life—if the yeshiva or traditional learning system was made more efficient, more rational, more sophisticated. Personally, I spend about 40 to 45 percent of my time in administration, and split the rest of the time equally between study (reading) and delivery of services (teaching, lecturing, writing). My typical work week runs well over seventy-five hours. Thank God for *Shabbos* (on which day I do read and study)!

Q. Rabbi, do you think that the role of the rabbi is an unchanging one, or do you believe that it is going to change in the years ahead? If so, how?

Greenberg. You have heard something about my belief that there is an ongoing transformation of the covenant. At every stage in the maturation, the Divine Partner in the covenant becomes more hidden, and the human becomes more active and responsible.

There is a rabbinic counterpart to this theory. According to rabbinic teaching, holiness is ever more widely present, but it is present in a more hidden fashion. Holiness is found not just in the Temple; it spreads to the land, to the Diaspora, to every place where people are. The ultimate logic of development is that the holiness is present everywhere, but is hidden in the secular. In the age of the manifest and visible God, holiness was found in the Temple. The counterpart teachers were the priest and the prophet—visible reflections of the manifest God. The ornate uniform of the priest and his genetic chosenness reflect God's electing will and God's "visible" presence. Ask the priest through the *urim* and the *tummim* (the breastplate), and you get a direct answer from God. Similarly, the prophet speaks the manifest word of God.

In rabbinic times, when God's presence has entered a more hidden phase, a priest is too sacramental to be credible; a prophet is reporting God's voice too manifestly to be heard. (It is almost like trying to broadcast on FM when you have an AM receiver.) The rabbi's appearance is secularized in comparison to the priest and the prophet. After all, anybody can be a rabbi; God does not have to choose the individual. One can volunteer, one can study to become eligible for the title. The word of God comes through human activity and interpretation, which is a "hidden" voice of God. In the past, the prophet declared: "Thus says the Lord." In contrast, the rabbi says: "In my best judgment, applying past models of divine instruction to this moment, this is what God wants of you or of me."

Today, we live in a time of even greater "hiddenness" of God. The Divine is calling on humans to take a greater role in creating or uncovering holiness. The sacred realm is even more masked; it is more widely present, but it needs to be uncovered by deeper digging. In these circumstances, what would be the model of the best teacher? Logic suggests that the teacher would also be more hidden. The rabbi today, especially when the rabbi speaks with rabbinic authority and style, often sounds like the priest or prophet did after the destruction of the Temple. They talk, but you do not hear them. The holiness is too visible. The self-evidence is in dissonance with the hiddenness of actual holiness today. It is almost as if the rabbis are on the wrong wavelength, so their broadcasts are not received.

In typical synagogues, the rabbi speaks as one endowed with the intrinsic authority of the tradition. People would not think of asking questions to the sermon-giver (by contrast to the university, as I have indicated). The ironic result is that the "self-evident" authority comes across as less credible. The authority that can be challenged is more hidden, but it is more credible because it is designed to be heard by contemporary receptors. In fact, the rabbi who has less competition and is less challenged (in the synagogue) is less heard and less effective as a teacher.

One of the concepts undergirding CLAL's work is that, in the age of God's hiddenness, the lay person becomes the natural exponent of what God asks of us. Hence, we seek to train lay people to know and speak for Jewish values and tradition. This does not mean that the lay person enjoys automatic wisdom. If the lay people do not learn, they will not be able to communicate anything. Knowledge is not bestowed by the holy Spirit. However, using their intelligence, through learning and study, lay people can become—should become—the spokesperson and teacher of God's word. When the lay person teaches, one avoids the interference generated by signals that are appropriate for God's manifest presence, but are not appropriate for God's hidden presence. The present-day audience is open to hear the message on the merits of its power. If it points to God's presence, if it commits the listener to holiness, it will be heard.

The hidden rabbis of this era are writers like Cynthia Ozick and Elie Wiesel, or public figures like Natan Scharansky and Alan

Dershowitz. They are modern-day rabbis, though they would be shocked to be designated as rabbis. But cut through the smoke-screen of their title—in fact, they are teaching Torah. Their work passes as secular activity—but that is its strength. By positioning themselves as secular, their words come across as being on the right wavelength. The further implication of this concept is that the lay people as a group have to become as educated, as vivid models as the rabbis have been classically. Then the lay people can become the Torah teachers of this era.

There is another great gain in credibility when a lay person teaches. If a physician and a rabbi come to teach me medical ethics, there is a credibility difference between them. Usually, the *posek* (halachic authority) is not a physician or steeped in medical knowledge. There is inevitably a certain abstract quality—sometimes a tone-deafness in hearing the problem—that shows up in the decisor's view. (This is said notwithstanding the explosion in medical ethics and my appreciation of the rabbis' medical *psakim.*) If the teacher–decisor is a rabbi, internally the physician wonders, "What does the *posek* really know? Has the decisor ever been in this situation, on the spot in a crisis? Does he really know how to guide me?"

A businessperson trusts a fellow businessperson much more than an outside theoretician, be it a rabbi in a yeshiva or a professor at Harvard who never has had to meet a payroll. When the physician meets a fellow physician who has gotten his or her hands dirty in exactly the same way that this physician has, when the businessperson or politician knows that the ethical–religious guidance is coming from a person who has faced the same temptations and pressures, then the credibility of the ruling is considerably greater. By this logic, in our time, the rabbi is less credible than the lay person.

Does this mean the rabbis are out of business? My answer is: In the age of secular holiness, when the lay person becomes the rabbi, then the wise rabbi does not cling to the inherited roles and perquisites of a rabbi. Rather, the wise cleric strives to become a rabbi's rabbi. The rabbi becomes the teacher, the enabler; the rabbi strives to give information. The rabbi empowers a lay person to be teacher on behalf of the rabbi. When the rabbi stands up and claims: "I am the official rabbi; take my word and do not argue," the rabbi loses the argument. The paradox is that when the rabbi gives up the claim to automatic authority, the rabbi gains more influence. This is how to become a rabbi's rabbi.

Q. Rabbi, as you look back, what do you feel have been your greatest achievements and your greatest disappointments in your work? What are your hopes and plans in teaching, in writing, in your work for the future?

Greenberg. I probably speak for my wife as well as for myself when I say that the most important accomplishment in our lives is our children. Not that the family is fully accomplished. The children are still making their own lives; it is too early to say what their final contribution to *tikkun olam* will be. Still, we love them very much and feel that we have raised five people who are truly *tzelem elokim.* (Not that there is not room for improvement; I am a Jewish parent, after all!) To have kept the chain of life going and to have created and nurtured five infinitely valuable, unique people is an accomplishment of cosmic import. I consider this my primary life accomplishment.

As a teacher, I am well aware that the Talmud says: "*Talmidim*—students—are like children," in terms of significance. I deeply appreciate and feel love for every student that I have raised and shaped. Over the years, there have been thousands who have studied with me. Often I think of my father, *zichrono livracha*'s, quotation: "This is my portion out of all my labor" (Ecclesiastes 2:10).

However, owing to my professional life, including the shift from academia to synagogue to academia to organization, I have not raised up really close student-disciples in the numbers that I yearned to achieve. The contacts have been transient and limited, for the most part. Still, I do feel a special sense of gratitude and gratification for the handful of close student-colleagues. If I could live my life over again, I would make a greater effort to work and teach in settings that would allow for extended, substantial learning and bonding.

Professionally speaking, it is too early to rank my accomplishment. I have achieved different goals at different times and have loved most of the work, but the outcomes have not always been what was planned. Recently, I met a couple who met and got married through Yavneh, a religious college students' organization that I helped set up in the early 1960s. I laughed to myself. Yavneh was primarily established to help Orthodox students cope with the challenges of college and to help develop a more intellectual, open, critical, sophisticated Orthodoxy. Yavneh made some contributions along those lines, although that vision of Orthodoxy lost out over the past thirty years. The Yavneh organization did not make it beyond the 1970s. Starting in 1967, I had pulled back from it owing to my other responsibilities. In my mind's eye, I saw Yavneh as a very limited accomplishment—that ended in failure. But who is to say that the official goals are the standard of accomplishment, rather than the *shidduchim* and the friendships that grew out of the organization?

One of the covenantal principles is that work is not finished in one lifetime or in one generation. For some of the issues I have worked on—including the challenge of developing a Judaism that can swim in the sea of modernity—it is too early to say whether or not the work has been successful.

I consider the teaching of students, together with my influence at Yeshiva University in the 1960s, as one of the highlights of my life. The crystallization of a Riverdale Orthodox community, and the creation of the SAR day school as a model of humane, loving, spiritually alive education based on respect for students and their individual uniqueness, are significant accomplishments. Care for each person and for those in need and for *clal Yisrael* has been a major feature of SAR. SAR is an open school designed to allow greater self-development; it has been a trailblazer in its respect for the individuality of the student. The spirit and model of SAR is one of the keystones of my life's work.

I have spent years writing, lecturing, and teaching about the lessons we should draw from the Holocaust and the importance of the Holocaust as a turning point for the Jewish people and the world. Communicating this message is a major challenge; it is a project that is not over yet. There have been significant accomplishments in this work. I have been least successful in the area that I consider central—repositioning the *halachah* as a method of *tikkun olam* and nurturing *tzelem elokim* in the light of the Shoah. While I have influenced many Jews and Christians, I failed with the institutional leadership of Orthodoxy. Yet I believe that, succeed or fail, it has been worth spending my life doing this work.

Whenever I start to add up such successes and contributions, I remind myself that projects of equal importance in my mind, such as creating a retreat center for the Jewish community, did not happen. Clearly, a lot of my accomplishment is not personal. The outcome depends on what people are ready for, and what the times support.

One of the major failures in my life is the Jewish community and its policy vis-à-vis assimilation. Notwithstanding an early alert on my part, notwithstanding that I changed my life's work to concentrate on this issue, I failed. The Jewish people now faces a grave threat of assimilation. The threat of physical security is subsiding (although not yet over); assimilation is *the* major threat. Meeting the challenge together, as a community, is the only way to be effective. But, instead of uniting, there is a growing polarization in confronting the issue. The structures of unity are eroding; a communal split is taking place before our very eyes. The community institutions are weak; the synagogue institutions are weakening. Instead of cooperating, they cling to their conflicts. Clearly, I have failed to get this message of cooperation and pluralism across.

As the community continues to polarize, there is weaker support from CLAL's leadership for this issue. Organizationally, the lay people humor me on this issue as little as they can get away with; they do not see the support for pluralism work out there. They do not think that much can be done to ameliorate the situation. The CLAL staff also thinks that this is my *shtick*—yet I am convinced that this is an absolutely central question. If tomorrow morning my life would end, the assessment would have to be that I have failed. I have not convinced enough people to do something about the problem. Instead of bringing the communities together, I have become somewhat marginalized in the Orthodox community. I cling to the hope that the tide will turn—that extremism will burn out, that the community will awaken and bring pressure to bear to solve the problems. Still, as of now, my work in this area is certainly a failure.

The decline of religious unity and the failure to create a retreat center are the glaring professional defeats of my life so far.

(I have a few years left, so I am hoping for more failures!) In coming to grips with age and the possibility of death, and what I have not accomplished, and what I can still accomplish, I grasp at the straw that some policies can still be achieved—or I cling to the consolation prize that a life lived intensely trying to pioneer must be marked by some failures. One could say that the importance of any life is measured by the importance of the failures!

People are starting to tell me: Write now, and get your ideas down for the ages. I would like to get my ideas on paper for the people that will come after me. But I am convinced that time is working against us as a people, so I must bear down now. Once Jews are children of assimilated Jews, it will be much harder to reach them—so I feel a great urgency to redouble CLAL's efforts now. I want to swing for the fences, if you will, rather than go for the bunt.

Let me apply this principle through a favorite teaching. Judaism teaches the triumph of life and that life is stronger than death. As humans get older, there is the risk of death taking over. Life becomes routinized, standardized. People repeat themselves. That is a form of death. Physically, people get weaker and do have more limitations. That is real. But the danger is that you want to play it safe because you are afraid to die. You want to make sure that when you retire you will have enough money. Professionally, you want to make sure that you will be comfortable rather than pushed aside. So you go along, afraid to rock the boat. Those are all forms of death in life.

An alternative approach is summed up in the *mitzvah* of *la'erev* (in the evening). In *Yevamot* 62B, the Talmud considers the *mitzvah* of *pru u'rvu* (be fruitful and multiply—Genesis 1:28). For me, this *mitzvah*, which grows out of creation, captures the central Jewish message of the triumph of life and the individual's task to contribute to that outcome. This is the context of the *mitzvah* of *la'erev*.

The Talmud asks what the minimum fulfillment of the commandment to be fruitful and multiply is. Two schools of rabbis disagree, but the conclusion of the tradition is that having two children of any gender is the minimum fulfillment of this instruction. I read this conclusion as a message. Every person must contribute in the struggle of life against death. If we do not have children, then death wins out. Therefore, the minimum task set for every human being is to love another—a spouse—and together, God willing, to have at least two children. This means that when these individuals die, they have ensured that there will be no less life in the world than when they came into existence. Since having a child generates a responsibility that is lifelong; takes over every minute of one's life; and involves physical effort, financial outlay, and psychological nurturing without limit, this commandment is more than a standard observance. It is the commitment of one's life to ensure that life will go on after one's death.

Then the Gemara challenges the two-children total. The Talmud quotes Isaiah 45:18: "The world was not created to be void; it was fashioned to be settled (*la'shevet.*)" ("Settled" means that civilization can build up the world so that the globe can sustain more life—then it should be filled with life.) Isaiah's interpretation means that God intends the world to be *filled* with *life.* Since the purpose is to fill the world, two children per family are not enough. A total of two implies that the balance of life and death will be static; neither death nor life will win out. From *la'shevet* ("to be settled"), we learn that it is a *mitzvah* for parents to have another child. The third child tilts the balance of the world toward life. Over generations, such a ratio will tend to fill the world with human beings and ensure that life wins out over death. (To the individual couple, having three children means that there will be more life in the world when the parents are finished than when they started.) Three-children families are the key to Jewish survival, too. If the Jewish birthrate in Diaspora were three per family (instead of 1.7 and dropping), there would be a lot less anxiety about all the other dangers, including intermarriage.

Now the Talmud comes back with another verse to challenge the concept that the commandment of *pru u'rvu* is fulfilled by having two—or even three—children. In Ecclesiastes 11:6, we are told: "In the morning sow your seed, and in the evening [*la'erev*] do not hold back your hand [from sowing it again] for you do not know which seed will prove seminal, this one or that one, or if both will be equally good." The Talmud then applies this principle twice. First it says that even if individuals have had children (presumably two or three) in their youth, they should have children again in their old age—for who knows which children will survive and have children themselves?

The Talmud then applies this principle of *la'erev* to the story of Rabbi Akiva. Akiva became the greatest teacher of his generation, with a following of 24,000 students. All the students were wiped out during the terrible period of the Roman persecutions and the plague that ravaged Judea before, during and after the Bar Kochba revolt. Akiva had to start teaching all over again. And these few students became the scholars whose teachings are the core of the Mishnah. Akiva's second effort, while small in numerical achievement, raised up the key people who created the heart of the Talmud, the core of rabbinic Judaism, the oral law of Jewish life. By not surrendering to death, the aged Rabbi Akiva created the students who became the life force of Judaism through the writings and teachings of the Mishnah.

Thus *la'erev* represents the second effort—perhaps even the final effort—of life in its struggle against death. This extra effort (when it proves successful) enormously widens the margin of life over death that this individual has created through his or her work. Thus, *la'erev* can be fulfilled by having children at a more advanced age—even after one has met the minimum requirement to be on the side of life in this cosmic struggle. Equally, one can teach students (the spiritual equivalent of parenting) or do some other life-shaping project at an age when most people surrender to the coming death and stop creating. Here again, the capacity to create anew in old age enormously increases the margin of life over death. Every individual is called to run this final stretch in the race of life; it is in each person's hands to increase the margin of life generated with their own life and efforts.

The *mitzvah* of *la'erev* is one of the central commandments of the Jewish tradition, in my view. To fulfill this *mitzvah*, one must renew oneself—almost be reborn—and take on tasks that are life-consuming, but which give meaning and value to our lives. *La'erev*—the new effort made at an older age—represents the extra margin of life over death. During that second phase of one's life, in one's forties, fifties, sixties, it would be easy to serve time.

The voice whispers: "Stand pat and play it safe"—but that means that death is getting stronger. By standing still, one provides the margin of death over life. If you are willing to renew in old age, to have family, to resume creativity, to pioneer in career (of course, you have to have health, *mazel*, and God's help), then you produce life when others are dying. Thus you increase the surplus of life over death.

La'erev is the *mitzvah* that I think about all the time. I am not trying to make light of whatever I have done up to now. But the real challenge for me—as for anybody else—is *la'erev*. I am in my sixties now. The question addressed to me—and to anyone else sixty years old—is: "Do you serve out your time or do you renew it?" Do you sow your seed again (whether it be new students, new teaching, new projects)?

In my own life thus far, my thinking has been enriched again and again. The Holocaust completely changed my thinking on so many topics in the 1960s and 1970s. Yet, somewhat to my surprise, in the early 1980s, my thinking about the Shoah changed dramatically. A whole new phase of life and thinking began. I loved teaching at Y.U., yet Riverdale Jewish Center and its rabbinate transformed my life focus and my thought. I was excited to build Jewish Studies at City College, yet CLAL brought remarkable new challenges into my life. Each renewal has enriched my thinking again.

At this point, I would not consider any of my accomplishments the final or the ultimate one. There is no one project about which I would say: This is what I really want to be remembered for. Although I cannot guarantee to each person the fulfillment of Robert Browning's promise, "The best is yet to be," I am confident that it is a religious calling to increase life again and to help the Jewish people meet the challenges that it is facing.

With a little help from God and some *mazel*, there is a real chance for peace in Israel over the next few years. Then the main challenge facing the Jewish people will be the renewal of spiritual and cultural life. (True, Israel will have the challenge of creating an economy and of winning peace with its neighbors. This will require incredible, taxing efforts.) Still, the central challenge facing Israel and the Diaspora will be the renewal of Judaism's capacity to nurture life, to guide living, and to enable the Jewish people to serve as a life-model to the rest of the world. I hope that, in the next decade or two, God will spare me to go on and make a contribution in that field. It is a worthy task to help the Jewish people renew its life and thereby inspire others to help life win over death.

Q. Thank you very much, Rabbi. I think you forgot to mention the many people you have helped in life, and who have been inspired through your teaching. I consider myself blessed to be one of them. I thank you very, very much.

Afterword: Bringing the Messiah . . . A Good, Steady Job

Shalom Freedman (Q). You speak of the post-Holocaust/rebirth of Israel era as a messianic moment in Jewish history. You have written that "the central paradigm of Jewish religion is redemption" (*The Jewish Way*, p. 18). Yet in my mind, I identify you with moderation and with pluralism (which implies limited claims and pragmatic accommodations). You have criticized Gush Emunim and Lubavitch for their messianism and lack of realism in historical terms. So which is it? Are you a messianist or are you a realist?

Rabbi Irving Greenberg. Both. (I hope.)

Q. But you can't have your cake and eat it too. If you are going to insist on plausible political scenarios for Israel's future and are ready to give up parts of the Holy Land to accommodate the Arabs, aren't you, by definition, giving up messianism? Is there any possibility of a messianic Kingdom of God in a land-poor, embattled, divided Eretz Yisrael?

Greenberg. Messianism is theologically, morally, and emotionally essential to our faith. At its heart, Judaism is a religion of redemption. One of the three primary stories which the Jewish people tells is the story of Creation which projects a perfect world which God seeks to create. In the first chapter of the Torah, God calls this world good not once but seven times and the seventh time God says that it is "very good" (i.e. perfect). (In biblical signifiers, seven is a marker of perfection). The world, according to Genesis 1, is being filled with emerging and differentiating life; the creation narrative is noteworthy for the absence of death, evil, war and oppression. Nature is marked by harmony, not strife, and the two humans are equal. Creation is blessed by God with life overflowing and bursting with vitality.

The historical world that we inhabit is scarred by evil, suffering, and death. Many humans are degraded by political, economic, and social exploitation; even the wealthy and powerful experience alienation, loneliness, and mortality. In Jewish tradition and in many other religions also there are numerous attempts to account for the contradiction between the world of Creation and the world of History. Whatever the explanations, Judaism insists that ultimately "both" worlds are true; neither is to be explained away or evaded. Eventually the two will be reconciled through the process of *tikkun olam.*

"The Jewish religion is focused on the divine assurance and human belief that the world *will* be perfected."[1] According to the Torah, the Jewish people and religion came into being to bring the divine blessing to fruition for all humanity. The prophets promised, in God's name, that the enemies of life including poverty, hunger, oppression, war, sickness and even death itself would be overcome (*cf.* Isaiah 25:8). Therefore, human efforts to perfect the world are not quixotic. The Jews are the avant garde serving as models, teachers, and coworkers with other humans to achieve *tikkun olam.*

Messianism expresses the conviction that life and good will triumph in this world. Then humans will be reconciled with God, with each other and with nature. Much of Judaism's impact on the world has come from the spread of its messianic vision of overthrowing the status quo. Messianism molded Christianity and gave it enormous appeal. Interestingly, although the concept was spiritualized in the course of being Christianized, there were recurring outbursts of worldly messianism in Christian culture along the way. Similarly the messianic hope affected Islam and (in secularized form) profoundly shaped and drove modern Western culture. It is compelling and essential to know that our move-

1. *The Jewish Way*, p. 18.

ments of redemption do not constitute pursuit of the impossible dream. So how can one be faithful to Judaism and not be a messianist?

Q. But isn't the Holocaust a direct contradiction to the messianic hope? I am reminded of Richard Rubenstein's argument in *After Auschwitz*, that in light of the Shoah the only Messiah is Death itself. While I strongly reject Rubenstein's Death of God theology, isn't it strange to talk of messianism in this period?

Greenberg. The Holocaust contradicts all of Judaism. When God's Kingdom is finally set up, we are told that "*lo yarayoo v'lo yashcheetu b'khol har kadshi*; they shall do no harm and not destroy [anywhere] in My whole Holy Mountain (=Earth)" (Isaiah 11:9). When the Kingdom of Night was set up, it was all death and destruction. It represented a victory for the evil which literally attacked (with intent to kill) all our principles. It wounded our beliefs and trashed our Torah. But the Jewish people responded by reaffirming faith and renewing its covenant. Such a reassertion grows out of tremendous groundedness in God and is driven by deep faith in and profound longing for the final redemption. Once we make this move, then we feel the impulse of messianism in more urgent form. The equilibrium of good and evil in the world has been upset by the Shoah. Therefore, in order to restore credibility to our story of redemption, we must have major breakthroughs—a massive infusion of good—to rebalance the world. This is the logic of messianism in our time.

After the other great tragedies of Jewish history, the same reaction occurred. The destruction of the Second Temple was followed within a generation by the Bar Kochba movement in which Rabbi Akiva himself proclaimed Simon ben Koziba to be the Messiah. The Expulsion from Spain stimulated kabbalistic messianism even as the Chmielnitski massacres provided the fallow ground for the rapid growth of the Sabbetai Sevi movement. Of course, every messianic movement so far has been proven to be premature (and caused many problems). Still the appearance of the movement shows that Judaism is alive and well. What a compliment to Judaism it is that our faith is still spawning would-be Messiahs—which it should be well and do until the real one comes.

Q. But you have stated publicly that Gush Emunim borders on false messianism and that Lubavitch represents failed messianism. Now you are praising them?

Greenberg. In 1966, I wrote an article citing Franz Rosenzweig's point that the false messianic movements of Jewish history were a sign of unbroken longing for redemption; therefore they were a sign of vitality. I complained that contemporary Jewry was so tyrannized by the mind set of modernity (e.g. secularity, rationality, empiricism, etc.) that it had failed to generate a mistaken messianic movement in response to the Holocaust. This was a sign that the iron grip of modernity's hand was around the throat of Judaism, choking its soul and paralyzing its capacity to respond.

Well, I was wrong! Years later it dawned upon me that my father, *zichrono livracha*, had called it right again. During my stormy adolescent years my father rejected my pietistic assault on Jewry's religious values. He insisted that instead of condemning I should study Jews' behavior and learn deeper truths from it. He would constantly quote the Gemara to me: *hanach lahem libnai Yisrael; im lav neviim haym, b'nai neviim haym.* Leave it to the Jewish people (and they will do it right)—for if they [the current Jews] are not prophets, they are the children of prophets (so their religious sensibility is still inspired and reflective of the will of God).

In the very next year—1967—Gush Emunim came into being—launched by people who perceived an eschatological breakthrough in the conquest of Eretz Yisrael. It launched a bold pioneering settlement wave and a movement to bring Israel to the geographic and spiritual level of the messianic Kingdom. Furthermore, in 1966 when I was complaining that Jewry was failing to respond, the Lubavitchers, unknown to me, had already begun their run to the messianic age. The spiritual ferment had begun under the previous Rebbe who saw in the suffering of the Shoah, "the labor pains of the Messiah." Starting in the 1970s Habad put together a series of spectacular organizational successes and public relations triumphs under the inspired leadership of Rabbi

Menachem M. Schneerson, *zichrono livracha.* This ignited a fever of redemption that turned into a full blast messianic frenzy focused on the Rebbe. Thus the Jewish people was proving that redemption hope was still alive. Personally, I deeply admired these two groups' drive, their vision and their relative freedom from the rigid constraints of modern culture.

Nevertheless, both Gush Emunim and Lubavitch went wrong in their excess. Going out of control is the built-in danger of all messianism. Hope keeps us alive under conditions of oppression and degradation; it gives us the strength to transcend the present realm and thus to persevere. But the redemption hope must be kept in dialectical tension with reality. If the dream becomes so buoyant that it pulls away from reality altogether, it disconnects from this world. This motivates the faithful to loftily dismiss present reality and to demand attainment of the impossible. Sometimes their exhilaration leads them to assault other people for the "crime" of living their regular lives; they want to punish normal people for being recalcitrant and delaying the end. If, on the other hand, hope is deflated and its party gives in to the present reality, then the dream is lost and the status quo is enshrined over all. Gush Emunim and Lubavitch failed to maintain the dialectic of affirming and challenging the reality situation. Both became living examples of runaway messianism with negative consequences for others, for themselves and for the holy cause which they sought to advance.

Gush Emunim's utopianism energized its members to renew the lagging spirit of *halutziut* (pioneering) and to build up the wastelands of Eretz Yisrael. They were able to reach out to non-observant Israelis and to create some of the rare settlement/neighborhoods in which secular and religious lived together in harmonious interaction. They were able to articulate the miraculous nature of Israel reborn and the profound religious significance of the third Jewish commonwealth. But that same fervor led them to excess. They began to consider the Arab majority on the West Bank as a problem to be overcome or pushed aside. They refused to give the needed moral weight to the question of whether one could impose Israeli rule (or even presence) on a resistant local population—without grave violations of democracy and of respect for the dignity of others. They refused to adequately consider the diplomatic/military/political situation which made it impossible for Israel to ignore Arab and Western positions. (In turn, those pressures would make it mandatory for Israel to give back territory.)

The Gush's tacit argument was: with God and Messiah behind us, Jews should not let themselves be bound by realistic and prudent political calculations. This appeal to a higher authority led them to act irresponsibly and turned them into a force for reckless political behavior. The inevitable conflict with reality factors (which could not be denied or wished away) started to foster the growth of extremist solutions in their midst. Racism, Kahanism, and flirting with "transfer" policies (e.g. expulsions and/or forced population movements) soon made their appearance. Had these policies been adopted, then the Israelis would have done unto others what was done so cruelly and unjustly to Jews over the course of our exile.

The lessons of Gush Emunim's experiences confirm a truth which we know already. Messianism can no longer be based on miraculous calculations that assume that the Messiah is irresistible and not bound by political considerations. Elie Wiesel already wrote in *The Gates of the Forest* that it is too late for an all powerful Messiah to come. Had the Messiah who could have overthrown the evil forces and redeemed the world existed then, the time to have come was then. Failure of an omnipotent redeemer to come to stop the Shoah then implies indifference and a colossal moral failure; for such a Messiah to come after the Holocaust would be obscene. It would be incumbent on every religious Jew to reject such a Messiah. However, a Messiah who wanted to come—but who could not take charge due to the power of evil and the status quo—deserves our compassion and help.

Because messianism is still our core value, because we burn with the suffering of humanity, we must do everything to bring this Messiah—as soon as possible. Bringing the Messiah is dependent on human intelligence, passion, and courage to help overcome the obstacles to perfection. The movement to bring this Messiah is bound by political considerations and human limitations. The Kingdom of God can only be created if we bring people together and spread knowledge of God. Such a Kingdom cannot be built on an Original Sin of expulsion or massacre of indigenous populations, God forbid. Jews will have to work with Arabs to bring peace between neighbors and break down the barriers to hatred and degrading stereotypes. Achieving such a reality would represent a truly messianic breakthrough. Admittedly this cooperation would be extraordinarily difficult to achieve but one should dare and dream messianically in this lifetime. As for Gush Emunim, they could not change the balance of power in the world. They did not try to change the dynamics of our relationship with the Arabs. Instead, they turned messianic longing into magical thinking; inevitably, they failed.

Q. Well, Habad's messianism seems to be built on their actual accomplishments especially in bringing Judaism to people all over the world and in bringing many people back to yiddishkeit. Why then are you critical of Lubavitch? Where did they go wrong? It would appear that they erred in taking the idea of Moshiach very seriously—but this is the very idea that you are promoting.

Greenberg. Habad's current wave of messianism grew out of World War II and the devastating impact of the Holocaust. For this response, I honor them. However, under the previous Rebbe, already the lesson of the Holocaust was read wrongly. The Shoah was understood as divine punishment for the sin of modernity and assimilation. This conception, in turn, grows out of the image of the all powerful God of History who pulls all the strings while powerless humans passively wait to be saved (except that they do *mitzvot* and other actions which kabbalistically move God and history.)

The limitations of this conception have already been pointed out in Tanach in parts of Isaiah, Jeremiah, and the Books of Lamentations and Job. Furthermore, alongside the affirmation that "*mipnei hateynu*—because of our sins, we were exiled from our land" the Rabbis developed other conceptions of divine suffering and human partnership—just as the Kabbalists developed theories of cosmic catastrophe—to account for Jewish exile. Modern Orthodoxy and Religious Zionism long ago grasped the idea that Jews must participate in their own liberation as part of a newly activist humanity that was trying to become an effective partner with God in *tikkun olam.* The nub of my essays on the third era of Jewish history is that God has voluntarily engaged in *tzimtzum* (self-limitation) in order to summon humans to partnership in realizing the Covenant. This theological stance makes clear that humans can use their freedom to inflict great evil. (Thanks to modern culture, they can inflict almost unlimited suffering—as the Nazis did in the Shoah.) This removes the theological basis of seeing the Holocaust as a divinely willed punishment for Jews.

Unfortunately, Habad paid the price for being culturally outside of modernity. They failed to reject this punishment theology as morally unacceptable, a libel on God and on the victims. They failed to recognize that the level of Divine control and miraculous intervention that they were positing was no longer true, historically or halachically. Yet the Hazon Ish (*cf.* Yoreh Deah, Hilchot Shekhitah, Siman 2) and Rabbi Joseph B. Soloveitchik (*cf.* "Kol Dodi Dofek" in B'sod Hayachid Ve-Hayachad, pp. 331–402, especially pp. 333ff, 354–362) each in his own way, in response to the Holocaust, recognized this very change. By contrast, Rabbi Menachem M. Schneerson affirmed that the Holocaust was the outcome of the Divine Surgeon cutting out a limb of the Jewish people (to eradicate the cancer of modernity)? In the Rabbi's teaching, the Shoah with all its intense suffering represented the pangs of labor of the Messiah's birth. The belief that the extreme (labor) pains come just before the birth gave Habad great dynamism—but it weakened their sense of realism. The remarkable series of accomplishments under Rabbi Schneerson's inspired leadership eventually led the Lubavitchers to a kind of inebriation with their success. This released a wave of glorification of the Rebbe as the Messiah.

The conviction that God was on their side and that whatever the Messiah decreed must be done (and will inexorably succeed) led Habad to take extreme political positions. Israel should not give back one inch of land, proclaimed the Rebbe. The foot soldiers of Lubavitch intervened heavily in Israeli politics, hamstringing Yitzhak Rabin's efforts to achieve peace. As in Gush Emunim, only more so, the apocalyptic urge led Habadniks to flirt with racist ideas and transfer policies. The lack of social contact with Gentiles (on a mutual and equal basis) leads to a one-sided moral stance (only Jewish needs are adequately weighed and only Jewish suffering gains full empathy).

Finally Lubavitch paid the price for their authoritarian structures and the lack of pluralism in the community. (Although Lubavitchers reach out to everyone, it is very much a one-sided conversation. They will not recognize non-Orthodox clergy in any serious way. They do not listen much to other Orthodox Rabbis either. There are no voices of dissent or criticism and, frequently, no non-Lubavitch media inside the community.) Thus the talk of their achievements became self-referential and uncritical.

Lubavitchers are fond of pointing out that the Rebbe fulfilled Maimonides' criteria for the true Messiah. "[If he] studies Torah and is busy with mitzvot [presumably teaches Torah and gets other Jews to do mitzvot as well -IG] . . . and will press *all of Israel* to go in the Torah's way and to strengthen its walls, and fights the battles of the Lord, then he has the presumption of being the Messiah."[2] In truth, the Rebbe deserves credit for reaching more Jews than any other Rabbi in this generation. In the early 1990s when I was asked: is the Rebbe the Messiah?, my answer was: I am rooting for him—because we need the Messiah. I prayed for his success because this generation needs such an outcome. But Habad is highly limited by its own internal value system which is profoundly interwoven with premodern culture. Therefore, it cannot penetrate deeply into the lives of the vast majority of modernized Jews—for their souls are equally profoundly interwoven with modern culture. Failure to listen to others, failure to get honest feedback, led the Habadniks to lose all perspective as to the vast majority of Jews *not* being reached by them. The painful contrast between rampant assimilation and Lubavitchers' claims for the Rebbe was a crushing proof that he was not in fact the Messiah for whom we longed. His death confirmed that bitter truth although most of Lubavitch (not just its continuing messianic wing) still has not come to grips with this reality.

Q. Some say that Habad's messianism has led them beyond the Jewish pale. Professor David Berger's critique of Habad reprinted

2. Maimonides, *Mishneh Torah*, Hilchot Melachim, ch. 11, p. 4.

in the Union of Orthodox Jewish Congregations of America's Jewish Action magazine, and Berger's statement adopted by the Rabbinical Council of America, the leading centrist Orthodox rabbinic organization, seem to assert that Habad has become a deviationist movement.

Greenberg. People are understandably worried that the Lubavitchers' talk (of a Messiah, e.g. the Rebbe, dying and then coming back by resurrection to lead the world into the messianic age) will give post facto credence to Christian claims for their religion. Nevertheless, I do not consider Habad to be a case of false messianism. As I have argued elsewhere, there have been two kinds of messianic movements in Jewish history so far. (The third kind—the final bringing of the true Messiah—has not happened yet.) Historically, there are cases of false messianism and failed messianism. A false Messiah preaches evil or reverses classic moral standards and undermines Jewish loyalty to Judaism. Such were the outcomes of the Sabbetai Sevi and Jacob Frank movements. Those two individuals are true examples of false Messiahs.

By contrast, Lubavitchers (as the Rebbe himself) teach good values—love your neighbor as yourself, learn Torah, increase *mitzvah* observance to bring the Messiah, etc. These are the values of life and goodness. Then Habad is clearly a case of failed messianism. Even if the group has been carried away by excess enthusiasm, should some years of bad judgment be allowed to wipe out the merit of decades of good teaching and remarkable devotion and construction of a better Jewish world? One's heart breaks that the Rebbe did not make it. But, as a Messiah, he is a failure—not a fraud.

There is nothing shameful about being a failed Messiah. Bar Kochba tried to be the redeemer; he won the support and approbation of Rabbi Akiva who asserted that this warrior was the Messiah. The crushing of the revolt did not lead Jewry to recategorize him as a wicked deviant or as a false Messiah. Maimonides makes clear that Bar Kochba's death proved decisively that he was not the Messiah. But Rambam is not in agreement with commentators who claim that Bar Kochba was found to be evil by the Rabbis.[3] In truth, most Rabbis would only dream of reaching the Lubavitcher Rebbe's scale of grandeur in achievement and failure.

I would draw a different conclusion from this sad failure. The lesson is that pluralism is essential to the healthy operation of any system, however good or even divinely inspired it is. Had there been genuinely open, two-way conversation with others, had there been a lively and independent debate within Habad, the Lubavitchers probably would have not lost their balance. *Tzimtzum*—self-limitation—is essential to prevent teachings from being extended too far and to save every worthy movement from going out of control. (This is a reprise of the eighteenth century political science debates over the merits of democracy versus revolutions bestowed by elites. Enlightened despots may well work more efficiently than democracies in the short run. However, dictatorships lack internal checks and control mechanisms—so when they go wrong, they go dreadfully wrong. Democracies inevitably outperform despotisms because self-limitation is almost impossible in total settings where alternate groups, forces, and voices are not allowed to exist.)

In sum, the inner dynamics of all positions—even of good views held by constructive groups—is that they tend to be constantly extended, when there are no critical or independent voices. When there are no clashing views, then the dynamic operates even more powerfully toward inevitable excess. Then good truths that operate constructively over their range of validity and effectiveness are pushed beyond those limits and often turn negative or even destructive. Therefore, outside groups and multiple voices are needed to keep (even) divinely ordained truths and religiously inspired movements within their proper boundaries. Far from undermining great truths, the forces of pluralism serve to keep them under control, supple, self-correcting and protected against excess.

In retrospect, the Lubavitchers (and all of us) were lucky that the Rebbe was such a good man. With his unchecked authority Rabbi Schneerson—especially after he became ill and reputedly

3. *Ibid*, ch. 11, para. 3, Commentary of Rabad.

was receiving steroids—could have given terrible instructions and might have been obeyed. Compare, *lehavdil elef alfei havdalot,* David Koresh, the self-anointed Messiah of the Branch Davidians who ultimately instructed his followers to die—and they obeyed. Thus he proved that he was a false Messiah, if any further proof was needed.

It must be said that Lubavitch has not yet grasped this important lesson of the need for opening up—although the continuing debate as to the messianic claims about the Rebbe may be the germ of some beginning pluralism. Thus far, the entire Orthodox community has failed to grasp how essential pluralism is to keep the Torah teachings on target and to protect the integrity of the community's moral views. This failure of understanding has led Orthodoxy to resort to political and other forms of suppression of dissenting views, within and without the community. This same psychology creates the tendency to delegitimate Habad rather than to criticize, debate, and try to clean up its excesses. The harsh response results in a lack of compassion for Habad's incredible effort and to an inability to grasp the pathos in this awesome failure.

Q. If the Rebbe couldn't be the Messiah and if Gush Emunim also failed, then who can succeed? Can anyone be the Messiah in light of the scope of evil in this world? Dare anyone try to become the Messiah in view of the excesses which messianism brings?

This reminds me of Rabbi David Hartman. He argues that since messianism is a constant source of extremism in Israeli politics and leads to dangerous, almost totalitarian attitudes toward Arabs, disbelievers, etc., it has become a threat in our time. He feels that the rabbinic/halachic tradition with its realism and pragmatism and restraint in history must be placed front and center again, for religious and secular alike. To accomplish this, must we repudiate messianism?

Greenberg. Anything that David Hartman says I take seriously because I greatly admire his work and consider him one of the most creative and relevant Jewish thinkers in our time. Let us also keep in mind that with his provocative formulations, in this area as in so many others, he is trying to shake us out of our complacency and force us to confront the depth of our own needed choices.

Still, my instinctive reaction is that the either/or formulation is too stark. The need to repudiate messianism reflects the powerful pull of runaway messianism. (As it were: Since we can't stop once we start, we must refuse to get started.) However, if we can break the stranglehold which miraculous messianism has on our imagination, then we can attain a more nuanced, more dialectical position, one which yokes together messianism and realism. This is my goal: to affirm messianism but to discipline its practitioners and thus prevent its excesses. As in a controlled explosion or controlled fusion, we can contain utopianism's explosive energy and direct it into realistic channels. Properly harnessed, it can power significant historical breakthroughs.

The paradigm of realistic messianism is modeled after the process of covenant, which is consistently dialectical. The covenant teachers: *not either/or* (either God does it all or humans are alone in a meaningless universe and make their own fate) *but both/and* (God and humans are in true partnership in which both must contribute and neither can/will do it alone). Judaism as a covenantal system requires us to dream realistically. The halachic way to redemption seeks revolutionary ends by conservative, gradualist means.

Applying these concepts to economic policy, the Torah tells us that six days a week we are to work in the world and it allows us to compromise with realities such as slavery, poverty, and inequality. But on Shabbat, we are commanded to reassert the perfectionist standard. For twenty-four hours, the slave (as the master) is free of labor. For six years, the Torah recognizes private property and tolerates the inequality of rich and poor. But in the seventh, sabbatical year, the land is thrown open. The poor can come and help themselves to its yield and the rich are denied the right to work their wealth (or even to control it). Thus the Torah affirms the dialectic; neither the ideal nor the real pole is repudiated. Note, however, that overall, the utopian/perfectionist thrust (Shabbat; Shmittah) powers the system. Eventually reality is remade in the image of the ideal; the weekday is the satellite of the Shabbat. Every day, pious Jews remind themselves to bring

Shabbat into the week. "Today is the first (second, third, etc.) day of the Sabbath. . . ."

After the Shoah, those who defy this total assault of death on life respond with an elemental reassertion of life that can only be described as messianic. It is particularly appropriate that the impulse to greatly increase perfection should drive the system of daily life while we feel the momentum of that stunning event and of the rebirth of Israel. Still, the process must be bound by reality.

On the one hand, God has self-limited and called humans to take a greater role in *tikkun olam.* The urgency of restoring the image of God to a messianic level gives humans a doubled responsibility. We know that we cannot do it alone but, together, humans and God can generate tremendous force. There is in fact a worldwide dynamic of improving life conditions and demand for access to a better life. There are remarkable accomplishments or even breakthroughs for human dignity in almost every area of human endeavor. The free market movement and capitalism are anti-perfectionist; yet in themselves, they are relentless forces for change and improvement of the economic situation. In turn, economic development typically leads to demands for social and political upgrading.

On the other hand, there was a clear signal in the Shoah that God would not intervene in the world process with miracles. Failure to think and work realistically led to devastating destruction of the weak and persecuted. The power of evil was more manifest than ever. Since future miscalculations can lead to more catastrophic outcomes, the enormous power of evil must never again be underestimated.

My conclusion is that people are capable of being driven by the exhilaration of hope while accepting the covenantal disciplines of the tenacious, unyielding step-by-step activity toward *tikkun olam.* Nothing less than this synthesis can do justice to the dream and the reality and eventually make them one.

Q. I won't deny that I am moved by your words of hope. But as you catalogued the failures, I also felt an increasing sense of despair. The question that emerges demands to be asked: Is it too late to bring the Messiah?

Greenberg. Given the pain, the suffering, the brokenness in the world, it will *never* be too late to bring the Messiah. The world needs the Messiah today as much as ever. Thus far, it has repeatedly proven to be too early to bring the Messiah. But we must keep on trying.

Q. Honestly now, if the world was not transformed by the death of the six million, will it ever change enough? If we have lost the momentum of the world's (temporary) guilty conscience and the profound life affirmation of the Jewish people, and Israel is still a small, embattled nation . . . if the Lubavitcher fire has been spent in vain, can we ever hope to achieve our goal? Should we not settle down and turn our backs on the dreams that unsettle our lives and tear us apart—in vain? Let us accept the hard reality and try to make the world a little better; let us settle for making life a little easier wherever we are!

Greenberg. Your question reflects the sadness of giving up the hope of a divinely bestowed cosmic breakthrough. It bespeaks the anxiety that we are not up to the job of *tikkun olam.* It expresses the unarticulated wish—if only God would step in again (as in biblical days) and do it all for us! Thereby you speak our deepest heartfelt yearnings. Still I would offer an alternate position.

For one, everybody overrates the power—and effect—of miraculous messianism. Years ago I speculated about an all-powerful, miracle-making Messiah who finally comes—and the world goes on with business as usual. At the risk of putting the narrative into a fixed mold (it should be kept in oral form and the characters rotated every few years to reflect current concerns), let me tell you the Messiah-already-come story:

> In the middle of the night, as foretold in prophecy, the whole world is suddenly flooded with light, a light so powerful that it penetrates into all rooms, all caves, even all underground installations in the world. Police emergency switchboards light up; newsrooms are inundated with calls. Rumor after rumor swirls through the population as anxiety builds.
>
> The President of the United States calls a midnight session of the National Security Council. Political and religious leaders

convene parallel meetings worldwide. As panic builds, only one piece of hard news emerges. CNN cameras show live that a wild-eyed rider on a pure white donkey has been spotted headed for the Dung Gate in Jerusalem.

President Clinton goes on national television to speak to the nation. My fellow Americans: Nitpickers and naysayers have challenged my election year promise to restore the classic American belief that every generation will do better than the last. The coming of the Messiah is categorical proof that my administration has achieved its goal to restore the American dream. I have contacted Newt Gingrich and Republican leaders and offered bipartisan cooperation to assure that the Messiah will come to the United States. My only condition is that the arrival be revenue neutral so that our agreement to balance the budget by 2002 is not undone. Hilary and I have sent a telegram inviting the Messiah to stay with us in Washington and sleep in the Lincoln bedroom. I categorically deny the false Republican allegation that Messiah will have to give $25,000 to the Democratic National Committee for that privilege. On the other hand, if coffee and breakfast at the White House is also requested for the redeemer, we have to show something for it.

At that, Hilary Rodham Clinton, sitting at the President's side, exclaimed: At last, we've arrived at the true "politics of meaning" that I've always searched for; I just knew it would come from the Jews. From now on, it's not just Michael Lerner and *Tikkun*, it's a learned Messiah and *Tikkun Olam*!

After meeting with his budget-hawks and Senate leaders as well, Newt Gingrich goes on the air. "We are deeply troubled by this blatant Democratic attempt to repudiate our contract with America! (Please note that the Messiah pretender is riding on a donkey!) Nothing alien can reverse the tide of shrinking government and greater reliance on the free market. The messianic kingdom sounds to us like a swollen bureaucracy overregulating business and improving environmental standards as if the Earth is meant to be a Garden of Eden! And why does Isaiah say that "he will judge the poor righteously"; it sounds like the old tired, discredited New Dealism to me. And what is Messiah's view on abortion? On reducing capital gains taxes? We are going to refuse to pass the budget for this boondoggle and, yes, we will close down the government of the Kingdom of God until it presents us with a balanced budget and tax cuts.

In the former Soviet Union, Leonid Brezhnev, resurrected,

goes on the air to denounce Messiah as a chauvinist, Zionist, imperialist plot to undermine Communism. He accuses Messiah of being a CIA spy and an accomplice of Natan Sharansky. He reads KGB documents showing that under interrogation, Yuli Edelshtein admitted that he was actively working to bring the Messiah.

On the other hand, Boris Yeltsin announces that he will issue a presidential decree rewriting the Constitution so the president shares power with the Messiah, as long as the free market reforms continue and Chechnya is not given its independence.

In China, the government closes Tiananmen Square. Jiang Zemin denounces this thinly disguised attempt by Taiwan to take over the mainland. The Politburo goes into emergency session. All broadcasts are stopped and the music for "the wind is blowing from the east" is played over and over again. Finally Mao Zedong, resurrected, goes on the air to announce the launching of another Great Leap Forward to overcome poverty before Messiah arrives. "Moshiach is an imperialist paper tiger," declares Mao. "Besides, he can't be the Messiah. I am the true Messiah. God is Mao's Rock—yes, Mao'z Tzur."

In Iraq, Saddam Hussein executes thirty officers including his son and brother-in-law for secret collaboration in a plot to overthrow Saddam Hussein and bring the Messiah. In Iran, Ayatollah Khomeini, resurrected, denounces President Khatami as a Zionist dog forced on Iran by the Messiah through feeding the voters an aphrodisiac chewing gum which led women to vote for a man who is attractive to women. After consulting with other Arab oil exporting nations, Saudi Arabia announces that the presumed Messiah is a barefaced attempt by Israel to stop the peace process. In retaliation, the Saudi announce an immediate oil boycott. The spokesman says: "We will bring Israel to its knees. Why, our spies report that Israel has only one day's supply of oil on hand. Yet it will take at least eight days to get a new supplier of oil."

Yasir Arafat angrily accuses Israel of another attempt to predetermine the final status of Jerusalem. "Anyone who sells land to the Messiah will be put to death for treason to the Palestinian national cause," he announces. Western observers indicate that while this action is a bit extreme, they understand where Arafat is coming from. They call upon the Israeli prime minister to make some meaningful concession to him in order to revive the peace process.

Back in America, ABC announces that it has secured an exclusive interview with the Messiah by Barbara Walters in return for a fee of $30 million. Michael Jordan announces that he will demand a one-year contract of $35 million minimum. "I am the man," says Michael. Dennis Rodman, his hair colored blue and white, challenges Messiah to a one-on-one rebounding contest. George Steinbrenner announces: at last, we have found a manager to whom I would give a lifetime contract!

At its national convention, the National Organization of Women, introduces a resolution to denounce the Messiah as a male chauvinist myth imposed on women to keep them down. Louis Farrakhan at a hastily called meeting of Nation of Islam denounces Messiah as a white, racist myth imposed on blacks to keep them subservient. However, both meetings break up in confusion when the first CNN camera closeup reveals that the Messiah riding through the Dung Gate is a black, handicapped woman. Louis Farrakhan then appears on Meet the Press and categorically denies that he is an anti-Semite. "That charge is part of a Jewish plot to use the media which they control to defame me." Revealing that he was a Shabbos goy as a child and that he really loves Jews, Farrakhan states: "I never said that Judaism is a 'gutter religion.' I said that it was a 'gooter' religion."

In the Jewish world, United Jewish Appeal (UJA) and the Council of Jewish Federations (CJF) announce that they are merging. Their first joint program will be a major gift, black tie dinner in the Garden of Eden, with the minimum gift of $1,000,000. The Wexner Heritage Foundation announces its new elite leadership training program to prepare the next generation of young Messiahs. However, Mort Klein issues a press release that research by the ZOA shows that the Messiah is a firm believer in peace now, and is therefore unfit to sit in the Conference of Presidents of Major Jewish Organizations.

In Israel, Prime Minister Netanyahu offers the Messiah the posts of Finance Minister and Minister of Infrastructure together—if he will support the coalition. The United Torah Judaism party announces that it will only go along with this offer, if the Messiah gives assurances that he will always rule on matters of personal status such as "who is a Jew," "who is a legitimate convert," *mamzerim*, etc. only in accordance with the directions of the traditional religious parties. However, when contacted, the Messiah rejects this demand on the grounds that the greatest danger to Jewry is not the *mamzerim* who are trying to get into the Jewish people but the ones who are in already.

In Rome, the Pope emerges from an all-night meeting,

> looking somewhat pale and nervously clutching his yarmulke. He reads the following unanimous declaration of the College of Cardinals. "The presumed Messiah is to be stopped at once and asked the following question. Is this his First Coming or his Second? If he says this is his First, he is to be dismissed as an imposter. If he says that it is his Second Coming, he is to be greeted with hosanahs and escorted triumphantly into Jerusalem."
>
> In the whole world, nobody is prepared to change their positions. Therefore, the Messiah sadly turns back to await the day when people are ready to join in perfecting the world with the Kingdom of God.

The point is obvious, if a bit heavy-handed. As Maimonides pointed out,[4] God does not miraculously transform human nature itself. According to human nature, it is . . . "impossible to go suddenly from one extreme to the other . . . it is . . . impossible for him [human] suddenly to discontinue everything to which he is accustomed." Therefore, divine wisdom allows for (and educates) humans to develop the capacity to respond properly to events in life. For this reason, says Maimonides, God did not lead the frightened, still psychologically enslaved Israelites by way of the land of Philistines. The Hebrews were not prepared to fight for their freedom.

As the Torah itself makes clear, the miracles of the Exodus, the Crossing of the Red Sea and at Sinai were of little avail. They were brushed off—if you will, "defeated"—by the Israelite slave mentality. I have argued earlier in this book that the prophets with all their miracles, revelations, and categorical demands failed in their primary mission to bring their contemporary Israelites to repentance. The Rabbis who educated, compromised, and gradually transformed the Jews made them into a committedly monotheist, law-abiding people who were faithful followers of the prophets.

The same principle applies to messianism. A miraculous Messiah who comes when people are not ready (or when people do not participate in their own liberation) will fail. Therefore, we

---

4. *Guide to the Perplexed,* (Part 3, Chapter 32, Friedlander translation, pp. 150 ff).

have not lost as much as people think in the Divine *tzimtzum* and (by God's will) the devolution of the covenantal task primarily to us in our time. On the contrary, it is our task to bring the Messiah. Then, in the very process of working for redemption, we and all who labor toward this goal become prepared to receive the redeemer. (Incidentally, the category "all who labor" means the Jewish people, but I believe that it includes massive numbers of Gentiles as well. We will need worldwide cooperation and breakthroughs to achieve this magnificent goal.)

We can do it. "If you will, it is no dream," said Theodor Herzl when he set in motion the Zionist movement that generated the most powerful messianic signal of our era.

Consider the following protomessianic accomplishments of the past five decades. One: The survivors arose from under the heel of unparalled degradation and recreated life. I know a woman who served on the undertaking detail in Auschwitz. After the war she married, had children, and built a beautiful home life for her family. Does that reflect any less tenacious or elemental a force for life than the actions of the daughters of Lot? According to Rabbi Soloveitchik, the daughters refused to yield to the universal death they saw around them. They even seduced their father because they would stop at nothing to recreate life. This imbued their action with cosmic and messianic significance and they were worthy of being the ancestors of the Messiah (via Ruth, David, etc.). Well, then, hundreds, thousands of survivors prove that the life force is no weaker in our time. Do not their actions make them equally worthy to be the ancestors of the Messiah?

Second, in the depths of the Holocaust, Jewish life was not worth $10 a head. (The Joel Brand mission offered a million Jews at that price and there were no takers.) In the summer of 1944, the lives of Jewish children were not worth two-fifths of a penny each to reduce their agony by gassing them before burning them.[5]

Through an extraordinary response involving creation of the state of Israel, political and community organizing, and major

5. *Cf.* I. Greenberg, "Cloud of Smoke, Pillar of Fire," in E. Fleishner, *Auschwitz: Beginning of a New Era?* pp. 7–11.

fundraising, the value of Jewish life was restored. It has been raised to its highest level in history. For the first time Gentiles in mass numbers pass as Jews (in the former Soviet Union and Ethiopia, for example) because they know that Jewish lives are worth more. Today, people are more likely to be rescued, or helped to survive, if they are Jews.

No individual or community could have done this incredible work alone. Through unity and coordination and an unspoken consensus that energized millions of people to engage tirelessly in countless daily actions, this milestone was achieved. It is a down payment on the messianic promise that all humans will be treasured, rescued, fed, and cared for as beings in the image of God. This achievement suggests what is possible if we apply ourselves across the board to the full range of the tasks of *tikkun olam.*

Third, the State of Israel has been reestablished. This in itself has messianic dimensions because the renewal of sovereignty and the ingathering of the exiles both fulfill prophecies of eschatological restoration. Jeremiah predicted that there would come an age in which the primary proof that God was alive would no longer be the original Exodus from Egypt (as it had been throughout Jewish and Christian history) but rather would be the New Exodus in a future restoration and covenantal renewal in which the whole world would come to know God.[6] Well, there is worldwide recognition of Jewry and Judaism—and, thereby, of God—because of the extraordinary significance of the Jewish return. It is striking that these achievements and Israel's attainment of (relatively) ethical power and the establishment of a just (if flawed) society as well as the restoration of the value of Jewish life—were accomplished through everyday, realistic, disciplined, all too human efforts undertaken by millions of individuals.

The overall significance of this accomplishment has been obscured by the tragic split in consciousness between secular and religious Jews, growing out of the cultural crisis of modernity and Judaism. The religious are prone to look for miraculous solutions;

6. *Cf.* Jeremiah ch. 16, v. 14–15, also 19–21. *Cp.* Jeremiah, ch. 23, v. 5–6, 7–8.

this generation's flawed, finite achievements are underestimated. (A notable exception is the Chief Rabbinate's prayer for Israel, which calls the Jewish state "the beginning of the flowering of redemption." This is just right. The validity of this phrase is not refuted by the current Chief Rabbinate's failure to apply this guideline to its policy or principles.) The religious often use messianic categories to judge contemporary leadership; by this standard the leaders are found wanting and dismissed. For their part, the secular are prone to miss the miraculous dimensions of Israel's existence. Since many are alienated from classic Jewish values and standards, they make little attempt to bring them into the twentieth century and to reunite the heritage and the *sitz im leben* of the Jewish people.

This leaves the present culturally impoverished and strengthens the forces of assimilation in Israel and worldwide.

Sometimes secular politicians sell the (hiddenly) miraculous present to get through the next election. Frequently, they give over the Israeli public square to anti-Zionist *haredim* in return for a few votes in the Knesset. I often think of the tragic missed opportunity of David Ben Gurion. Maimonides writes that the would-be Messiah must accomplish two goals to become the actual redeemer. One, to fight Israel's (the Lord's) battles and win ("the only difference between the current historical situation and the messianic age is that Israel is liberated from its servitude to [foreign] governments").[7] Two, to study Torah, engage in *mitzvot,* and move all of Israel to walk in the Torah's way. Says Rambam, "If he did all this and succeeded, and [re]built the Temple in its place and gathered the dispersed of Israel, then this one is certainly the Messiah."[8]

Ben Gurion had reached two-thirds of the Messianic signposts. But he was so alienated from the tradition that it never occurred to him to bring it to bear in Israel. He could have integrated the tradition into life and the people with the tradition. Instead, the Labor party used the government institutions and economic and cultural power to strip Sephardim of their

---

7. *Mishneh Torah,* Hilchot Melachim, ch. 12, para. 1.
8. *Ibid,* ch. 11, para. 4.

traditional ways of living—inflicting a loss of self-respect and values that damaged them for generations. When the Sephardim (especially Yemenites) came to Israel filled with messianic expectations, Ben Gurion's party used this appeal to get their votes. They shamelessly played and sang the classic messianic song "*David Melech Yisrael Chai Vekayam* . . . David, King of Israel, is alive and well" as an election anthem. They garnered the Sephardic votes; they won the elections; but they blew the Messianic possibility for a mess of pottage. In this past decade, the aftershock of those behaviors has generated an upsurge of fundamentalism out of a belated Sephardic backlash. Still, whatever the failures to grasp the full significance of what is happening in Israel, we must not lose sight of Rabbi Soloveitchik's profound insight. This is an eschatological knock on the door of history.

All these Jewish accomplishments occur in the context of a global surge toward the messianic ideals. There is, in fact, a worldwide rise in the standard of living which allows for greater human dignity. The concept of human equality and value has spread remarkably (now spilling over to include women, non-whites, etc. as never before). World religions such as Christianity are engaged in a remarkable self-critique and have opened up to genuine repentance. This involves renouncing supercessionist claims and working to end the Othering of other peoples and the degradation or stereotyping of other ways of life. However unfinished the transformation is within Christianity and however limited in other religions, this process is under way on an unprecedented scale. It offers the hope that religion can become a force for unification of humankind while preserving the variety and uniqueness of its varied traditions.

The victory of democracy, however incomplete, opens up the prospect that the process of *tikkun* is now self-reinforcing and building up momentum. Medical breakthroughs are being achieved at every level; they raise the possibility of correcting flaws in the fundamental operations of the life processes. All this creates an environment in which messianism becomes more plausible. People everywhere are energized by the dream of perfection and motivated to stretch for transformational breakthroughs.

I conclude that far from having missed our opportunity, we have made significant strides toward its realization. Ironically, the persistent use of the category of the perfect to measure our achievement of perfection is a constant source of confusion (and a recurrent factor in failing to grasp what can be done). We continue to use the old lens of miraculous, bestowed redemption to view the new (renewed) realistic messianic accomplishments. Inevitably this leads to misjudgements. I am reminded of Rabbi Norman Lamm's comments after the Yom Kippur war. When he saw how flawed and vulnerable Israel was, he decided that he would no longer recite the words in the prayer for Israel that it was "the beginning of the flowering of our redemption." Lamm correctly saw that Gush Emunim's runaway messianism had blocked Israel from pursuing potential peace and compromise. Lamm recognized that the arrogance engendered by the 1967 triumph had blinded Israel to its vulnerability to Arab counter-attack. But Lamm failed to see that a humanly wrought redemption was bound to be flawed; inevitably, its achievements would be distorted from time to time. This did not prove Lamm's conclusion that Israel was a false "beginning of the flowering . . ." It actually *proved* that Israel was a true "beginning" but not yet the conclusion "of the flowering of our redemption."

The expectation of perfection bespeaks the miraculous redeemer, divinely bestowed, untouched and uncorrupted by human hands who ends all the misery and transforms the earth into a paradise overnight. By this standard, the Orthodox expect a totally observant leader and a government of Israel that is traditional in all its practices—and are disappointed. (They forget that in the present official state of *halachah*, such a government would be nonviable. Many injustices would be encased in the system and perpetuated instead of being perfected as they need to be.)

By this same standard, the secularists are disillusioned that all the dysfunctional side effects of modernity are not yet corrected in Israel and that the religious friction and coercion continues. (They forget that Jews can participate in the present reality yet can imagine—and bring into being—a transformation. However, secular culture is not yet up to the job and needs to be itself liberated and perfected.)

Ask yourself what kind of Messiah should come now . . . if we are bringing the Messiah by our human efforts . . . if the redeemer is coming after the Holocaust . . . if we fully appreciate the tremendous inertial resistance of the status quo? The answer is obvious. This redeemer can only come as the outcome of enormous wrestling with God and humans alike. Like Jacob, this Messiah will have been stretched to the limit. Like the patriarch, this one will come to us limping and wounded out of this struggle.

This Messiah has endured our suffering and, not surprisingly, is broken by the Shoah. (Who other than a monster would not be?) Still this redeemer has renewed love and covenantal commitment in order to achieve redemption—so with Rabbi Nachman, we can say: no Messiah is so whole as a broken Messiah. This redeemer bears our sicknesses. (How can it be otherwise if we are bringing the redemption?)

Translate this portrait of the Messiah into contemporary situational terms and one understands that the flaws and failures of our redemptive process are the marks of its integrity and viability. If the Messiah is sometimes cut off from the land of the living through the sins of our people, then out of anguish and devotion, we must fight the matter through together and overcome. It will take the efforts of all of us, together. We will have to heal all Jews and not just our favorite kind. We will have to overcome the divisiveness that cripples our efforts and distorts our needed understanding. We will need to reach out to Gentiles. . . .

Q. What are the hallmarks of this messianic effort that will signal that we are getting there?

Greenberg. More than anything else, the true signal would be to accomplish breakthroughs in restoring the Image of God of all humans. It will take extraordinary political, economic, social, and cultural efforts to uphold the infinite value, equality, and uniqueness of every human being. It will take equally remarkable religious and halachic efforts to reach higher levels of dignity for women, for Gentiles, for the handicapped and the outcasts (*cf.* Isaiah ch. 53) as well as for sinners and the poor and the persecuted for whom we are told the Messiah has a special feeling (*cf.* Isaiah ch. 11).

Q. But what if after all this, we don't succeed? You must admit that in light of our experience so far, failure is a potential, if not likely, outcome?

Greenberg. We will never give in. Rather than yield the dream, we would hound God and energize people until it is accomplished. The very definition of Israel is that we wrestle with God and with humans—even when our heart is pounding, our muscles straining, our joints at the point of bursting—until we overcome. It is our honor, our privilege, our *shlichut* (mission).

Q. And for this honor we have suffered such persecutions and killing . . . and please forgive me, but I don't think that the "honor" and "privilege" answers the question, what if we fail again in this generation?

Greenberg. As Jews, our return for being the watchman to bring the Messiah to the world has been to be murdered and persecuted. Our pay for being humanity's avant garde has been abysmal. Our risk and suffering for serving as God's witnesses have proven to be staggering. But we love our mission. It provides us with a good, steady job!

And now you know why God puts on *tefillin* every day. In God's *tefillin,* it is written—so that neither God nor anyone else should ever forget, even for a single day—"Who is like your people, Israel? It is a nation, unique in the whole world."[9]

9. (1 Chronicles 17:21—as stated in TB Berachot 6A.)

Index

About the Authors

Rabbi Irving Greenberg is the Founding President of CLAL—The National Jewish Center for Learning and Leadership, an organization dedicated to the renewal of *clal Yisrael*—the unity and totality of the Jewish people. He has been a pioneer in leadership education and a leading figure in intra-Jewish dialogue and the development of pluralism. An Orthodox rabbi and Harvard Ph.D., Rabbi Greenberg has been a seminal thinker in confronting the Holocaust as an historical transforming event and Israel as the Jewish assumption of power and the beginning of a third era in Jewish history. Rabbi Greenberg has published articles and monographs on Jewish thought and religion, and a book, *The Jewish Way*, a philosophy of Judaism. He is currently President of CHAverIm Kol Yisrael/Jewish Life Network, a Michael and Judy Steinhardt Foundation, which develops new institutions and projects in religion, education, and culture to strengthen the inner life of American Jewry.

Shalom Freedman is a writer on Jewish subjects who has lived and worked for many years in Israel. He has published four previous books, *Seven Years in Israel: A Zionist Storybook*, a book of poems, *Mourning for My Father*, a work of Jewish thought, *Life as Creation: A Jewish Way of Thinking about the World*, and *In the Service of God*, a book of interviews with Torah teachers in Jerusalem.